AMERICAN CUT GLASS

PRICE GUIDE

BOOK 1

INTRODUCTION

This Price Guide was written with the antique dealer, mail order dealer, beginning and advanced collector, traders, and individuals in mind. I felt there was a need for a price guide that covered the complete range of cut glass from the $5.00 piece to the $2,000.00 piece. I have pictured and valued over 1500 pieces of cut glass. My book is made up of the type of pieces that are available in any antique show, dealers shop or flea market in the U.S. The prices shown are what each piece sold for originally and the value today shown in script. The value shown is an average of the asking prices I have seen at major antique shows and shops in a large part of the U.S. in the past two years. It has been fun and I hope my experience will help you.

ALPHA LEE EHRHARDT

First printing, Sept. 1973
HEART OF AMERICA PRESS
P.O. Box 9808, Kansas City, Mo. 64134

ISBN 9-913902-04-7

<u>HOW TO READ THE PRICES</u>

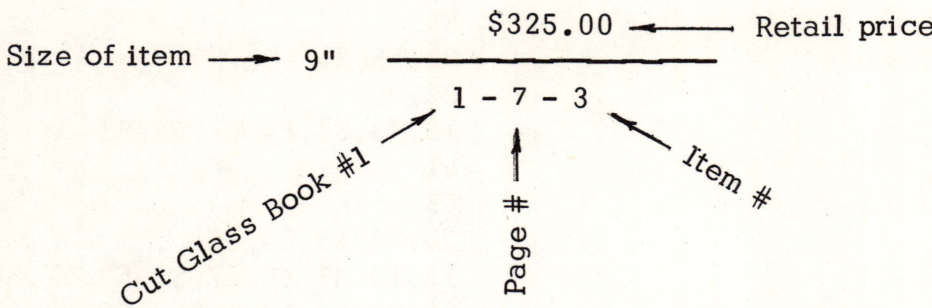

I used this method so as to perhaps help mail order dealers and their buyers understand each other better.

ALPHA LEE EHRHARDT

For the collector or dealer who would like more detailed information on cut glass, how made, makers, etc., I would recommend the following books:

AMERICAN CUT AND ENGRAVED GLASS, by Albert C. Revi, $15.00.
Published by Thomas Nelson, Inc., Nashville, Tennessee.

AMERICAN CUT GLASS, by Michael and Dorothy Pearson, $12.50.
Published by Vantage Press, 120 West 31st Street, New York, N.Y.

LIBBY GLASS 1818-1968. The Toledo Museum of Art, Toledo, Ohio

There are many other reprints, price guides, etc. that are available from most antique book dealers.

4

PREFACE

 **I**T IS AN OLD SAYING that the best kind of friendship in business is based on the best business relations, hence we retain the good will and co-operation of our customers in always seeking to conduct all transactions with due regard to their interests.

If the most careful buyers in the field, having tried our goods, found them satisfactory and re-order, it is convincing proof of the superiority of our catalog—in illustrating only merchandise of refined quality and workmanship at lowest prices.

The Success, Growth and Reputation of our Company, with the acknowledged leadership in its field, not only evidences the efficiency of our methods, but firmly establishes our position as America's largest distributors of goods in our line.

Such progress is the combined result of Co-operation, Facilities, Efficiency and Fair Dealing.

Thus we are enabled to enjoy the proud distinction of a reputation for reliability and honesty extending to all parts of the world.

We wish to convey to our friends and patrons our thankful appreciation of their generous support and take pleasure in presenting this issue of a book which, without question, is the most complete and authentic Jewelers' Catalogue published.

THE OSKAMP, NOLTING COMPANY

Cincinnati, - - - - - - Ohio, U. S. A.

SPECIAL NOTICE!

UNSETTLED BUSINESS CONDITIONS PREVAILING

CONDITIONS brought about by the European war, and which must prevail for an indefinite period, even after the termination of the war, caused an extraordinary increase in the cost of material and other supplies entering into the manufacture of all classes of goods, and in addition there has been experienced by all manufacturers an advanced cost in labor.

We are quoting prices in our catalogue on the conditions and advanced cost which prevails at the time our catalogue has gone to press.

Should the manufacturers request an advance on any of their products after the issue of this catalogue, our prices will be governed accordingly and subject to such advance without further notice.

However, any reductions in prices made by the manufacturers on any subsequent date, our customers will receive the benefit of such reductions.

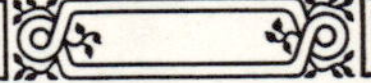

THE OSKAMP, NOLTING COMPANY
Cincinnati, Ohio, U. S. A.

Genuine American Cut Glass Punch Bowls and Sherbet Glasses

PRICE EACH

Cut Glass Footed Bowl. Fine Combination Floral and Mitre Cutting. Height, 8½ inches. Diameter of Bowl, 8 inches.
No. 9246 ....$12.00

Footed Punch Cup. Mitre Cutting and Floral Engraving. To Match Bowl No. 9250.
No. 9249........$4.25 Each

Cut Glass Footed Punch Bowl. Fine Combination Floral and Mitre Cutting. Can be Used as Separate Bowl or Compote.
No. 9247— 9 inches................$14.00
No. 9248—10 inches.................. 21.00

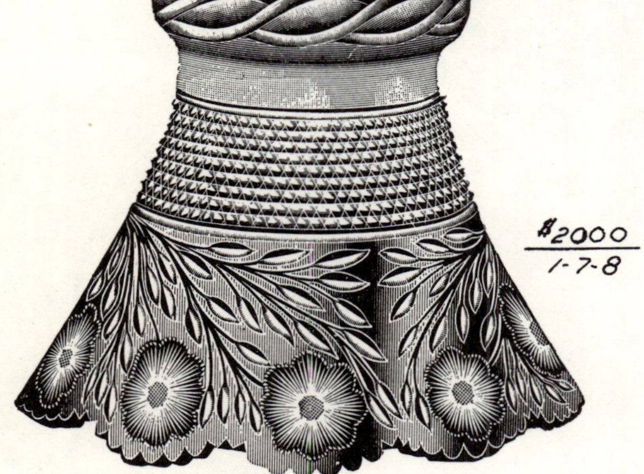

Large Punch Bowl. Mitre Cutting and Floral Engraving. Diameter, 14 inches. See Footed Cup No. 9249 to Match.
No. 9250 ....$150.00

Cut Glass Lemonade or Punch Cup. Illustration One-Half Size.
No. 9251....................$1.75 Each
To Match Punch Bowls on Page 572

Cut Glass Lemonade or Punch Cup. Illustration One-Half Size.
No. 9252.......................$1.75 Each

Cut Glass Footed Sherbet. Height, 3¼ inches. Finely Cut.
No. 9253.......$2.75 Each

Cut Glass Footed Sherbet. Height, 3¼ inches. Finely Cut.
No. 9254.......$2.75 Each
To Match Punch Bowl on Page 572

Genuine American Cut Glass Fruit or Nut Bowls
PRICE EACH

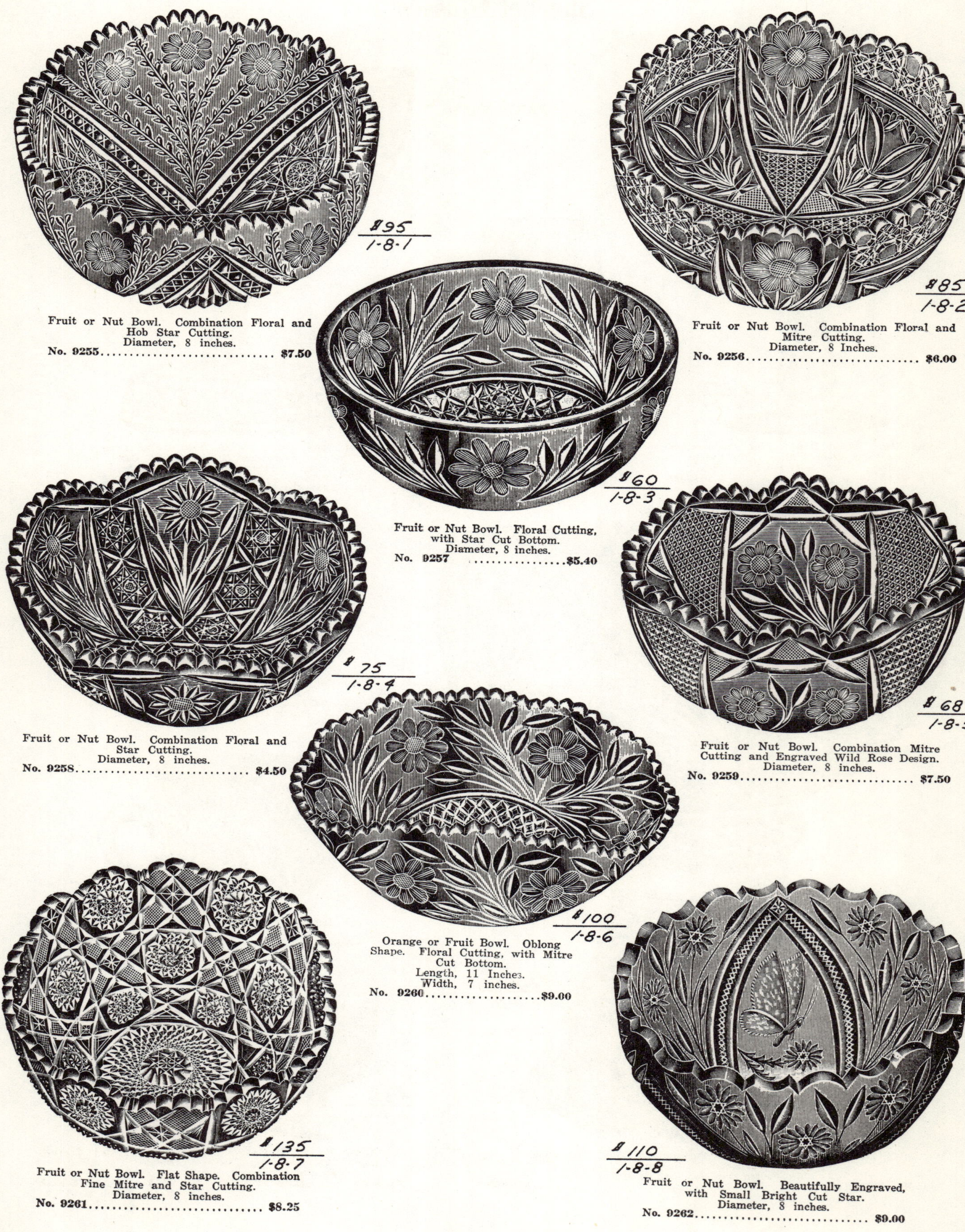

Fruit or Nut Bowl. Combination Floral and Hob Star Cutting.
Diameter, 8 inches.
No. 9255.............................$7.50

Fruit or Nut Bowl. Combination Floral and Mitre Cutting.
Diameter, 8 Inches.
No. 9256.............................$6.00

Fruit or Nut Bowl. Floral Cutting, with Star Cut Bottom.
Diameter, 8 inches.
No. 9257 ....$5.40

Fruit or Nut Bowl. Combination Floral and Star Cutting.
Diameter, 8 inches.
No. 9258.............................$4.50

Fruit or Nut Bowl. Combination Mitre Cutting and Engraved Wild Rose Design.
Diameter, 8 inches.
No. 9259.............................$7.50

Orange or Fruit Bowl. Oblong Shape. Floral Cutting, with Mitre Cut Bottom.
Length, 11 Inches.
Width, 7 inches.
No. 9260...................$9.00

Fruit or Nut Bowl. Flat Shape. Combination Fine Mitre and Star Cutting.
Diameter, 8 inches.
No. 9261.............................$8.25

Fruit or Nut Bowl. Beautifully Engraved, with Small Bright Cut Star.
Diameter, 8 inches.
No. 9262.............................$9.00

Genuine American Cut Glass Fruit or Nut Bowls

PRICE EACH

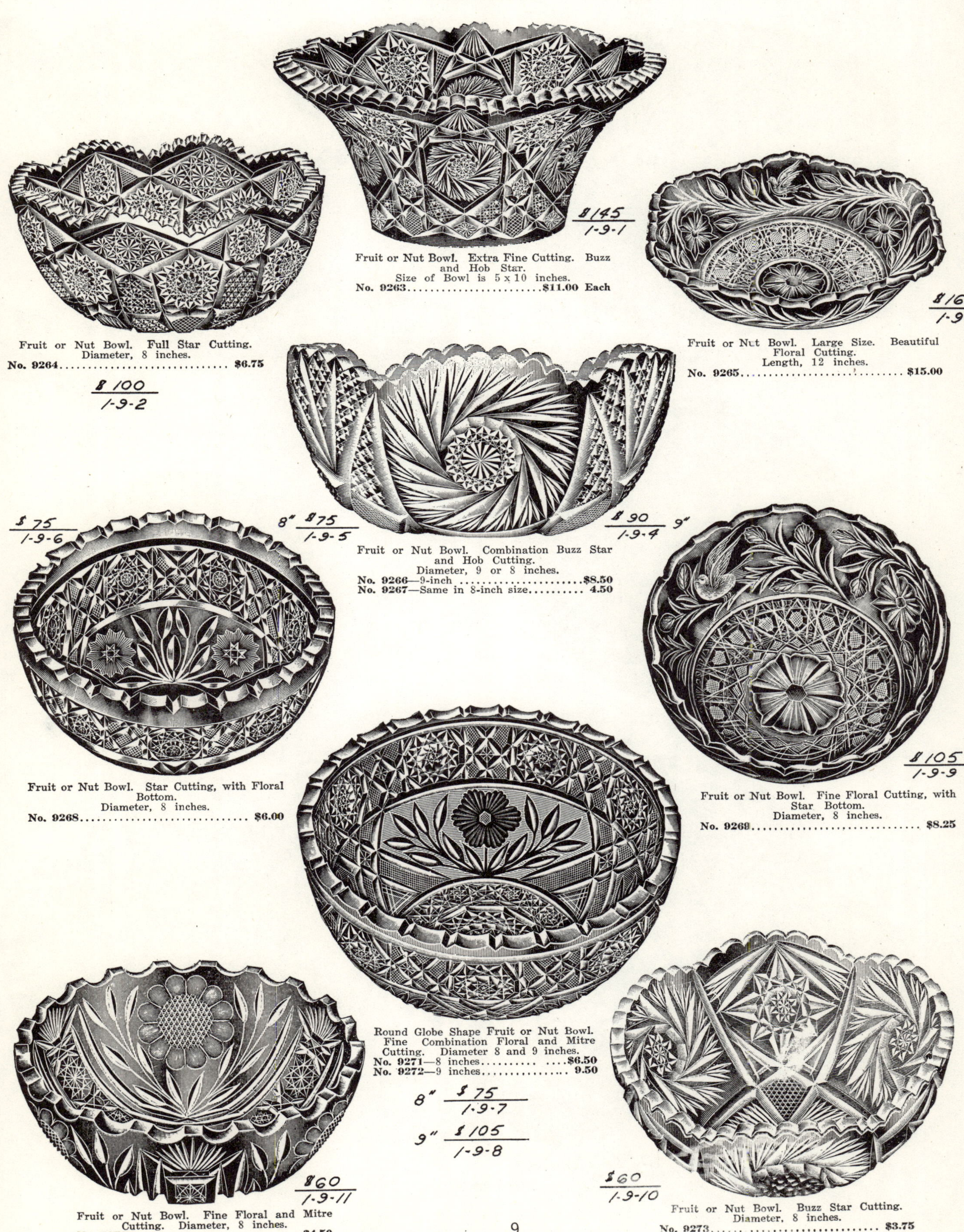

Fruit or Nut Bowl. Extra Fine Cutting. Buzz
and Hob Star.
Size of Bowl is 5 x 10 inches.
No. 9263.................$11.00 Each

8 145
1-9-1

Fruit or Nut Bowl. Full Star Cutting.
Diameter, 8 inches.
No. 9264..........................$6.75

8 100
1-9-2

Fruit or Nut Bowl. Large Size. Beautiful
Floral Cutting.
Length, 12 inches.
No. 9265..........................$15.00

8 160
1-9-3

Fruit or Nut Bowl. Combination Buzz Star
and Hob Cutting.
Diameter, 9 or 8 inches.
No. 9266—9-inch $8.50
No. 9267—Same in 8-inch size.......... 4.50

8" *8 75* / *1-9-5*   *8 90* 9" / *1-9-4*

8 75
1-9-6

Fruit or Nut Bowl. Star Cutting, with Floral
Bottom.
Diameter, 8 inches.
No. 9268...........................$6.00

Fruit or Nut Bowl. Fine Floral Cutting, with
Star Bottom.
Diameter, 8 inches.
No. 9269.............................$8.25

8 105
1-9-9

Round Globe Shape Fruit or Nut Bowl.
Fine Combination Floral and Mitre
Cutting. Diameter 8 and 9 inches.
No. 9271—8 inches.............$6.50
No. 9272—9 inches.............. 9.50

8" *8 75* / *1-9-7*

9" *8 105* / *1-9-8*

Fruit or Nut Bowl. Fine Floral and Mitre
Cutting. Diameter, 8 inches.
No. 9270.............................$4.50

8 60
1-9-11

Fruit or Nut Bowl. Buzz Star Cutting.
Diameter, 8 inches.
No. 9273............................$3.75

8 60
1-9-10

Genuine American Cut Glass Fruit Bowls and Berry Sets

Orange or Fruit Bowl. Oval Shape. Full Star Cutting.
Length of Bowl is 11¾ inches. 8 inches Wide.
No. 9276...$8.50 Each

8" $90 / 1-10-1   9" $130 / 1-10-2

Large Fruit or Nut Bowl. Combination Floral and Star Cutting.
Comes in 8 and 9-inch Size.
No. 9274—8 inch...$6.75 Each
No. 9275—9 inch... 9.75 Each

4½" $35 / 1-10-4 $70 / 1-10-5

Berry Set. Fine Floral Cutting. Set Consists of one 8-inch Bowl and
Six Berry Dishes. 4½ inches Wide and 2 inches High.
No. 9277...$16.50 Per Set

$160 / 1-10-6

Genuine American Cut Glass Bowl. Combination Hob Star and Engraved
Strawberry Pattern. Diameter, 8 inches.
No. 9278...$13.50 Each
See No. 9279 Plates to Match.

$70 / 1-10-7

Genuine American Cut Glass Nappy or Berry Dish.
Combination Hob Star and Engraved Strawberry Pattern.
No. 9279...$5.25 Each
See No. 9278 Bowl to Match.

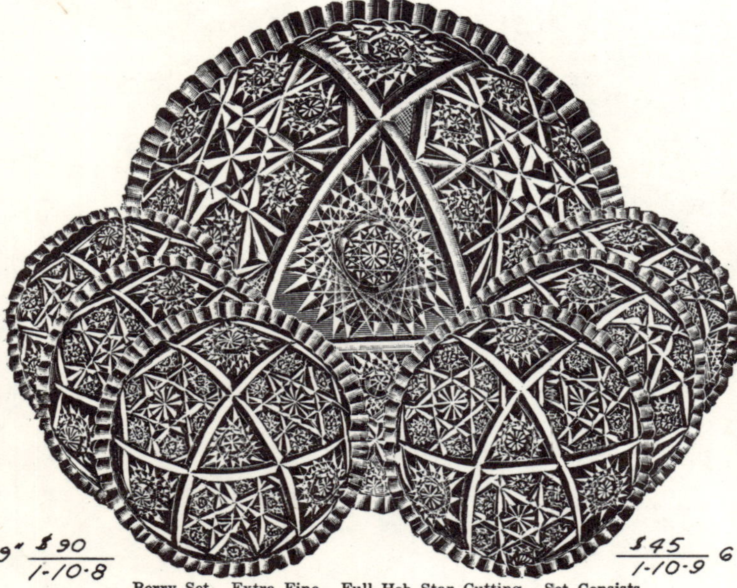

9" $90 / 1-10-8 $45 / 1-10-9 6"

Berry Set. Extra Fine. Full Hob Star Cutting. Set Consists
of 9 inch Bowl and Six Berry Dishes (Diameter, 6
inches). All Well Cut.
No. 9280...$30.00 Per Set

$175 / 1-10-10

Round Globe Shape Fruit or Nut Bowl.
Star Cutting.
Diameter, 9 inches.
No. 9281...$13.50 Each

PRICE EACH

Celery Tray. Fine Combination Floral and Engraved Fruit and Butterfly. Length, 11 inches.
No. 9282 .... $7.50

Celery Tray. Beautifully Engraved Pattern. Length, 11½ inches; Width, 4½ inches.
No. 9283 .... $7.50

Celery Dish. Combination Floral and Mitre Cutting. Length, 12 inches; Width, 4½ inches.
No. 9284 .... $6.00

Celery Tray. Combination Floral and Mitre Cutting. Length, 11 inches; Width, 4½ inches.
No. 9285 .... $4.95

Large Celery Tray. Combination Floral and Star Cutting. Length, 12 inches; Width, 4½ inches.
No. 9286 .... $5.25

Cut Glass Celery Dish. Fine Combination Floral and Mitre Cutting. Length, 11 inches; Width, 4½ inches.
No. 9287 .... $4.50

Celery Tray. Heavy Star and Mitre Cutting. Length, 11¼ inches.
No. 9288 .... $5.25

Cut Glass Celery Dish. Extra Fine Cutting. Length, 12 inches.
No. 9289 .... $4.75

Cut Glass Celery Dish. Combination Floral and Star Cutting. Length 11 inches.
No. 9290 .... $5.00

Cut Glass Celery Dish. Deep Hob Star Cutting. Length, 10½ inches.
No. 9291 .... $4.00

GENUINE AMERICAN CUT GLASS ICE CREAM AND CELERY TRAYS

PRICE EACH

Large Ice Cream or Cake Dish. Combination Mitre and Floral
Cutting. Length, 14 inches; Width, 7½ inches.
No. 9292 . . . . $9.75

Cut Glass Celery Combination Floral and Mitre Cutting.
Length, 12½ inches.
No. 9293 . . . . $9.50

Celery Tray. Heavy Star and Mitre Cutting.
Length, 9 inches.
No. 9294 . . . . $5.25

Cut Glass Celery Dish. Fine Floral Cutting.
Length, 11 inches.
No. 9295 . . . . $4.00

Cut Glass Celery Dish. Buzz Star Cutting.
Length, 12 inches.
No. 9296 . . . . $3.75

Celery Tray. Combination Floral and Mitre Cutting.
Length, 11½ inches.
No. 9297 . . . . $3.75

Celery Tray. Combination Floral and Mitre Cutting.
Length, 10¾ inches.
No. 9298 . . . . $3.50

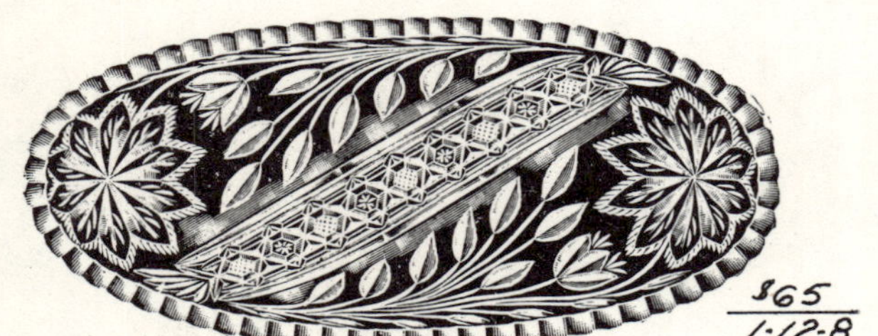

Celery Tray. Combination Pattern. Cut with Two Handsome Flowers
and Panel of Mitre. 10¾ inches long; 4½ inches wide; 1¾ inches deep.
No. 9299 . . . . $3.25

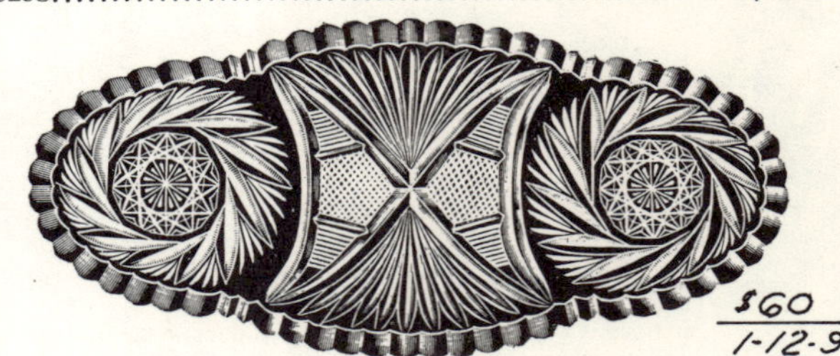

Celery Tray. Fancy Buzz Star Cutting.
Length, 10½ inches.
No. 9300 . . . . $3.00

Genuine American Cut Glass Nappies, Cake Plates and Ice Cream Set

PRICE EACH

R $60
1-13-1

WH $70
1-13-2

Cut Glass Round and Handle Nappy.
Beautifully Engraved Design.
Diameter, 6 inches.
No. 9301—Round.................$3.75 Each
No. 9302—With Handle..........$3.90 Each

$65
1-13-3

Cut Glass Deep Nappy.
Sunflower Floral Cutting.
Diameter, 8 inches.
No. 9303.........................$5.25 Each

R $50
1-13-4

WH $60
1-13-5

Cut Glass Round and Handle Nappy.
Star and Mitre Cut Panel, Floral Bottom.
Diameter, 6 inches.
No. 9304—Round.................$2.25 Each
No. 9305—With Handle.........$2.40 Each

$55
1-13-6

Two Handled Nappy. 6 inches in Diameter,
2 inches Deep. Cut in a Handsome
Floral Combination Pattern. Two
Flowers and Scalloped Edge.
No. 9306.................$3.00 Each

$185
1-13-7

Cut Glass Cake or Sandwich Plate. Beautiful
Floral and Mitre Cutting.
Diameter, 10 inches.
No. 9307........................$6.75 Each

$65
1-13-8

Cut Glass Double Handle Nappy. All Star
Cutting. Diameter, 6 inches.
No. 9308.......................$3.25 Each

$200
1-13-9

Cut Glass Cake or Sandwich Plate. Fine Combination Mitre and
Floral Cutting. Diameter, 10 inches.
No. 9309.........................$7.50 Each

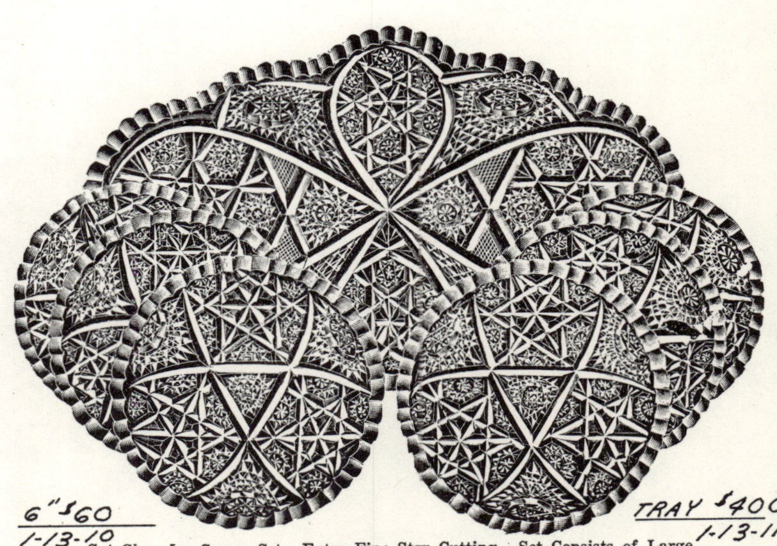

6" $60
1-13-10

TRAY $400
1-13-11

Cut Glass Ice Cream Set. Extra Fine Star Cutting. Set Consists of Large
Ice Cream Tray, 14 x 8½ inches, and Six Ice Cream
Plates, 6 inches in Diameter.
No. 9310........................$31.00 Per Set

GENUINE AMERICAN CUT GLASS NAPPIES, CHEESE AND CRACKER DISH, INDIVIDUAL BUTTER AND SALTS

Cut Glass Footed Salt.
Fine Star Cutting.
No. 9311....................$13.00 Dozen

Cut Glass Cheese and Cracker Dish.
Floral Design.
No. 9316.........................$9.00 Each

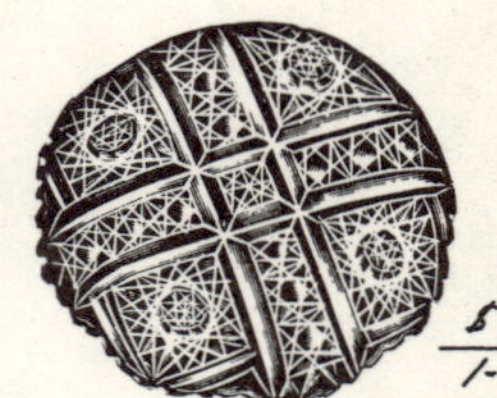

Cut Glass Individual Butter Plates.
Rich Cutting.
Diameter, 3¼ inches.
No. 9313....................$13.20 Per Dozen

Cut Glass Salt Dip.
Star Cutting.
No. 9312....................$9.00 Dozen

Cut Glass Individual Butter Plates.
Diameter, 3¼ inches.
No. 9314....................$15.40 Per Dozen

Cut Glass Two-Handle Bon Bon or Jelly Dish.
Combination Floral and Star Cutting.
Width, 9½ inches.
No. 9317....................$2.25 Each

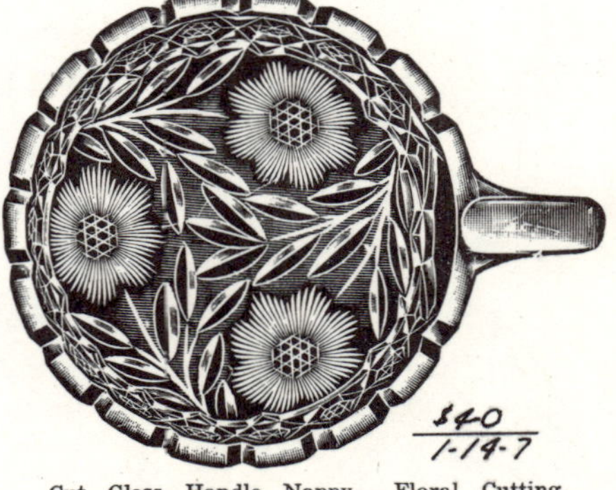

Cut Glass Handle Nappy. Floral Cutting.
Diameter, 6 inches.
No. 9318....................$2.25 Each

Cut Glass Individual Butter Plates.
Rich Cutting. Diameter, 3¼ inches.
No. 9315....................$20.90 Per Dozen

Cut Glass Handle Nappy. Fine Buzz and Hob
Star Cutting. Comes in 5 and 6 inches.
No. 9319—5 inches, Round......$1.80 Each
No. 9320—6 inches, Round.......2.00 Each
No. 9321—6 inches, with Handle..2.15 Each

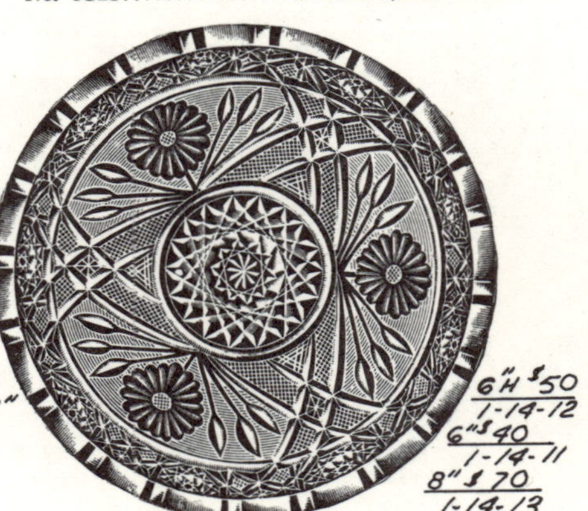

Cut Glass Nappy. Fine Combination Floral
and Mitre Cutting. Comes in 6-inch
Round and with Handle and 8-inch Round.
No. 9322—6-inch, Round..........$2.80 Each
No. 9323—6-inch with Handle.....2.95 Each
No. 9324—8-inch, Round..........5.50 Each

Cut Glass Nappy. Combination Floral and
Star Cutting.
Diameter, 6 inches.
No. 9325—Round.................$2.75 Each
No. 9326—With Handle..........$2.90 Each

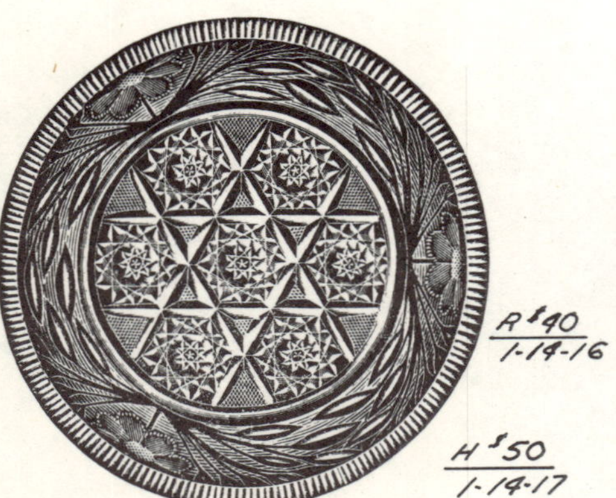

Cut Glass Nappy. Combination Floral and
Star Cutting.
Diameter, 6 inches.
No. 9327—Round.................$2.40 Each
No. 9328—With Handle..........$2.55 Each

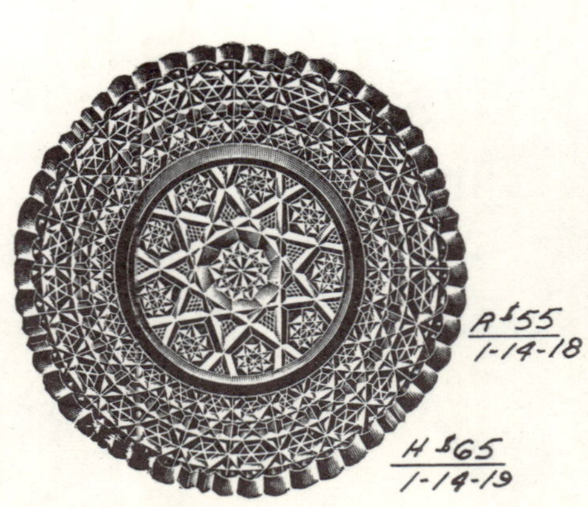

Cut Glass Nappy. Extra Fine Star and
Diamond Cutting. Comes with
or without Handles. Diameter,
6 inches.
No. 9329—Without Handle........$2.75 Each
No. 9330—With Handle..........$2.75 Each

Cut Glass Nappy. Beautiful Fruit and
Butterfly Cutting. Diameter, 6 inches.
No. 9331..........................$3.50 Each

Genuine American Cut Glass Spoon Trays, Domino Sugar and Olive Dishes

PRICE EACH

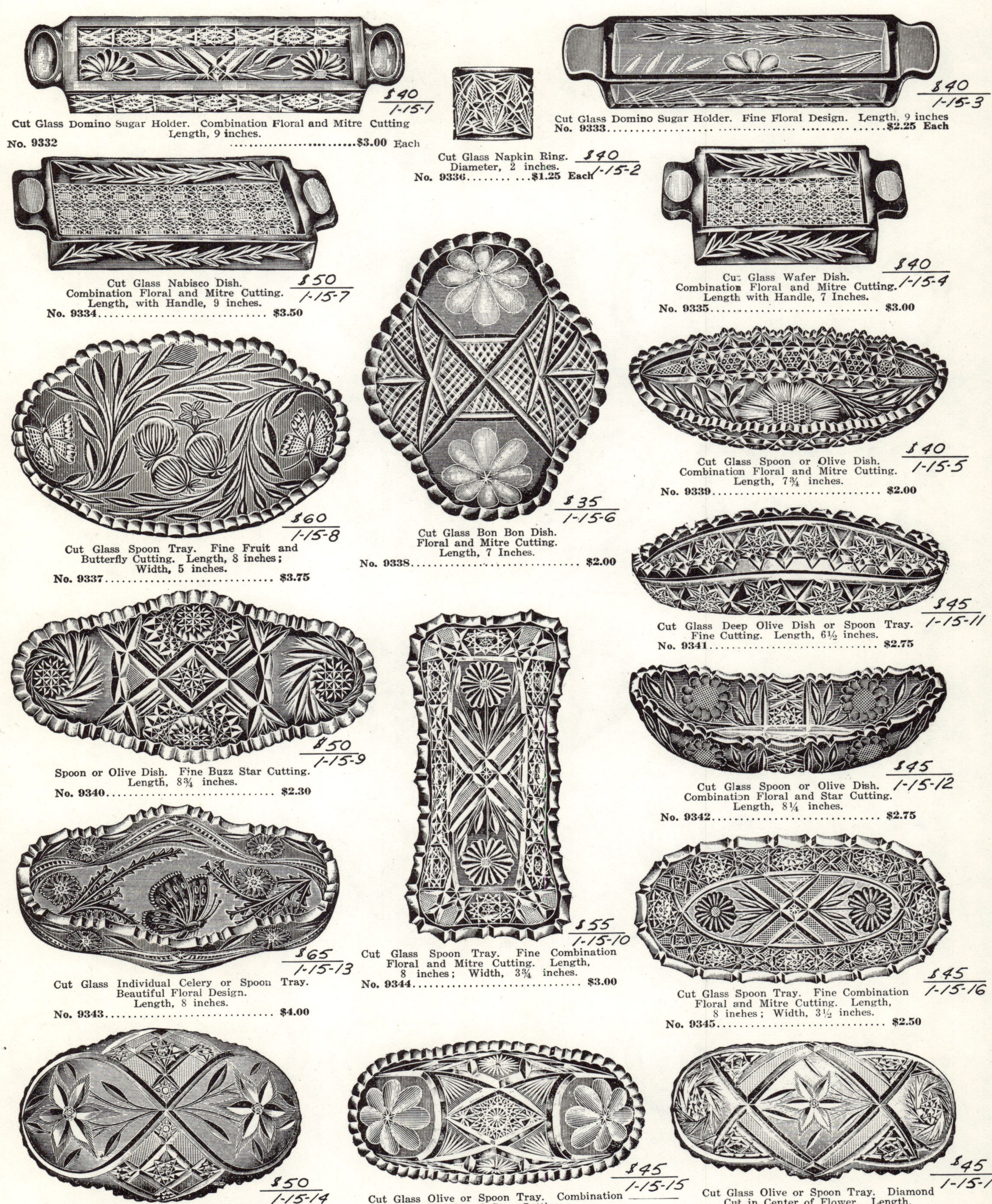

Cut Glass Domino Sugar Holder. Combination Floral and Mitre Cutting. Length, 9 inches.
No. 9332 ....$3.00 Each

Cut Glass Napkin Ring. Diameter, 2 inches.
No. 9336 ....$1.25 Each

Cut Glass Domino Sugar Holder. Fine Floral Design. Length, 9 inches
No. 9333 ....$2.25 Each

Cut Glass Nabisco Dish. Combination Floral and Mitre Cutting. Length, with Handle, 9 inches.
No. 9334 ....$3.50

Cut Glass Wafer Dish. Combination Floral and Mitre Cutting. Length with Handle, 7 inches.
No. 9335 ....$3.00

Cut Glass Spoon Tray. Fine Fruit and Butterfly Cutting. Length, 8 inches; Width, 5 inches.
No. 9337 ....$3.75

Cut Glass Bon Bon Dish. Floral and Mitre Cutting. Length, 7 inches.
No. 9338 ....$2.00

Cut Glass Spoon or Olive Dish. Combination Floral and Mitre Cutting. Length, 7¾ inches.
No. 9339 ....$2.00

Cut Glass Deep Olive Dish or Spoon Tray. Fine Cutting. Length, 6½ inches.
No. 9341 ....$2.75

Spoon or Olive Dish. Fine Buzz Star Cutting. Length, 8¾ inches.
No. 9340 ....$2.30

Cut Glass Spoon or Olive Dish. Combination Floral and Star Cutting. Length, 8¼ inches.
No. 9342 ....$2.75

Cut Glass Individual Celery or Spoon Tray. Beautiful Floral Design. Length, 8 inches.
No. 9343 ....$4.00

Cut Glass Spoon Tray. Fine Combination Floral and Mitre Cutting. Length, 8 inches; Width, 3¾ inches.
No. 9344 ....$3.00

Cut Glass Spoon Tray. Fine Combination Floral and Mitre Cutting. Length, 8 inches; Width, 3½ inches.
No. 9345 ....$2.50

Cut Glass Pickle or Olive Dish. Diamond Cut in End Flowers. Length, 8 inches.
No. 9346 ....$3.10

Cut Glass Olive or Spoon Tray. Combination Floral and Star Cutting. Length, 8 inches.
No. 9347 ....$2.00

Cut Glass Olive or Spoon Tray. Diamond Cut in Center of Flower. Length, 8 inches.
No. 9348 ....$2.50

Genuine American Cut Glass Sugar and Cream Sets

PRICE EACH

Cut Glass Sugar and Cream Set. Floral Cutting with Star Cut Bottom.
No. 9349 .... $5.25

Cut Glass Sugar and Cream Set. Fine Sunburst Cutting.
No. 9350 .... $4.50

Cut Glass Sugar and Cream Set. Combination Mitre and Floral Cutting.
No. 9355 .... $5.25

Cut Glass Sugar and Cream Set. Fine Combination Mitre and Floral Design.
No. 9351 .... $4.50

Cut Glass Sugar and Cream Set. Fine Buzz Star Cutting.
No. 9352—Per Set $3.75

Cut Glass Sugar and Cream Set. Buzz Star and Mitre Cutting.
No. 9356 .... $6.00

Cut Glass Sugar and Cream Set. Combination Floral and Mitre Cutting.
No. 9353 .... $3.75

Cut Glass Sugar and Cream Set. Floral Design.
No. 9354 .... $3.45

Cut Glass Sugar and Cream Set. Fine Floral Design.
No. 9357 .... $5.00

Genuine American Cut Glass Sugar and Cream Sets

PRICE PER SET

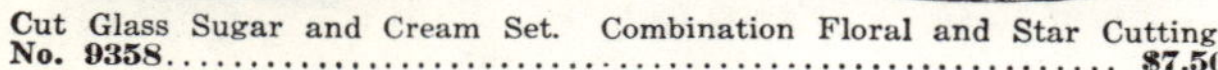

Cut Glass Sugar and Cream Set. Combination Floral and Star Cutting.
No. 9358.. $7.50

Cut Glass Sugar and Cream Set. Combination Floral and Mitre Cutting.
No. 9359.. $7.00

Cut Glass Sugar and Cream Set.
Floral and Butterfly Design.
No. 9363...................... $6.50

Cut Glass Sugar and Cream Set. Beautiul Engraved Design.
No. 9360.. $8.25

Cut Glass Sugar and Cream Set.
Combination Foral and Mitre Cutting.
No. 9364........................... $8.00

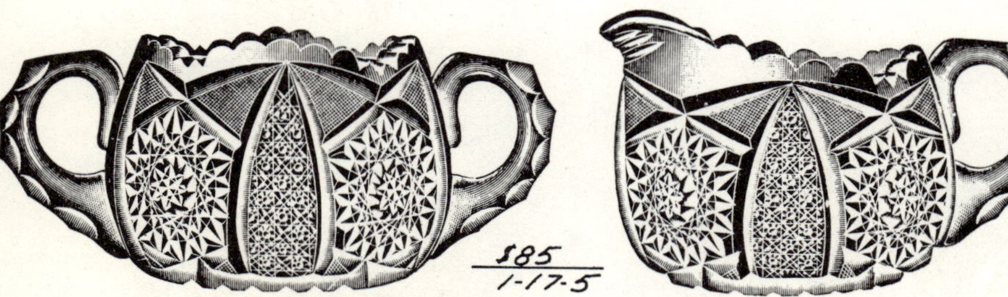

Cut Glass Sugar and Cream Set. Fine Hob Star Cutting.
No. 9361.. $6.00

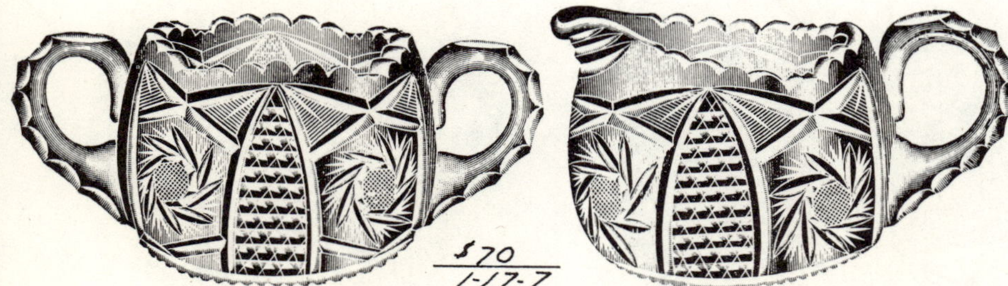

Cut Glass Sugar and Cream Set. Buzz Star and Mitre Cutting.
No. 9362.. $6.00

Cut Glass Sugar and Cream Set.
Floral and Mitre Cutting.
No. 9365.................................. $3.75

Genuine American Cut Glass Mayonnaise Sets, Spoon Holders and Sugar Sifter

PRICE EACH

$105
1-18-1

Mayonnaise Set. Bowl and Plate.
Engraved Flowers and Bird.
Diameter of Bowl, 4¾ inches;
Plate, 6¼ inches.
No. 9369.................. $9.25

$125
1-18-2

Cut Glass Double Handle Spoon
Holder. Fine Cutting.
Height, 4½ inches.
No. 9366.............$7.00 Each

$90
1-18-3

Cut Glass Spoon Holder.
Height, 4 inches.
No. 9367..............$4.50 Each

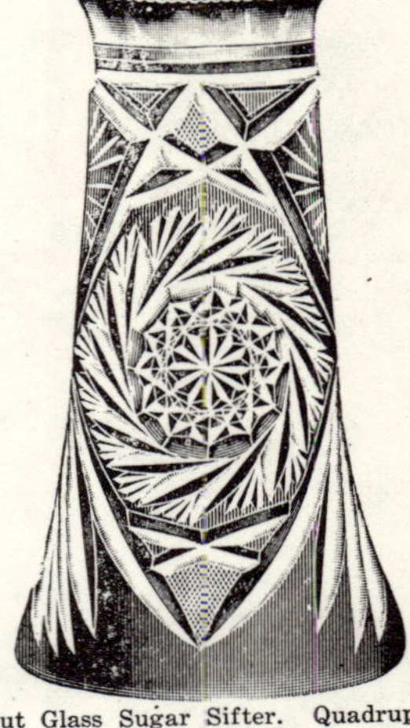

$125
1-18-4

Cut Glass Sugar Sifter. Quadruple
Silver Plated Top.
Height, 5¾ inches.
No. 9368..............$5.50 Each

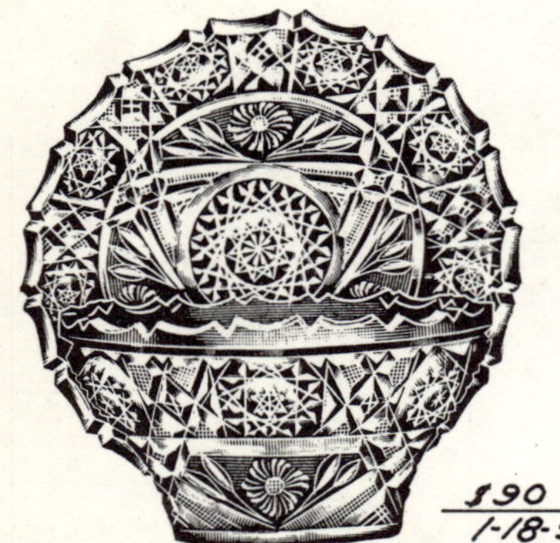

$90
1-18-5

Cut Glass Mayonnaise Bowl and Plate. Fine
Combination Floral and Mitre Cutting.
Diameter of Bowl is 5 inches; Plate, 6 inches.
No. 9370............................. $6.00

$90
1-18-6

Cut Glass Mayonnaise Set. Combination
Floral and Mitre Cutting. Height of Bowl is
2¾ inches. Diameter of Plate, 7 inches.
No. 9371............................. $5.50

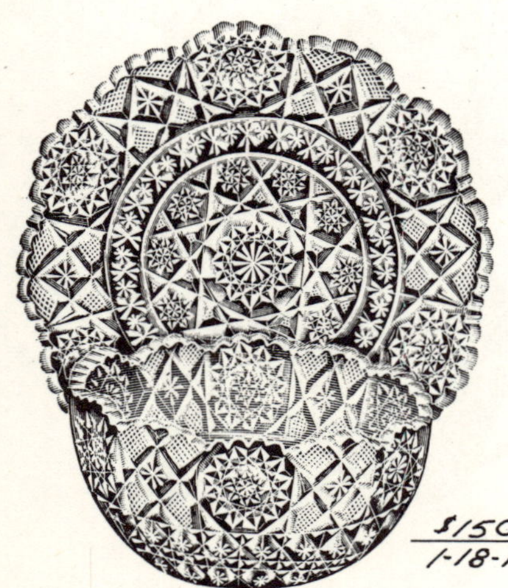

$70
1-18-7

Cut Glass Mayonnaise Set. Bowl and Plate.
All Floral Design. Diameter of Bowl is
5 inches; Plate, 6 inches.
No. 9372............................. $4.25

$100
1-18-8

Cut Glass Footed Mayonnaise or Compote.
Combination Hob and Buzz Star Cutting.
No. 9373................................. $5.50

$90
1-18-9

Cut Glass Mayonnaise Set. Bowl and Plate.
Combination Floral and Mitre Cutting.
Diameter of Bowl is 5 inches; Plate
6 inches.
No. 9374............................. $5.25

$150
1-18-10

Cut Glass Mayonnaise Set. Heavy Star and
Mitre Cutting. Diameter of Bowl is
5 inches; Plate, 7 inches.
No. 9375................................. $8.10

$275
1-18-11

Cut Glass Butter Plate or Cheese Dish, with
Cover. Diameter of Plate is 8 inches.
No. 9376.............$9.50 Per Set

$200
1-18-12

Cut Glass Ice or Butter Tub and Plate. Fine
Hob Star and Floral Cutting. Diameter
of Plate is 7 inches. Diameter
of Tub is 4¾ inches.
No. 9377.............$8.75 Per Set

Genuine American Cut Glass Oil or Vinegar Cruets

PRICE EACH

Cut Glass Oil or Vinegar Cruet. Floral Cutting.
No. 9378 . . . . $3.50
$40
1-19-1

Cut Glass Oil or Vinegar Cruet. Combination Floral and Mitre Cutting.
No. 9379 . . . . $6.00
$70
1-19-2

Cut Glass Oil or Vinegar Cruet. Combination Floral and Mitre Cutting.
No. 9380 . . . . $6.00
$60
1-19-3

Cut Glass Oil Cruet. Fine Floral Cutting. Height, 7¾ inches.
No. 9382 . . . . $4.50
$60
1-19-4

Cut Glass Salad Dressing Bottle. Height, with Stopper, 7½ inches. Floral Cutting.
No. 9383 . . . . $4.50
$50
1-19-5

Crystal Glass Salad Dressing Bottle. Floral Cutting.
No. 9381 . . . . $3.75

The Princess Oil or Vinegar. Mitre Cutting and Engraved.
No. 9384 . . . . $6.25
$85
1-19-6

Cut Glass Vinegar or Oil Cruet. Extra Fine Cutting. Capacity, ½ Pint.
No. 9385 . . . . $6.00 Each

Cut Glass Oil or Vinegar Cruet. Fine Floral Cutting.
No. 9386 . . . . $4.80
$90
1-19-7
$70
1-19-8

Cut Glass Oil or Vinegar Cruet. Beautiful Engraved Design.
No. 9387 . . . . $6.00
$90
1-13-9

Oil or Vinegar Cruet. Combination Floral and Mitre Cutting. Height, with Stopper, 8½ inches.
No. 9388 . . . . $5.50
$75
1-19-10

Cut Glass Oil or Vinegar. Globe Shape Sunflower Floral Cutting.
No. 9389 . . . . $4.50 Each
$55
1-19-11

Cut Glass Oil or Vinegar Combination Floral and Mitre Cutting.
No. 9390 . . . . $4.00
$50
1-19-12

Cut Glas Vinegar or Oil. Extra Fine Cutting.
No. 9391 . . . . $3.50 Each
$45
1-19-13

Cut Glass Oil or Vinegar Cruet. Height, 7 inches.
No. 9392 . . . . . $3.50 Each
$60
1-19-14

Cut Glass Vinegar or Oil Cruet. Height, 7 inches.
No. 9393 . . . . $3.50 Each
$65
1-19-15

Genuine American Cut Glass Flower Bowl, Compotes and Footed Nappies
PRICE EACH

The Very Latest in Table Decoration.
Large Cut Glass Flower Bowl.
Beautiful Cutting with Blackberry and Leaves.
Diameter of Bowl, 14 inches.
No. 9394 .... $45.00

Cut Glass Footed Bowl. Combination Flora
and Mitre Cutting.
Diameter of Bowl is 8 inches.
No. 9395 .... $6.00

Cut Glass Compote or Jelly Dish.
Floral Cutting.
Diameter of Bowl is 5 inches.
No. 9396 .... $2.75

Cut Glass Footed Nappy. Fine Floral Daisy
Cutting. Comes in 6 and 7 inches.
No. 9397—6-inch $3.00
No. 9398—7-inch 4.50

Cut Glass Three Footed Nappy. Fine Floral
and Mitre Cutting. Comes in 6 and 7 inch.
No. 9399—6-inch $3.75
No. 9400—7-inch 4.75

Cut Glass Compote. Combination Floral and
Mitre Cutting. Height, 5 inches.
Diameter of Bowl, 6 inches.
No. 9401 .... $4.50

Cut Glass Footed Nappy. Floral Cutting.
Diameter 6 inches.
No. 9402 .... $3.30

Cut Glass Compote. Combination Floral and
Mitre Cutting.
Diameter of Bowl, 6½ inches.
No. 9403 .... $3.00

Cut Glass Footed Bowl or Nappy.
Combination Daisy Cutting.
Diameter, 8 inches; Height, 3¾ inches.
No. 9404 .... $9.50

Cut Glass Compote. Buzz and Hob
Star Cutting.
Height, 4¼ inches; Diameter, 5 inches.
No. 9405 .... $3.50

Genuine Anerican Cut Glass Baskets and Flower Bowls

Cut Glass Hand Basket. Fine Combination Floral and Mitre Cutting. Comes in 6 and 8 inch.

No. 9406—6-inch...................... $4.50
No. 9407—8-inch...................... 7.50

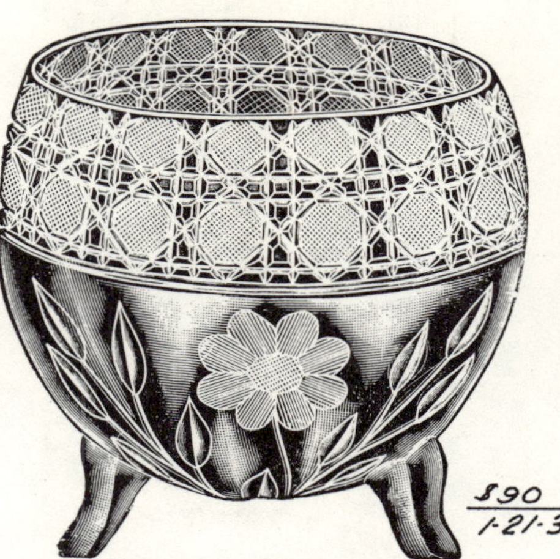

Cut Glass Jardiner or Bowl. Combination Floral and Mitre Cutting. Diameter, 8 inches; Height, 3¾ inches.
No. 9408............................. $9.00

Cut Glass Basket. Floral Cutting. Twist Handle. 6¼ inches Long.
No. 9409............................. $4.10

Cut Glass Footed Flower Bowl. Floral Cutting. Diameter, 6 inches.
No. 9410............................. $5.25

Cut Glass Footed Flower Bowl. Full Floral Cutting. Diameter, 11½ inches.
No. 9411............................. $10.50

Cut Glass Footed Flower Bowl. Floral Cutting. Diameter, 6 inches.
No. 9412............................. $5.25

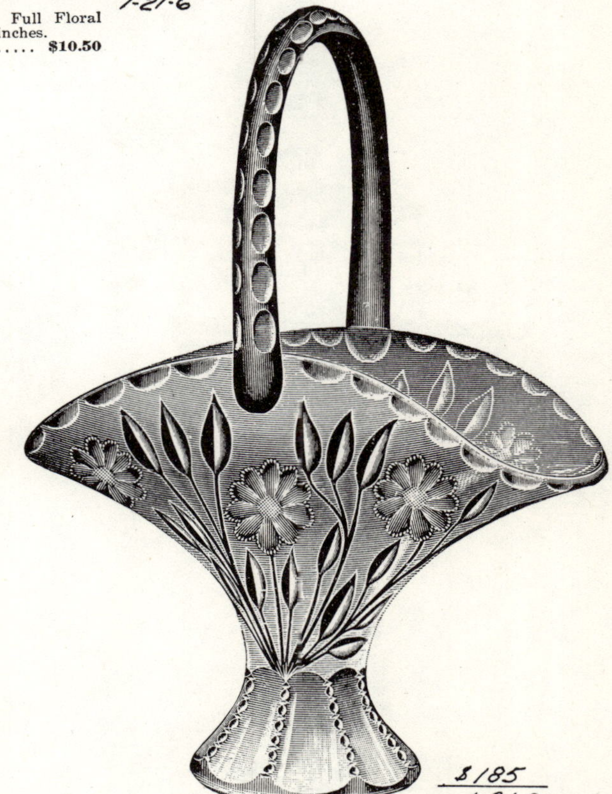

Cut Glass Basket. Floral Cutting. Length, 10 inches.
No. 9413............................. $18.00

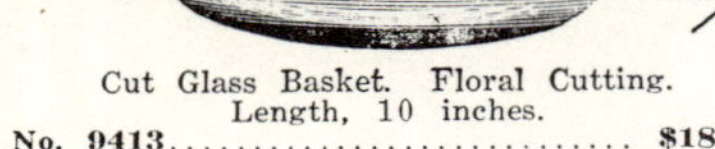

Cut Glass Basket. Full Floral Cutting. Length, 10 inches.
No. 9414............................. $13.50

GENUINE AMERICAN CUT GLASS COMPOTES
PRICE EACH

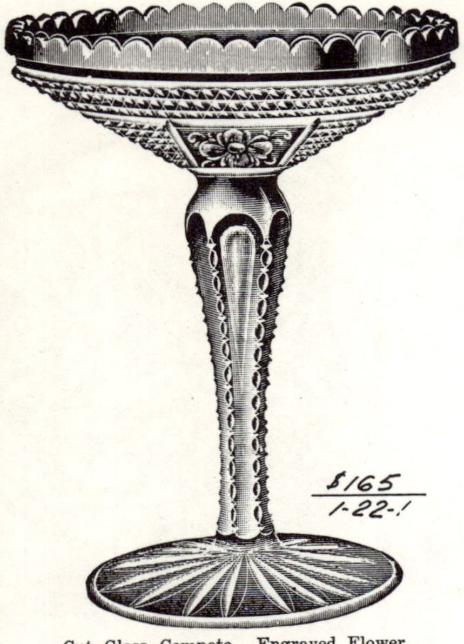

Cut Glass Compote. Engraved Flower.
Diameter, 7 inches.
No. 9415............................ $15.00

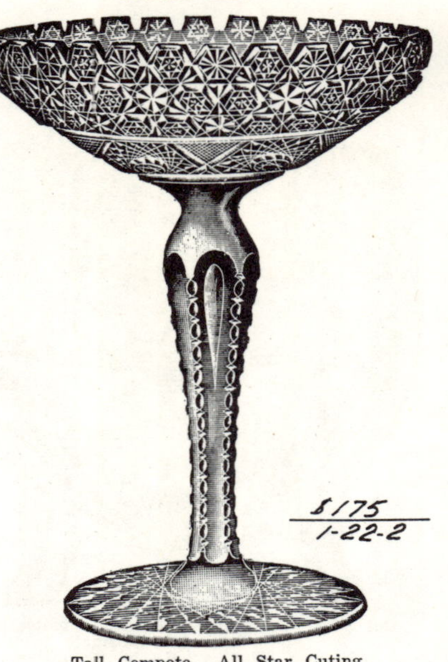

Tall Compote. All Star Cuting.
7-inch Dish.
No. 9416............................ $13.00

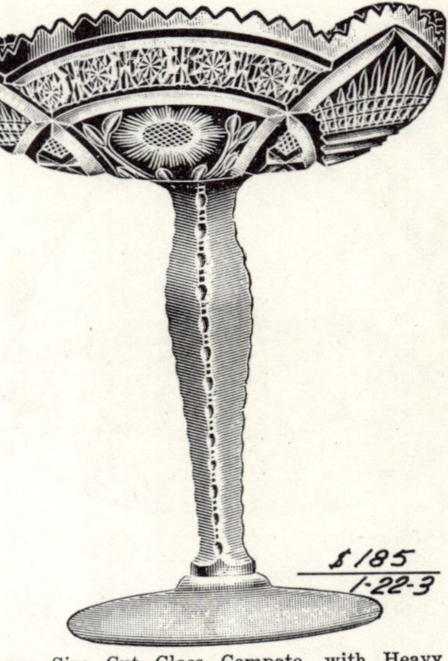

Large Size Cut Glass Compote, with Heavy
Cutting and Engraved Mat Finished
Flower. Height, 11 inches; Bowl, 9 inches.
No. 9417............................ $15.50

Cut Glass Compote. Fine Floral and Mitre
Cutting. Height, 8½ inches. Width
of Bowl, 8 inches.
No. 9418............................ $9.00

Cut Glass Deep Compote. Extra Fine Cutting.
Diameter, 6½ inches.
No. 9419............................ $7.50

Cut Glass Deep Compote. Blackberry
Pattern. Height, 8 inches; Diameter
of Bowl, 6 inches.
No. 9420............................ $9.00

Cut Glass Compote. Fine Combination Floral
and Mitre Cutting. Height, 7 inches.
Diameter of Bowl, 6 inches.
No. 9421............................ $6.00

Cut Glass Deep Compote. Combination Floral
and Mitre Cutting. Height, 8 inches;
Diameter of Bowl, 6 inches.
No. 9422............................ $7.50

Cut Glass Compote. Fine Combination Floral
and Mitre Cutting. Eeight, 7 inches.
Diameter of Bowl, 5 inches.
No. 9423............................ $5.25

Genuine American Cut Glass Compotes

PRICE EACH

Cut Glass Compote. Combination Floral and Mitre Cutting. Height, 8 inches. Diameter, 6 inches.
No. 9424 .... $7.50

Cut Glass Compote. Full Floral Cutting. Height, 8 inches. Diameter, 6 inches.
No. 9425 .... $4.10

Cut Glass Compote. Buzz Star Cutting. Diameter, 6 inches.
No. 9426 .... $4.00

Cut Glass Compote. Combination Floral and Mitre Cutting. Height, 6¼ inches. Diameter of Bowl, 5 inches.
No. 9427 .... $3.75

Cut Glass Compote. Full Floral Cutting. Height, 8 inches; Bowl, 6 inches.
No. 9428 .... $4.00

Cut Glass Compote. Sunflower Floral Cutting. Height, 7 inches. Bowl, 5 inches.
No. 9429 .... $4.50

Cut Glass Compote. Fine Floral Cutting. Diameter 5 inches.
No. 9430 .... $3.75

Cut Glass Compote. Fine Hob Star Cutting. Step Foot. Diameter, 6 Inches
No. 9431 .... $3.50

Cut Glass Compote. Floral Cutting. Height, 6 inches. Bowl, 4½ inches.
No. 9432 .... $2.50

Cut Glass Puff Jar.
Floral Cutting.
Diameter, 4 inches.
No. 9434...$3.75 Each
(See No. 9447 Cologne
to Match)

Cut Glass Hair Receiver.
Floral Cutting.
Diameter, 4 inches.
No. 9435...$3.75 Each

Cut Glass Puff Jar.
Matt Finish Buzz Star.
Diameter, 3½ inches.
No. 9436....$3.60 Each

Cut Glass Hair Receiver.
Matt Finish Buzz Star.
Diameter, 3½ Inches.
See No. 9455 Cologne to
Match.
No. 9437....$3.00 Each

Bureau or Dresser Set. Fine Combination Floral and Mitre Cutting. Set
consists of 10-inch Tray, 5-inch high Hair and Puff
Box, and 8-oz. Cologne Bottle.
No. 9433—Set Complete...$22.00

Cut Glass Glove Box. Beautiful Floral Cutting
with Butterfly on Lid. Length, 9 inches.
Width, 4½ inches.
No. 9438.............................. $15.00

Cut Glass Dresser Set. Floral Engraving. Set
Consists of 9¾-inch Tray, 3¾-inch Puff
Jar and Hair Receiver, Cologne and
Salve Jars.
No. 9439—Complete.................. $22.50

Cut Glass Cologne Bottle.
Fine Buzz Star Cutting.
No. 9440—4 oz.
size $3.00
No. 9441—6 oz.
size 3.75

Cut Glass Cologne Bottle.
Cacapity, 2 Ounces.
Buzz Star Cutting.
No. 9442.........$2.75

Cut Glass Hair Receiver.
Prism Cutting.
No. 9443............$4.00

No. 9444—Salve Box.

No. 9444—Cologne

Cut Glass Dresser Set. Beautiful Floral Cutting. Set Consists of Tray,
Puff Box, Hair Receiver, Cologne and Salve Jar. Tray Is
11½ Inches Long, 8½ Inches Wide. Puff
Jar and Hair Receiver 3½
Inches in Diameter.
No. 9444—Set Complete $24.00

No. 9444—Hair Receiver.

No. 9444—Puff Box.

Crystal Glass Cologne Bottle. Floral Cutting.
No. 9445.........$2.70

Crystal Glass Cologne Bottle. Floral Cutting.
No. 9446.........$2.70

Cut Glass Cologne Bottle. Floral Cutting. 6-oz. Size.
No. 9447.........$4.00

Cut Glass Cologne Bottle. Fine Cutting. Height, 6½ inches.
No. 9448.........$7.50

Cut Glass Cologne Bottle. Floral Cutting. Comes 4 and 6-oz. Size.
No. 9449—4-oz....$3.40
No. 9450—6-oz.... 4.25

Cut Glass Cologne Bottle. Illustration Half Size.
No. 9451.................$4.00

Cut Glass Puff Jar. Buzz Star Cutting. Comes in Two Sizes.
No. 9452—Height, 2¾ Inches.$2.75
No. 9453—Height, 3¾ Inches. 4.50

Cut Glass Covered Bon Bon Dish. Fine Star Cutting. 3-Inch Size.
No. 9454.................$3.50

Cut Glass Cologne Bottle. Mat Finish. Buzz Star Cutting. 6-Ounce Size.
No. 9455.................$3.75

Cut Glass Cologne Bottle. Engraved Blackberry Design. 4-Ounce Size.
No. 9456.................$6.75

Cut Glass Footed Puff Jar and Hair Receiver to Match. Combination Engraved and Mitre Cutting. Diameter, 5½ Inches.
No. 9457—Puff Jar.........$8.25
No. 9458—Hair Receiver...... 8.25

Cut Glass Jewel Case. Hinge Lid. Combination Floral and Mitre Cutting. Comes in Two Sizes.
No. 9459—6 Inch ....$ 9.75
No. 9460—7-Inch 13.50

Cut Glass Cologne Bottle. Engraved Butterfly Design. 8-Ounce Size.
No. 9461.................$7.50

Cut Glass Jewel Case. Floral Cutting. Hinge Lid. Comes in Two Sizes.
No. 9462—6-Inch ....$ 8.25
No. 9463—7-Inch 10.50

Cut Glass Jewel Case. Hinge Top. Engraved Floral Design. Diameter, 7½ Inches.
No. 9464.................$15.00

Cut Glass Puff Jar. Floral Cutting. Diameter, 4½ Inches.
No. 9465.................$5.00
Hair Receiver to Match.
No. 9465½.................$5.00

Cut Glass Water Pitcher or Jug. Extra Fine Buzz Star Cutting. Capacity, Four Pints.

No. 9466.......................... $11.50

$140
1-26-1

Cut Glass Water Set. Eight Pieces. Extra Fine Hob Star and Diamond Cutting. Entirely New. Four-Pint Jug, Six Tumblers and Mirror Tray.

No. 9471—Set, Complete $34.50
No. 9471—Four-Pint Jug, Each 16.50
No. 9471—Tumblers, Each 2.00

$195
1-26-2

$30 EA
1-26-3

Cut Glass Tumbler. Buzz Star Cutting. Height, 3⅞ Inches.

No. 9467................ $1.25 Each

$16
1-26-4

Cut Glass Tumbler. Hob Star and Mitre Cutting. Height, 3⅞ Inches.

No. 9468................ $2.25 Each

$27
1-26-5

Cut Glass Tumbler. Buzz Star and Mitre Cutting. Height, 3⅞ Inches.

No. 9469............. $1.75 Each

$22
1-26-6

Cut Glass Tumbler. Floral Cutting. To Match Jug No. 9472.

No. 9473............. $1.25 Each

$17
1-26-7

Cut Glass Water Set. Eight Pieces. Four-Pint Jug. Six Tumblers and 14-Inch Plateau. Handsome Sunflower Design.

No. 9470—Set, Complete $26.00
No. 9470—Jug, Each 10.50
No. 9470—Tumblers, Each 1.50

$155
1-26-8

$22 EA
1-26-9

Cut Glass Jug or Water Pitcher. Floral Cutting. Capacity, 4 Pints. See Tumbler No. 9473 to Match.

No. 9472.................................. $7.50

$145
1-26-10

Genuine American Cut Glass Water Sets, Jugs and Tumblers

PRICE EACH

Cut Glass Tumbler. Combination Floral and Mitre Cutting. To Match Jug No. 9479.
No. 9480—Each $1.25

Cut Glass Tumbler. Engraved Butterfly Pattern. To Match Jug No. 9477.
No. 9478—Each $2.25

Cut Glass Water Set. Combination Floral and Mitre Cutting. 3-Pint Jug and Six Tumblers.
No. 9474—Per Set $20.00

Cut Glass Water Set. Fine Mat or Grey Finished. Spinning Star. 4-Pint Jug. Six Tumblers and Mirror Plateau.
No. 9475—Per Set $22.00

Cut Glass Jug or Water Pitcher. Engraved Butterfly Design. Capacity, 4 Pints. See Tumbler No. 9478 to Match.
No. 9477—Each $13.50

Cut Glass Jug or Water Pitcher. Combination Floral and Mitre Cutting. Capacity, 4 Pints. See Tumbler No. 9480 to Match.
No. 9479—Each $8.25

Cut Glass Water Set. Combination Floral and Mitre Cutting. 4-Pint Jug and Six Tumblers.
No. 9476—Per Set $18.00

Cut Glass Water Set. Eight Pieces. Four-Pint Jug, Six Tumblers and 14-Inch Plateau.
No. 9481—Set, Complete $23.00

Cut Glass Jug or Water Pitcher.
Combination Floral and Mitre Cutting.
See Tumbler No. 9484 to Match.
Capacity, 4 Pints.
No. 9483................................. $9.75

Cut Glass Tumbler.
Combination Floral and
Mitre Cutting. See
Jug No. 9485 to Match.
No. 9486—Each $2.00

Cut Glass Tumbler.
Flared Top.
Height, 4½ Inches.
No. 9487—Each $1.50

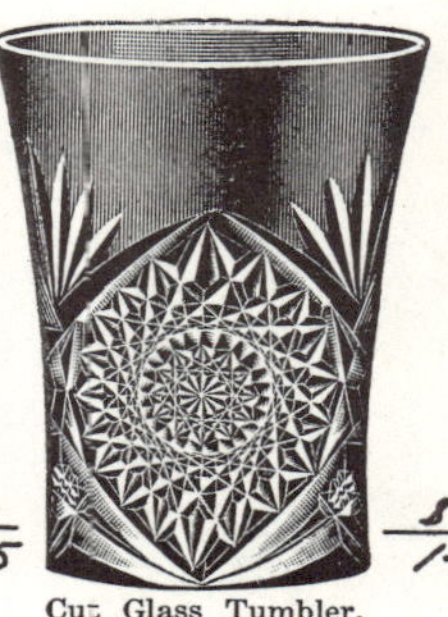

Cut Glass Tumbler.
Flared Top.
Height, 4½ Inches.
No. 9488—Each $1.50

Cut Glass Tumbler.
Hob Star Cutting.
Height, 3⅞ Inches.
No. 9489—Each $1.25

Cut Glass Tumbler.
Combination Floral and
Mitre Cutting.
To Match Jug No. 9483.
No. 9484—Each $1.50

Cut Glass Jug or Water Pitcher.
Combination Floral and Mitre Cutting.
Capacity, 4 Pints.
See Tumbler No. 9486 to Match.
No. 9485........................... $15.00

Cut Glass Water Set. Eight Pieces. Two-Quart Jug, Six Tumblers and 14-Inch Mirror Plateau.
No. 9482—Per Set, Complete $22.00

GENUINE AMERICAN CUT GLASS JUGS AND TUMBLERS

PRICE EACH

Cut Glass Jug or Water Pitcher.
Engraved Blackberry Design.
Capacity, 4 Pints.
No. 9490............................$15.00
See No. 9491 Tumbler to Match.

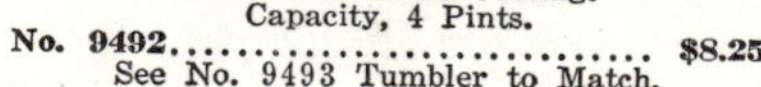

Cut Glass Water Pitcher. Fine Combination
Floral and Mitre Cutting.
Capacity, 4 Pints.
No. 9492............................$8.25
See No. 9493 Tumbler to Match.

Cut Glass Water Pitcher. Fine Combination
Floral and Mitre Cutting.
Capacity, 4 Pints.
No. 9494............................$12.00
See No. 9495 Tumbler to Match.

Cut Glass Tumbler.
Engraved Blackberry Design.
Matches Jug No. 9490.
No. 9491............$3.00

Cut Glass Tumbler.
Combination Floral and
Mitre Cutting.
Matches Pitcher No. 9492.
No. 9493............$1.25

Cut Glass Tumbler.
Fine Combination Floral and
Mitre Cutting.
Matches Pitcher No. 9494.
No. 9495............$1.50

Cut Glass Tumbler.
Fine Combination Floral and
Mitre Cutting.
Matches Jug No. 9497.
No. 9498............$1.50

Cut Glass Tumbler.
Fine Combination Floral and
Mitre Cutting.
Matches Jug No. 9499.
No. 9500............$1.00

Cut Glass Water Pitcher or Jug.
Extra Fine Buzz Star Cutting.
Capacity 4 Pints.
No. 9496............................$7.50

Cut Glass Jug or Water Pitcher.
Combination Floral and Mitre Cutting.
Capacity, 4 Pints.
No. 9497............................$11.00
See Tumbler No. 9498 to Match.

Cut Glass Jug or Water Pitcher.
Combination Floral and Mitre Cutting.
Capacity, 4 Pints.
No. 9499............................$6.00
See Tumbler No. 9500 to Match.

Genuine American Cut Glass Jugs and Tumblers to Match

Cut Glass Water Pitcher. Extra Fine Cutting. 4-Pint Size.
No. 9501—Each $12.00
$140 / 1-30-1

Cut Glass Pitcher or Jug. Fine Hob Star Cutting. 4 Pint Size.
No. 9502—Each $13.00
$155 / 1-30-2

Cut Glass Water Pitcher or Jug. Combination Mitre Cutting and Engraved Wild Rose. 4-Pint Size.
No. 9503—Each $12.00
See Tumbler No. 9508 to Match.
$190 / 1-30-3

Cut Glass Tumbler. Hob Star Cutting. Height, 3⅞ Inches.
No. 9506—Each......$1.50
$18 / 1-30-4

Cut Glass Tumbler. Buzz and Hob Star Cutting. Height, 3⅞ Inches.
No. 9507—Each......$1.50
$18 / 1-30-5

Cut Glass Tumbler. Combination Mitre and Engraved Wild Rose. To Match Jug No. 9503.
No. 9508—Each......$2.00

Cut Glass High Ball Glass. Straight Buzz Star Cutting. Height, 4¼ Inches.
No. 9509—Each......$1.40
$28 / 1-30-6

Cut Glass Tumbler. Buzz Star Cutting.
No. 9510—Each......$0.80
$22 / 1-30-7

$14 / 1-30-

Cut Glass Jug or Water Pitcher. Combination Floral and Mitre Cutting. Capacity, 4 Pints.
No. 9504—Each..................$9.00
$120 / 1-30-9

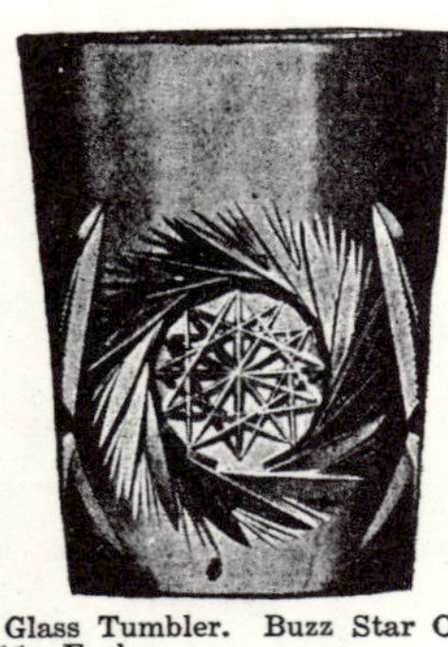

Cut Glass Tumbler. Buzz Star Cutting.
No. 9511—Each $1.00
$13 / 1-30-10

Cut Glass Tumbler to Match Pitcher No. 9505. Buzz Star and Thistle Cutting.
No. 9512—Each $1.10
$14 / 1-30-11

Cut Glass Water Pitcher. Extra Fine Buzz Star and Thistle Cutting. Three-Pint Size.
No. 9505—Each $7.00
See Tumbler No. 9512 to Match.
$100 / 1-30-12

Genuine American Cut Glass Water Sets

Water Set. Eight Pieces. Fine Cutting. Carafe, Six Tumblers and 14-Inch Plateau.
No. 9513—Water Set, Complete $14.50

No. 9514............$10.00 Each
Cut Glass Handle Carafe.
Quart Size. Fine Star Cutting.

Cut Glass Carafe. Extra Fine Hob Star Cutting. Capacity, 2 Pints.
No. 9515........................$6.00 Each

Cut Glass Carafe. Extra Fine Buzz Star Cutting. Capacity, 2 Pints.
No. 9516........................$6.50 Each

Cut Glass Carafe. Fine Hob Star Cutting.
No. 9517........................$7.50 Each

Cut Glass Water Set. Eight Pieces. Fine Buzz Star Cutting. Carafe, with Six Tumblers and Tray.
No. 9518—Set, Complete $16.00

Cut Glass Carafe. Fine Buzz Star Cutting.
No. 9519........................$5.50 Each

GENUINE AMERICAN CUT GLASS LIQUOR SETS

PRICE EACH

$50 / 1-32-1

Genuine American Cut Glass Liquor Glass. Grape Pattern. Engraved Leaves.
No. 9520.........$2.25
See Decanter No. 9521 to Match.

$250 / 1-32-2

Liquor Bottle. Fine Combination Floral and Mitre Cutting. Quart Size.
No. 9522.........$18.00
See No. 9523 Tumbler to Match.

$18 / 1-32-3

Liquor Glass. Fine Combination Floral and Mitre Cutting. Matches Bottle No. 9522.
No. 9523.........$1.50

$175 / 1-32-4

Liquor Bottle. Buzz Star Cutting. Height, including Stopper, 10½ inches.
No. 9524 ... $9.00 Each

$25 / 1-32-5

The Princess. Liquor Glass. Mitre Cutting and Engraved. To Match No. 9526 Decanter.
No. 9525....$2.00 Each

$350 / 1-32-6

Genuine American Cut Glass Decanter. Grape Design. Engraved Leaves. Quart Size.
No. 9521.................$16.50

$175 / 1-32-7

$16 EA / 1-32-8

Cut Glass Liquor Set. Decanter and Six Glasses. Mat Finished Buzz Star, with Mirror Plateau.
No. 9521½—Per Set..............................$22.00

$250 / 1-32-9

The Princess. Decanter. Mitre Cutting and Engraved. One-Quart Size.
No. 9526.................$15.50

$210 / 1-32-10

Cut Glass Decanter. Combination Daisy Cutting. Quart Size.
No. 9527.................$18.50
See No. 9528 Tumbler to Match.

$24 / 1-32-11

Cut Glass Liquor Tumbler. Combination Daisy Cutting.
No. 9528.........$2.25 Each
No. 9527 Decanter to Match.

$18 / 1-32-14

Liquor Glasses. Fine Buzz Star Cutting.
No. 9529.........$1.25 Each
To Match Decanter No. 9530.

$200 / 1-32-12

$22 EA / 1-32-13

Cut Glass Liquor Set. Decanter and Six Glasses, Extra Fine Cutting. With a Mirror Plateau. Height of Decanter Is 11 Inches; Glasses, 2⅝ Inches.
No. 9531—Complete Set $24.50

$180 / 1-32-15

Cut Glass Decanter. Extra Fine Buzz Star Cutting. Quart Size.
No. 9530.................$9.50
See Glass No. 9529 to Match.

Genuine American Cut Glass Ice Tea Set, Ice Tea Tumblers and Assorted Styles of Goblets

PRICE EACH

$50
1-33-1

Cocktail.
Cut Glass Cocktail Glass.
Buzz Star Cutting.
No. 9532.......$2.45 Each

$60
1-33-2

Cut Glass Saucer—
Champagne.
Buzz Star Cutting.
No. 9533.......$2.75 Each

$65
1-33-3

Cut Glass Goblet.
Buzz Star Cutting.
No. 9534......$2.75 Each

$50
1-33-4

Cut Glass Claret.
Buzz Star Cutting.
No. 95|35......$2.45 Each

$50
1-33-5

Cut Glass Wine.
Buzz Star Cutting.
No. 9536.......$2.45 Each

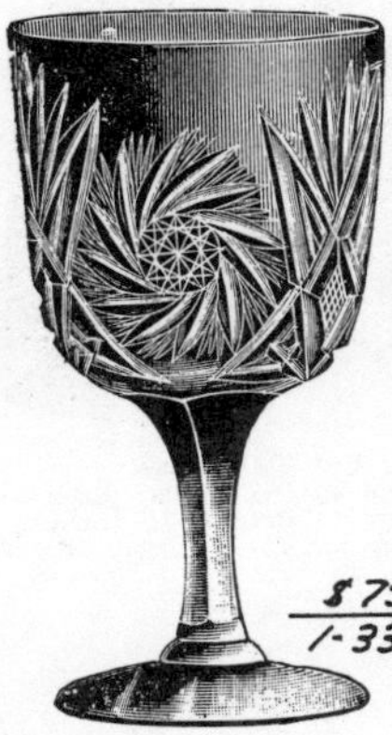

$75
1-33-8

Cut Glass Goblet.
Fine Cutting.
Height, 6 Inches.
No. £537.............$3.00 Each

$75
1-33-6

$12 EA
1-33-7

Cut Glass Ice Tea Set.   Crystal Glass Fern Decoration.   Pitcher, Six
Glasses and Tray.
No. 9539—Per Set $12.75

$50
1-33-9

Cut Glass Wine Glass.
Fine Cutting.
Height About 3 Inches.
No. 9538..............$1.75 Each

$16
1-33-10

Cut Glass Ice Tea Tumbler.
Fine Buzz Star Cutting.
No. 9540...................$1.50

$23
1-33-11

Cut Glass Ice Tea Tumbler.
Combination Floral and Mitre
Cutting.
No. 9541...................$2.25

$17
1-33-12

Cut Glass Ice Tea Tumbler.
Fine Floral Cutting.
No. 9542...................$1.50

$20
1-33-13

Cut Glass Ice Tea Tumbler.
Buzz Star Cutting.
Height, 5½ Inches.
No. 9543...................$1.90

GENUINE AMERICAN CUT GLASS VASES

PRICE EACH

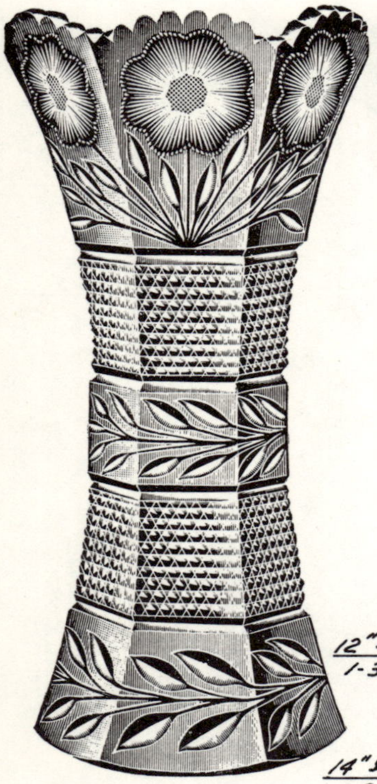

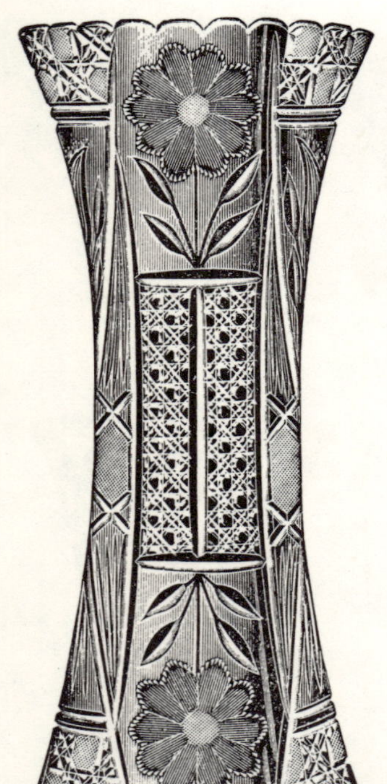

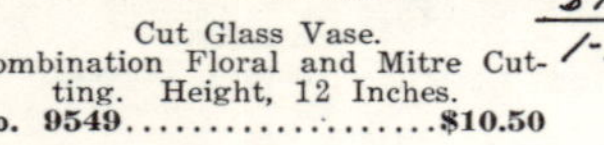

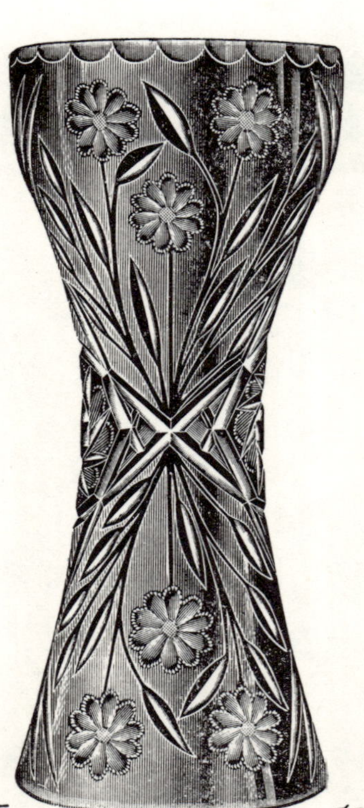

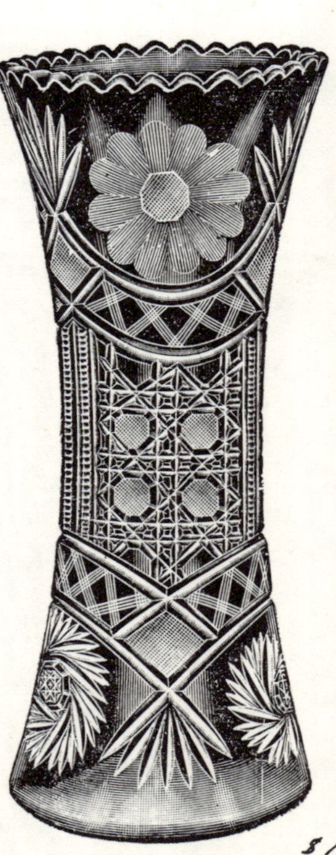

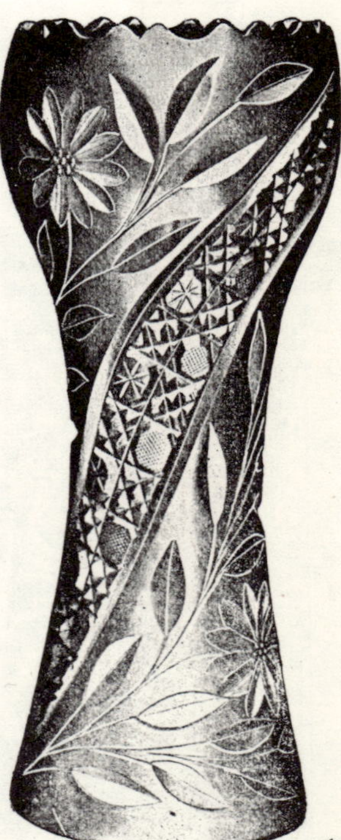

The Princess. Octagon Shaped Vase. Mitre Cutting and Engraved.
Comes in 12 and 14-Inch.
No. 9544—12 Inches.......$20.00
No. 9545—14 Inches....... 29.00

Cut Glass Vase. Engraved Blackberry Design. Height, 12 Inches.
No. 9546.................$22.50

Cut Glass Vase. Combination Floral and Mitre Cutting. Height, 12 Inches.
No. 9547.................$12.00

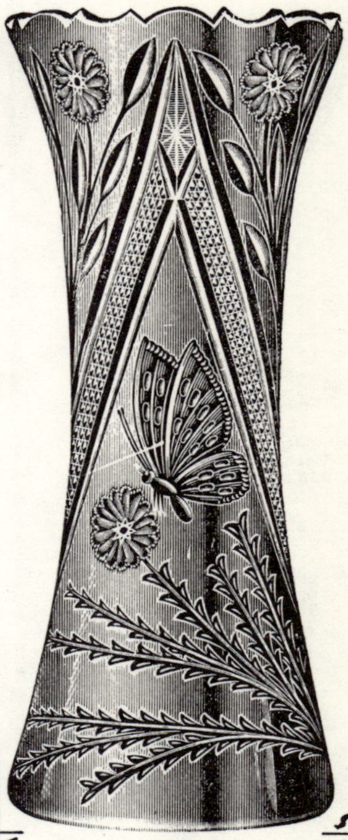

Cut Glass Vase. Floral and Mitre Cutting. Engraved Butterfly. Height, 12 Inches.
No. 9548.................$13.50

Cut Glass Vase. Combination Floral and Mitre Cutting. Height, 12 Inches.
No. 9549.................$10.50

Cut Glass Vase. Floral and Buzz Star Cutting. Height, 12 Inches.
No. 9550.................$7.50

Cut Glass Vase. Floral and Buzz Star Cutting. Height, 12 Inches.
No. 9551.................$10.50

Cut Glass Vase. Combination Floral and Mitre Cutting. Height, 12 Inches.
No. 9552.................$7.00

Cut Glass Vase.
Floral and Mitre Cutting.
Comes in Four Sizes.
Height, 16 Inches.

$40 / 1-35-1
$50 / 1-35-2
$80 / 1-35-3
$110 / 1-35-4

No. 9553— 6-Inch $3.00
No. 9554— 8-Inch 4.50
No. 9555—10-Inch 6.75
No. 9556—12-Inch 9.00

Cut Glass Vase.
All Floral Cutting.
Height, 12 Inches.

$90 / 1-35-5

No. 9557....................$6.75

Cut Glass Vase.
Combination Floral and Mitre Cutting. Height, 12 Inches.

$115 / 1-35-6

No. 9558....................$8.25

Cut Glass Vase.
Fine Buzz Star Cutting.
Height, 12 Inches.

$135 / 1-35-7

No. 9559....................$9.50

Cut Glass Vase.
All Floral Cutting.
Height, 16 Inches.

$160 / 1-35-8

No. 9560....................$11.25

Cut Glass Cylinder Vase.
Floral and Mitre Cutting.
Height, 12 Inches.

$90 / 1-35-9

No. 9561....................$9.00

Cut Glass Vase. Cylinder Shape.
Floral and Star Cutting.
Height, 12 Inches.

$120 / 1-35-10

No. 9562....................$11.00

Cut Glass Cylinder Vase.
Full Floral Cutting.
Height, 12 Inches.

$85 / 1-35-11

No. 9563....................$7.50

GENUINE AMERICAN CUT GLASS VASES

PRICE EACH.

Large Cut Glass Vase.
Floral and Mitre Cutting.
Height, 12 Inches.
No. 9564.................$18.00

$250
1-36-1

Large Cut Glass Vase.
Floral and Mitre Cutting.
Engraved Butterfly.
Height, 12 Inches.
No. 9565.................$24.00

$275
1-36-2

$60
1-36-3

Cut Glass Vase.
Fine Hob Star and Daisy Cutting.
Height, 7 Inches.
No. 9566.................$4.00

$110
1-36-4

Cut Glass Trumpet Shape Vase.
Floral Design.
Height, 12 Inches.
No. 9567.................$6.00

Cut Glass Vase.
Fine Buzz Star Cutting.
Height, 7 Inches.
No. 9568.................$3.50

$
1-36-5

Cut Glass Vase. Fine Floral Design.
Height, 18 Inches
No. 9570.................$16.50

$245
1-36-7

Cut Glass Vase. All Floral Cutting
Trumpet Shape. Height, 6 Inches.
No. 9569.................$2.00

$55
1-36-6

Cut Glass Vase.   Floral Cutting.
Height, 6 Inches.
No. 9571.................$2.25

$40
1-36-8

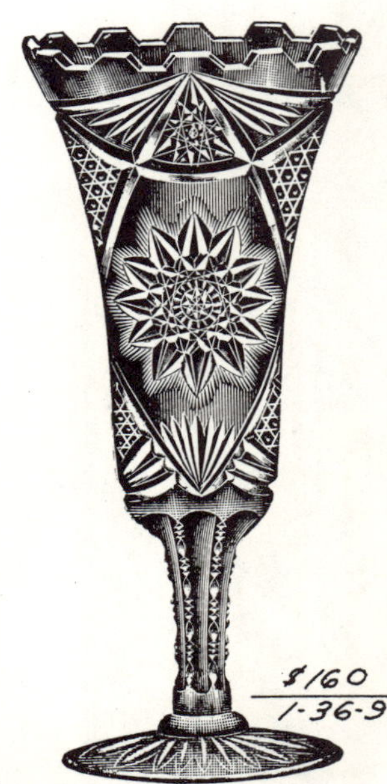

Cut Glass Footed Flower Vase.
Fine Diamond Star Cutting.
Height, 14 Inches.
No. 9572.................$10.50

$160
1-36-9

Cut Glass Bell Shape Vase.
Rich Cutting.
Comes in 8 to 16 Inches.

No.		
No. 9573— 8 Inches		$ 4.00
No. 9574—10 Inches		5.00
No. 9575—12 Inches		7.50
No. 9576—14 Inches		10.50
No. 9577—16 Inches		13.75

$60 8"
1-36-10

$80 10"
1-36-11

$100 12"
1-36-12

$160 14"
1-36-13

$200 16"
1-36-14

PRICE EACH

$70
1-37-1

Cut Glass Fern Dish.
Floral Decoration. Metal Lining.
Diameter, 9 Inches.
No. 9578............................$11.25

$80 8"
1-37-2
$110 10"
1-37-3
$150 12"
1-37-4

Cut Glass Vase. Extra Fine Star and
Hob Nail Cutting.
Comes in Three Sizes.
No. 9583— 8-Inch ....$ 5.00
No. 9584—10-Inch 8.00
No. 9585—12-Inch 11.00

$65
1-37-5

Cut Glass Fern Dish.
Floral Decoration. Metal Lining.
Diameter, 9 Inches.
No. 9579............................$3.75

$20
1-37-7

Cut Glass Toothpick Holder.
Height, 2¾ Inches.
No. 9586............................$2.25

$65
1-37-6

Cut Glass Fern Dish.
Floral and Mitre Cutting.
Diameter, 8 Inches.
No. 9580............................$8.00

$85
1-37-8

Cut Glass Fern Dish.
Floral and Mitre Cutting. Metal Lining.
Diameter, 8 Inches.
No. 9581............................$6.50

$125

Cut Glass Call Bell.
Fine Buzz Star Cutting.
No. 9587............................$3.45

$95
1-37-9

Cut Glass Fern Dish.
Fine Cutting. Metal Lining.
Diameter, 8 Inches.
No. 9582............................$7.50

$110
1-37-10

Crystal Glass Basket. Floral Engraved.
Size, 10 Inches.
No. 9588............................$8.00

$225
1-37-12

Cut Glass Cigar or Tobacco Jar. Extra Fine
Hob Star and Diamond Cutting.
Height, 6 Inches.
No. 9589............................$16.00

Cut Glass Salt Dips, Salt and Pepper Shakers and Cologne Bottles

Cut Glass Individual Salt Dip.
Diameter, 1¾ inches.
No. 9647.........$4.00 Per Dozen

Cut Glass Individual Salt Dip.
Diameter, 1⅛ inches.
No. 9648.........$3.00 Per Dozen

Cut Glass Individual Salt Dip.
Diameter, 1⅛ inches.
No. 9649.........$3.50 Per Dozen

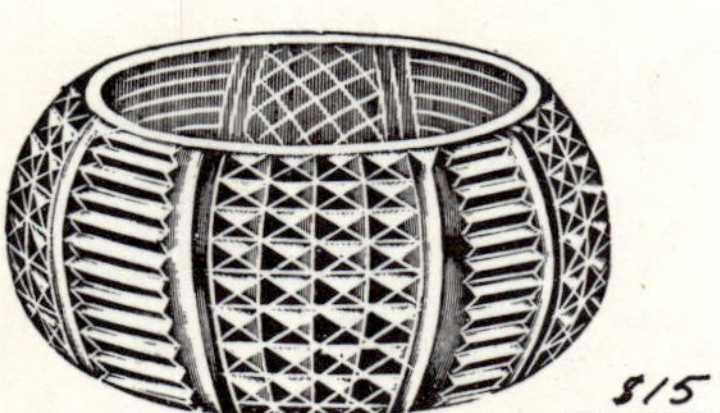

Cut Glass Individual Salt Dip.
Diameter, 2 inches.
No. 9650.........$5.00 Per Dozen

Imported Cut Glass Cologne, Bright
Floral Cutting.   Comes in
4 and 6 ounces.
No. 9652—4-oz.........$2.00 Each
No. 9653—6-oz.........$2.25 Each

Cut Glass Individual Salt Dip.
Plain Finish. Diameter, 1⅞ inches.
No. 9651.........$5.50 Per Dozen

Cut Glass Salt and Pepper
Shakers.   Sterling Silver
Tops.   Height, 3 in.
No. 9654.........$2.75 Per Pair

Cut Glass Salt and Pepper Shaker.
Sterling Silver Tops.
Height, 3¼ inches.
No. 9655.........$2.00 Per Pair

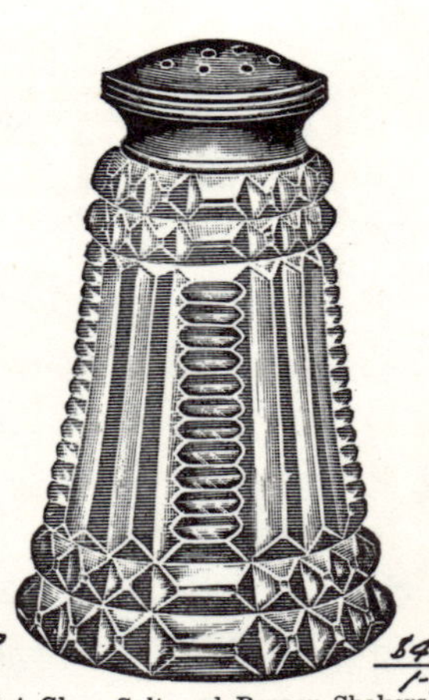

Cut Glass Salt and Pepper Shakers.
Sterling Silver Tops.
Height, 3¼ inches.
No. 9656.........$2.00 Per Pair

Cut Glass   Salt and Pepper
Shakers.   Sterling Silver
Tops.
No. 9657.........$1.75 Per Pair

Cut Glass Salt and Pepper Shakers.
Glass Top.   Sterling Silver
Band. Height, 2⅞ inches.
No. 9658.........$1.25 Per Pair

Cut Glass Salt and Pepper Shakers.
Glass Top.   Sterling Silver
Band. Height, 2¾ inches.
No. 9659.........$1.50 Per Pair

Cut Glass Salt and Pepper Shakers.
Glass Top.   Sterling Silver
Band. Height, 2¾ inches.
No. 9660.........$1.25 Per Pair

Cut Glass Salt and Pepper Shakers.
Glass Top.   Sterling Silver
Band. Height, 2¾ inches.
No. 9661.........$1.50 Per Pair

Cut Glass Puff Jars, Hair Receivers, Mustard Knife Rests and Tooth Pick Holders

PRICE EACH

Glass Puff Jar. Quadruple Silver.
Plated Top. French Grey Finish.
No. 9662 ....$1.50 Each
Hair Receiver to Match.
No. 9663 ....$1.50 Each

Glass Puff Jar. Quadruple
Silver Plated Lid.
French Grey Finish.
No. 9664 ....$1.50 Each
Hair Receiver to Match.
No. 9665 ....$1.50 Each

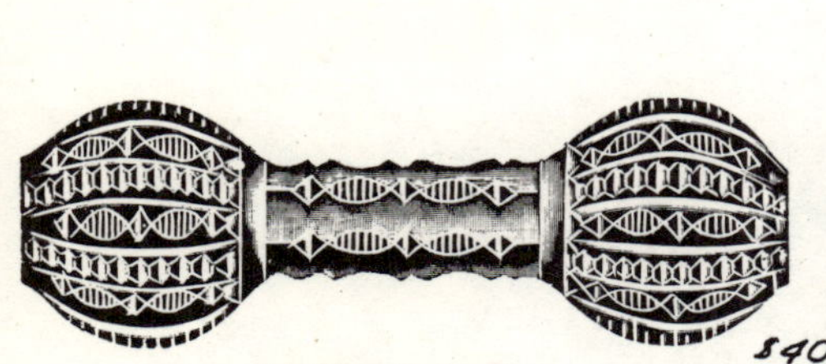

Cut Glass Knife Rest.
No. 9666—4¼ Inches ....$1.25 Each

Cut Glass Mustard, with Lid.
Height, 2½ inches.
No. 9668 .... $1.75

Cut Glass Mustard, with Lid.
Height, 2¾ inches.
No. 9669 .... $1.75

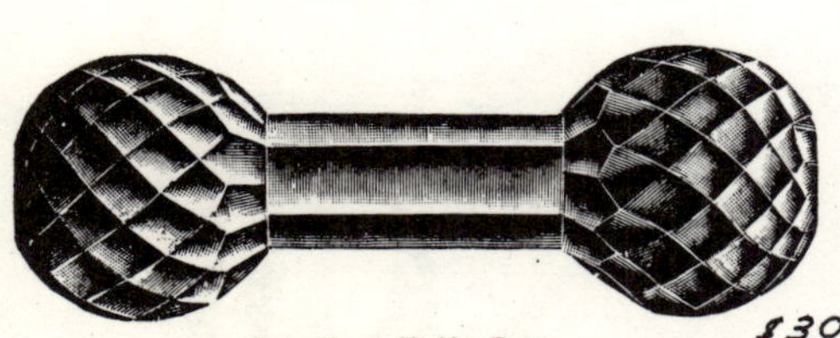

Cut Glass Knife Rest.
No. 9667—3½ inches ....$0.75 Each

Cut Glass Tooth Pick Holder.
Height, 2¾ inches.
No. 9670 .... $0.75

Cut Glass Tooth Pick Holder.
Length, 3¾ inches.
No. 9671 .... $1.25

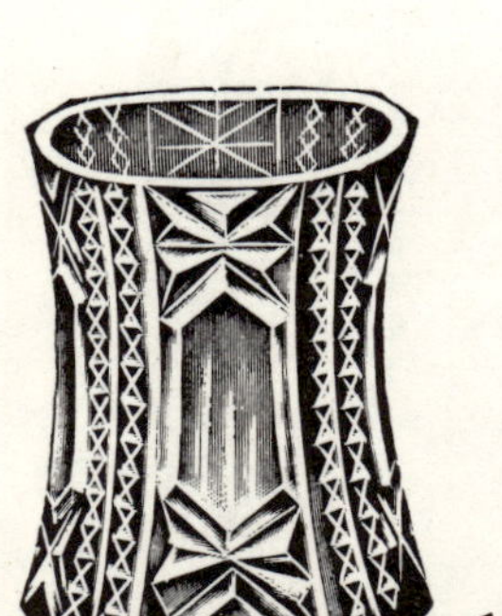

Cut Glass Toothpick Holder.
Illustration ¾ Size.
No. 9672 ....$0.60 Each

Cut Glass Toothpick Holder.
Illustration ¾ Size.
No. 9673 ....$0.68 Each

Tooth Pick Holder. Engraved and
Mitre Cutting. Height, 2 inches.
No. 9674 ....$0.84 Each

Cut Glass Toothpick Holder.
Height, 2¾ inches.
No. 9675 .... $0.80

CUT GLASS ELECTROLIERS

PRICE EACH

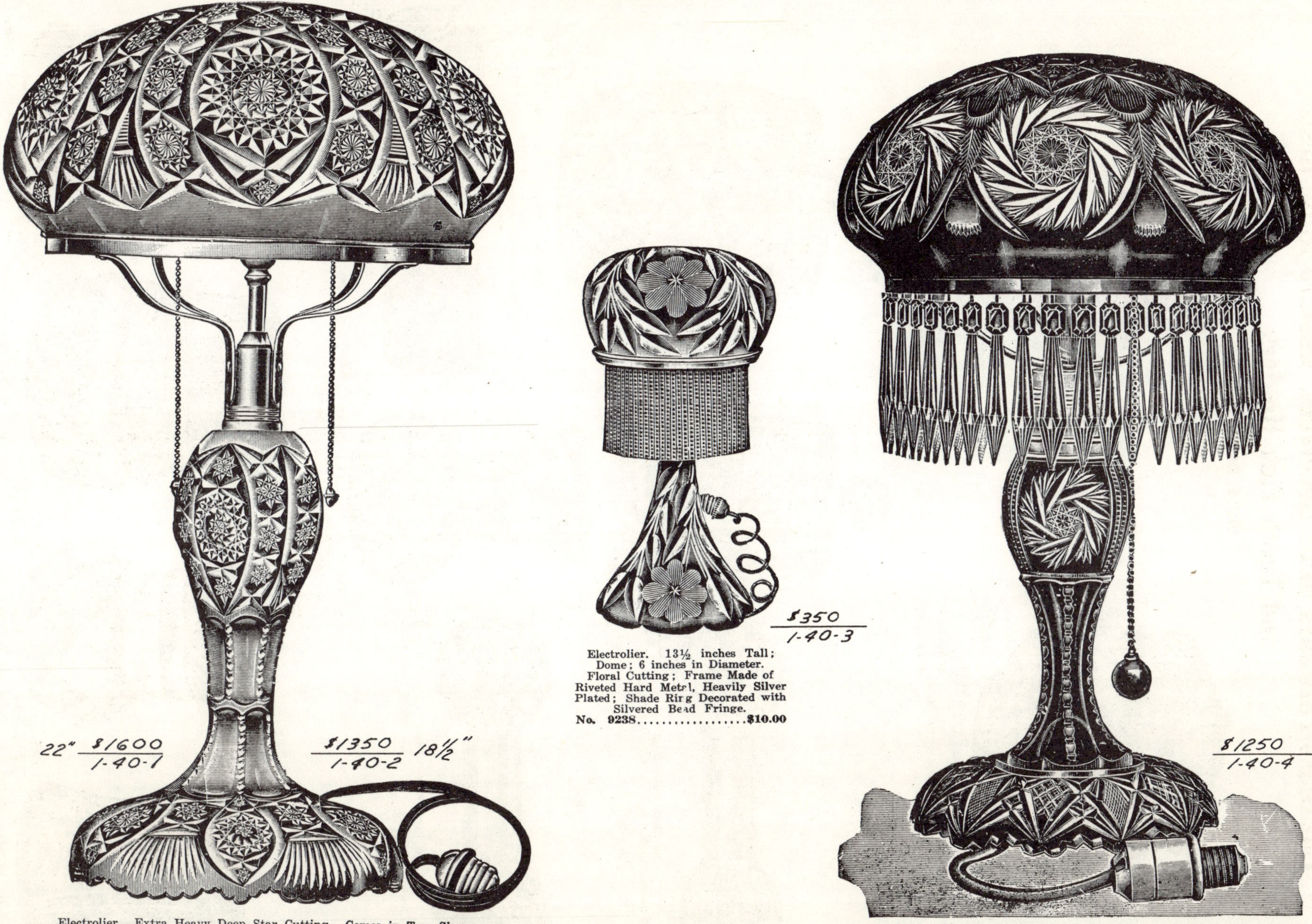

Electrolier. Extra Heavy Deep Star Cutting. Comes in Two Sizes, with Complete Socket.
No. 9236—22 in. high, 12-in. Shade..........................$70.00
No. 9237—18½ in. high, 10-in. Shade............................ 68.00

Electrolier. 13½ inches Tall; Dome; 6 inches in Diameter. Floral Cutting; Frame Made of Riveted Hard Metal, Heavily Silver Plated; Shade Ring Decorated with Silvered Bead Fringe.
No. 9238..................$10.00

Electric Lamp. Cut Glass Shade and Foot. Comes Complete with Socket. Height, 16¾ inches. Diameter of Dome, 10 inches.
No. 9239 ....$45.00

Genuine American Gut Glass Footed Punch Bowls and Sherbet Glasses

PRICE EACH

Cut Glass Footed Punch Bowl. Mitre and Fancy Buzz Star Cutting.
Height, 9¾ inches. Diameter, 10 inches.
No. 9240 ....$21.00

The No-Peg Footed Punch Bowl. Extra Fine Cutting. The Peg
Fitting is Not Used on This Bowl. Instead the Foot is Fitted into
a Groove Cut in the Bottom of Bowl.
This permits the Independent use of both bowl and base.
The latter is used as a Compote or Vase (see illustration). Bowl
comes in 10 and 12 inches in diameter.
No. 9241—10 Inch..$30.00
No. 9242—12 Inch..44.00

Illustration Shows Foot of Bowl No. 9241 as a Compote.

Illustration Shows Bowl No. 9241 Used Independently of Base.

Footed Punch Bowl. Fine Mitre and Hob Star Cutting.
Diameter, 12 inches.
No. 9243 ....$82.50

Cut Glass Footed Sherbet
Cup. Extra Fine Cutting.
To Match Bowl No. 9243.
No. 9245............$4.25

Footed Punch Bowl. Hob Star Cutting.
Diameter, 10 inches.
No. 9244 ....$21.00

Royal Pattern—Very Highest Quality Genuine Cut Glass

American made, real Cut Glass. Made of the purest clear lead potash blanks. This pattern is cut on the very heaviest blanks used for deep cutting, polished and finished with exceptional brilliancy. It is quality throughout, entirely new and exclusive in style of cutting. Guaranteed to please the most critical eye. **ALL PRICES NET.**

ROYAL CUT GLASS COMPOTE

No. **M2110** Royal Compote. Height, 7½ in.; diameter, 5⅞ in. Notched stem and cut bottom. Ea., net..$6.53

$130
1-42-1

ROYAL CUT GLASS OIL BOTTLE

No. **M2108** Royal Oil Bottle. Height, 7 in. Cut stopper and bottom, and cut handle. Each, net $5.51

$110
1-42-2

ROYAL CUT GLASS BOWL

No. **M2104** Royal Bowl. Diameter, 8 in.; 3⅜ in. high. Each, net............$5.73

$155
1-42-3

ROYAL CUT GLASS VASE

No. **M2107** Royal Vase. Height, 12 in. Cut bottom. Ea., net..$14.10

$175
1-42-4

Jug $195
1-42-5

TUMB $30
1-42-6

No. **M2115** Royal Water Set. Set consisting of one 4-pint jug, six 8-ounce tumblers, and 14 in. beveled and beaded edge plateau, silver plated frame. Per set, net.$25.76
No. **M2116** Royal Jug, 4 pint. Each, net.................................11.70
No. **M2117** Royal Tumblers; capacity, 8 ounces. Per set of six, net...........9.64
No. **M2118** Plateau, 14 in. Each, net...5.64

Royal Pattern—Very Highest Quality Genuine Cut Glass

American made, real Cut Glass. Made of the purest clear lead potash blanks. This pattern is cut on the very heaviest blanks used for deep cutting, polished and finished with exceptional brilliancy. It is quality throughout, entirely new and exclusive in style of cutting. Guaranteed to please the most critical eye. **ALL PRICES NET.**

ROYAL CUT GLASS BON BON
No. **M2106** Royal Bon Bon. Length, 6½ in.; width, 5 in. Ea., net...**$2.07**

$65
1-43-1

ROYAL CUT GLASS MAYONNAISE SET
No. **M2114** Royal Mayonnaise Set. Diameter of bowl, 6¼ in., and plate, 7¼ in. Both pieces have cut bottoms. Per set, net....**$5.98**

$180
1-43-2

$75
1-43-3

ROYAL CUT GLASS NAPPY
No. **M2111** Royal Handled Nappy. Diameter, 6 in. Each, net...**$2.73**

ROYAL CUT GLASS SPOON TRAY
No. **M2105** Royal Spoon Tray. Length, 7½ in.; width, 3½ in. Each, net...........**$2.40**

$75
1-43-4

$100
1-43-5

ROYAL CUT GLASS CELERY TRAY
No. **M2113** Royal Celery Tray. Length, 11½ in.; width, 5½ in. Each, net **$4.61**

ROYAL CUT GLASS SUGAR AND CREAMER
No. **M2112** Royal Sugar and Creamer. Sugar bowl measures 6½x2⅞ in., and creamer, 5⅝x3 in. All cut bottom. Per pair, net...**$5.93**

$130
1-43-6

ROYAL FERN DISH
No. **M2109** Royal Fern Dish. Diameter, 8 in. Fitted with a removable silver plated lining. Finest piece of workmanship. It is all over deep cut on the very best quality full potash leaded blanks and has a finish that sparkles like a diamond. Price each, net **$7.52**

$100
1-43-7

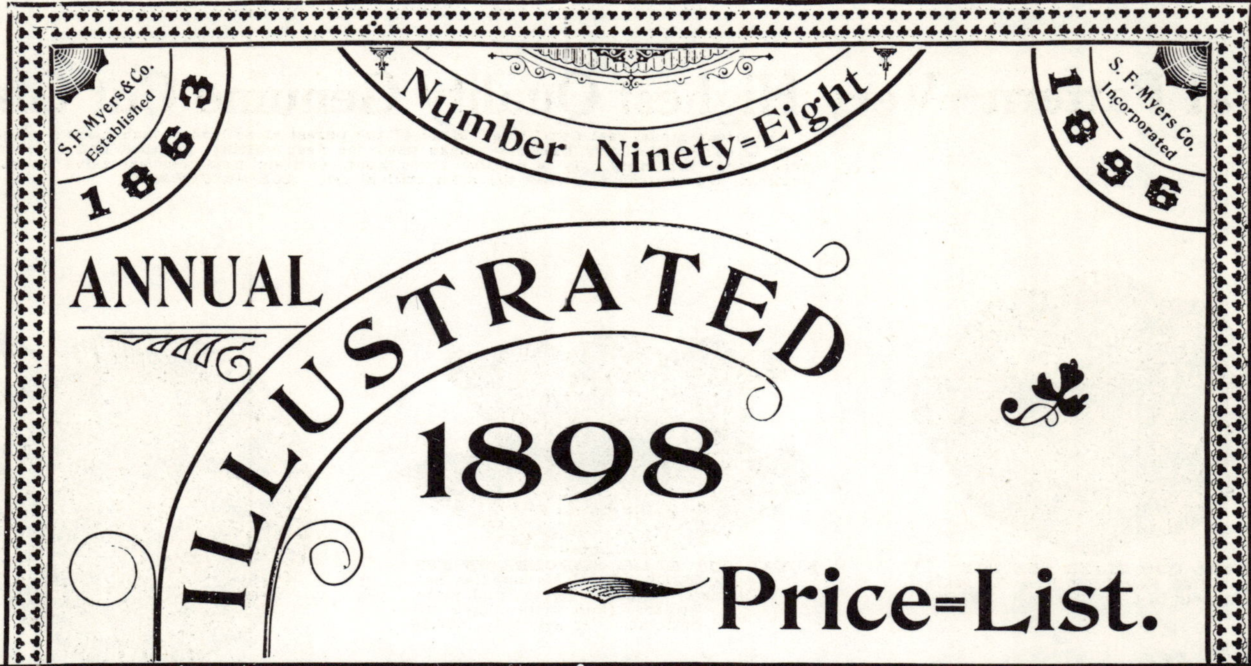

S. F. Myers & Co.
Established
1863
Number Ninety=Eight
S. F. Myers Co.
Incorporated
1896
ANNUAL
ILLUSTRATED
1898
Price=List.

Published by
S. F. Myers Co.

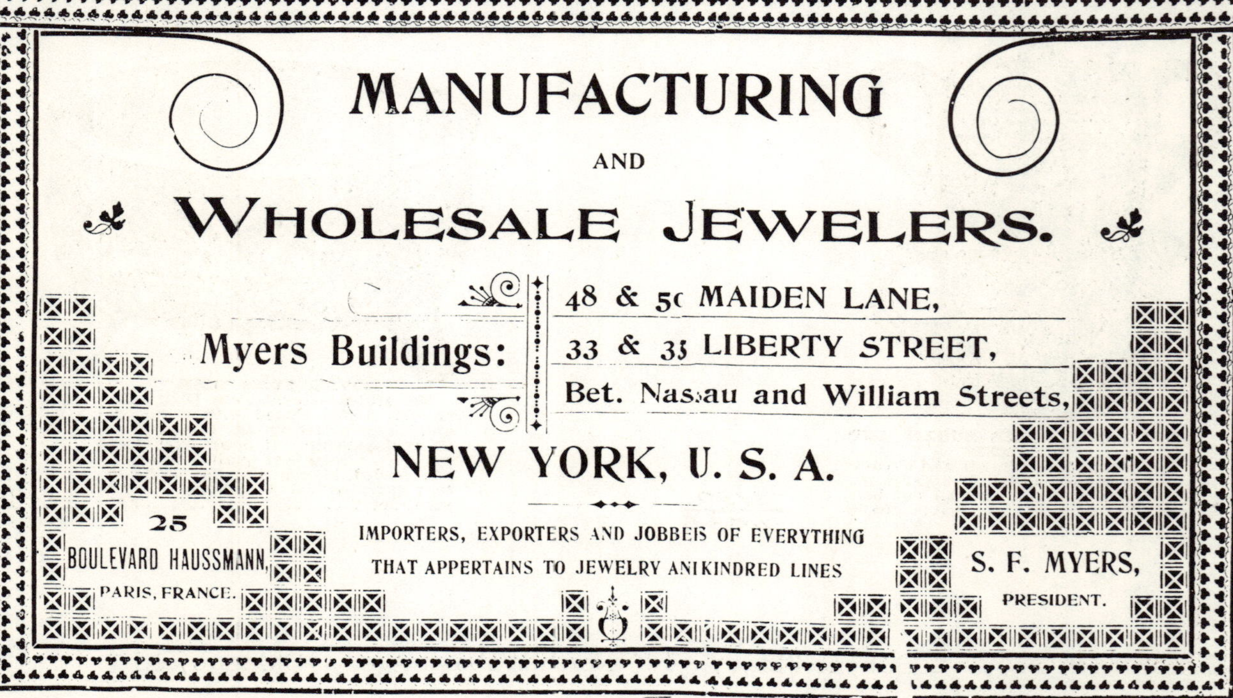

MANUFACTURING
AND
WHOLESALE JEWELERS.
Myers Buildings:
48 & 50 MAIDEN LANE,
33 & 35 LIBERTY STREET,
Bet. Nassau and William Streets,
NEW YORK, U. S. A.
25
BOULEVARD HAUSSMANN,
PARIS, FRANCE.
IMPORTERS, EXPORTERS AND JOBBERS OF EVERYTHING
THAT APPERTAINS TO JEWELRY AND KINDRED LINES
S. F. MYERS,
PRESIDENT.

TO THE TRADE.

Many consumers know that Prices in ███████ catalogues are LIST, and subject to a long discount, usua'ly 5o per cent. To overc██████his fact, and to assure the dealer a fair profit, **The Retail Discount Sheet Annexed** may remain in the book, if desired, *this part being removed.* **The diff rence between 50 per cent and 60 per cent. straight allows a profit of 25 per cent.** besides the cash discounts mentioned.

WHOLESALE

DISCOUNTS AND TERMS.

Every quotation in this Catalogue, No. 98, for 1898, IS A LIST PRICE

...AND SUBJECT TO A UNIFORM...

WHOLESALE OR TRADE DISCOUNT OF

60% Off,

BESIDES THE FOLLOWING DISCOUNTS FOR CASH:

Spot Cash (Cash with order),	10 per cent.
Imm diate Cash (Cash on receipt of goods, **NO TIME**),	10 per cent.
On all C. O. D. shipments,	7 per cent
On all bills paid in 10 days,	6 per cent.
On all bills paid in 30 days,	5 per cent

Our regular open account time limit is 30 days, less 5 per cent. off.

On very active accounts we permit all invoices to average as of the last day of the current month, thus practically allowing on monthly settlements 45 DAYS AVERAGE time, with the 30-day discount, or on semi-monthly settlements the 10-day discount.

Unless arranged otherwise we bill goods on above open account terms.

No new accounts opened, as a rule, unless accompanied by satisfactory business references.

No new accounts opened for less than Three Dollars. Remit cash for smaller orders.

All accounts payable at our office in New York, or subject to draft at maturity.

Remit in New York or London exchange, or add cost of exchange to country checks.

On orders amounting to One Dollar or less we allow no cash discount.

A deposit required on all C. O. D. orders. No orders filled C. O. D. that do not exceed Five Dollars in value. Remit for small amounts. Any excess will be returned with invoice. C. O. D. orders amounting to over Twenty Dollars shipped free of return charges.

A deposit required on all special job orders.

With the exception of silverware we, as a rule, invoice all goods at their net prices, subject to cash discount only.

Do not fail to visit us when convenient. Advise us of any change in address. Address all communications to the company. Order blanks, with or without copying ink, and addressed envelopes free on application.

All our publications prepaid – pay no charges on same. Advise us if contrary.

Do not lose or mislay this discount sheet. No discounts appear in the catalogue.

Respectfully,

S. F. MYERS CO., 48 and 50 Maiden Lane, New York.

Genuine American Cut Glass Ware.

Richly Engraved, Exclusive, Exquisite Designs, Heavy Weights. Made Only for the Best Trade. In All Respects Far Superior to the Many Imitation Foreign Makes. List Prices Each.

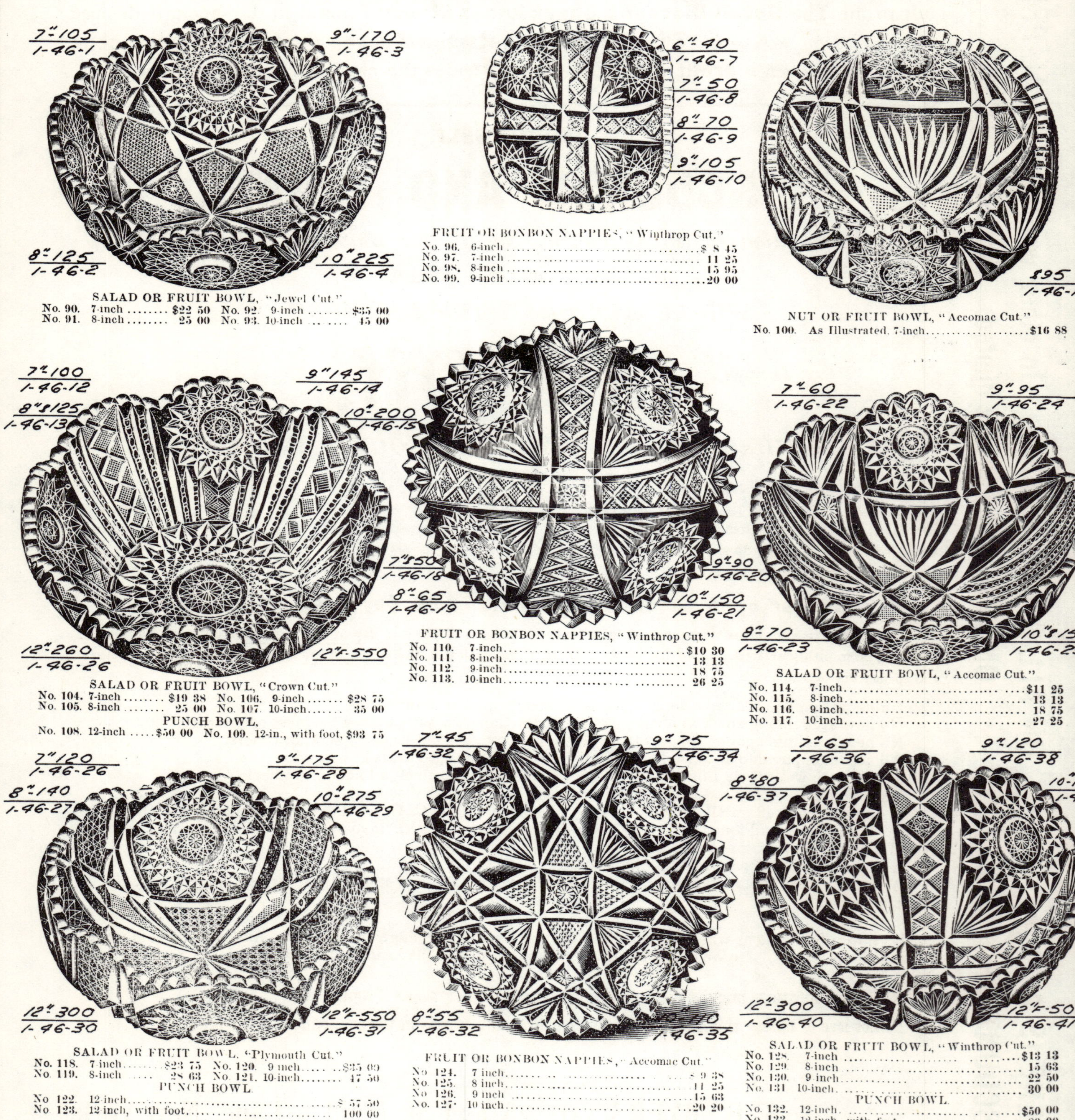

SALAD OR FRUIT BOWL, "Jewel Cut."

No. 90. 7-inch .... $22 50   No. 92. 9-inch $35 00
No. 91. 8-inch .... 25 00   No. 93. 10-inch 45 00

FRUIT OR BONBON NAPPIES, "Winthrop Cut."

No. 96. 6-inch .... $ 8 45
No. 97. 7-inch 11 25
No. 98. 8-inch 15 95
No. 99. 9-inch 20 00

NUT OR FRUIT BOWL, "Accomac Cut."

No. 100. As Illustrated. 7-inch $16 88

SALAD OR FRUIT BOWL, "Crown Cut."

No. 104. 7-inch .... $19 38   No. 106. 9-inch $28 75
No. 105. 8-inch .... 25 00   No. 107. 10-inch 35 00

PUNCH BOWL,

No. 108. 12-inch ..... $50 00   No. 109. 12-in., with foot, $93 75

FRUIT OR BONBON NAPPIES, "Winthrop Cut."

No. 110. 7-inch $10 30
No. 111. 8-inch 13 13
No. 112. 9-inch 18 75
No. 113. 10-inch 26 25

SALAD OR FRUIT BOWL, "Accomac Cut."

No. 114. 7-inch $11 25
No. 115. 8-inch 13 13
No. 116. 9-inch 18 75
No. 117. 10-inch 27 25

SALAD OR FRUIT BOWL, "Plymouth Cut."

No. 118. 7-inch .... $23 75   No. 120. 9-inch $35 00
No. 119. 8-inch .... 28 63   No. 121. 10-inch 47 50

PUNCH BOWL

No. 122. 12-inch .... $ 57 50
No. 123. 12-inch, with foot 100 00

FRUIT OR BONBON NAPPIES, "Accomac Cut."

No. 124. 7-inch .... $ 9 38
No. 125. 8-inch 11 25
No. 126. 9-inch 15 63
No. 127. 10-inch 20 20

SALAD OR FRUIT BOWL, "Winthrop Cut."

No. 128. 7-inch $13 13
No. 129. 8-inch 15 63
No. 130. 9-inch 22 50
No. 131. 10-inch 30 00

PUNCH BOWL

No. 132. 12-inch $50 00
No. 133. 12 inch, with foot 80 00

Genuine American Cut Glass Ware.

Richly Engraved, Exclusive, Exquisite Designs, Heavy Weights. Made Only for the Best Trade.   In all Respects Far Superior to the Many Imitation Foreign Makes.
List Prices Each and Per Set.

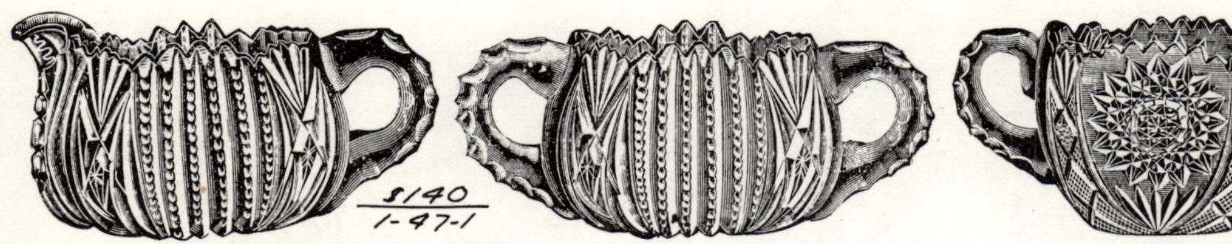

SUGAR AND CREAM SET, "Accomac Cut."
No. 142   As Illustrated.   Per set $18 75

SUGAR AND CREAM SET, "Winthrop Cut."
No. 144   As Illustrated.   Per set $13 75

HANDLE BONBON NAPPY, "Winthrop Cut."
No. 146   As Illustrated.   5 inch $6 58
No. 147   As Illustrated.   6 inch........ .... 7 50

HANDLE NAPPY, "Accomac Cut."
No. 150   As Illustrated.   5 inch $5 63
No. 151   As Illustrated.   6 inch.............. 6 58

JELLY OR ORANGE DISH, "Winthrop Cut."
No. 154   As Illustrated.   Length 9 inch $13 75
No. 155   As Illustrated.   Length 12 inch............ 26 25

OLIVE OR BONBON. "Accomac Cut."
No. 162   As Illustrated.   Length 8½ inch........ $8 75

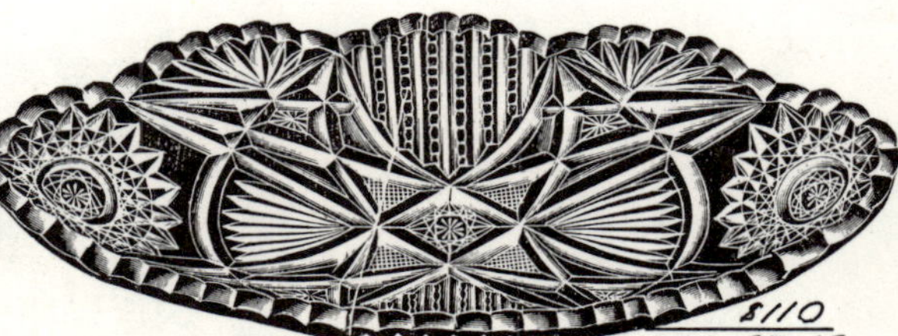
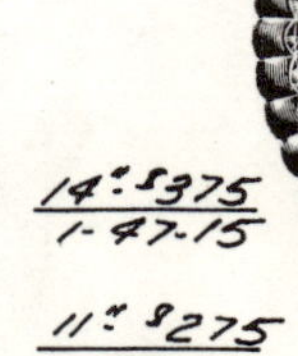

CELERY TRAY, "Accomac Cut."
No. 164   As Illustrated.   Length 11½ inches.....................$11 25

PLATE OR SAUCER, "Montague Cut."
No 158   5 inch $4 38
No. 159   6 inch 5 00

PLATE OR SAUCER, "Accomac Cut."
No. 160   5 inch $4 38
No. 161   6 inch...... .. .. 5 00

ICE CREAM TRAY, "Accomac Cut."
No. 166   Length 14 inches, width 8 inches. $37 50
No. 167   Length 11 inches, width 7 inches.... ...... 27 50

CELERY TRAY, "Winthrop Cut."
No. 168   As Illustrated.   Length 11¼ inches.........................$20 00

ICE CREAM TRAY, "Montague Cut."
No. 170   Length 14 inches, width 8 inches...............$37 50
No. 171   Length 11 inches, width 7 inches........................ 27 50

GENUINE AMERICAN CUT GLASS WARE.

Richly Engraved, Exclusive, Exquisite Designs, Heavy Made, Only for the Best Trade. In all Respects Far Superior to the Many Imitation Foreign Makes.
LIST PRICES EACH AND PER DOZEN.

TUMBLER, "Angelic Cut."
No. 173   Per Doz.. $26 25
Capacity, ½ Pint.

TUMBLER, "Winthrop Cut."
No. 174   Per Doz.. $45 00
Capacity, ½ Pint.

TUMBLER, "Montauk Cut."
No. 175   Per Doz.. $30 00
Capacity, ½ Pint.

TUMBLER, "FAN CUT."
No 172   Per Doz.............$8 13
Capacity, ½ Pint.

WATER PITCHER OR JUG, "Accomac Cut."
No. 176   Capacity, 2 Pints............. $16 88
No. 177   Capacity, 3 Pints............. 21 25
No. 178   Capacity, 4 Pints............. 26 25

ICE TUB WITH HANDLE, "ACCOMAC CUT"
No. 179   As Illustrated.   Bowl, 6 inches diameter $20 00

CLARET JUG, "WINDSOR CUT."
No. 186   Capacity, 3 Pints......... $45 00

CARAFE OR WATER BOTTLE, "Crown Cut."
No. 181   Capacity, 1 Quart..........$16 88

CARAFE OR WATER BOTTLE, "Winthrop Cut."
No. 182   Capacity, 1 Quart......$13 13

TANKARD JUG, "ACCOMAC CUT."
No. 183   Capacity, 2 Pints........... $16 88
No. 184   Capacity, 3 Pints........... 21 25
No. 185   Capacity, 4 Pints........... 26 25

CARAFE OR WATER BOTTLE, "Montauk Cut."
No 189 ....$11 25
Capacity, 1 Quart.

CARAFE OR WATER BOTTLE, "Carmen."
No. 188 ....$7 50
Capacity, 1 Quart.

CARAFE OR WATER BOTTLE, "Angelic Cut."
No 187 ....$7 50
Capacity, 1 Quart.

DECANTER, "Winthrop Cut."
No. 190 ....$23 75
No. 191   Same, with Handle......... 26 25
Capacity, 1 Quart.

Genuine American Cut Glass Ware.

Richly Engraved, Exclusive, Exquisite Designs, Heavy Made, Only for the Best Trade In all Respects Far Superior to the Many Imitation Foreign Makers. List Prices Each and Per Dozen.

VASE, "CARMEN CUT."
No. 199 Height, 7 in. $6 88
No. 200   "   8 in. 9 38
No. 201   "   10 in. 13 13
No. 202   "   12 in. 16 88

CHEESE DISH, "ACCOMAC CUT."
No. 203   With Cover and Plate, $37 50

CALL BELL.
No. 196.........$5 00
Height, 5½ inches.

ROSE GLOBE.
No. 192   6 inches, as Illustrated, $20 00
No. 193   7   " 26 25
No. 194   8   " 33 75

VASE.
No. 53........$6 88
Height, 6¾ inches.

SPOON HOLDER, "CARMEN CUT."
No. 204   As Illustrated, 4½ in $15 00

CREAM PITCHER, "ACCOMAC CUT."
No. 207   Capacity, ½ Pint.....$11 25
No. 208   "   1   " 13 13

SUGAR SIFTER.
33 Chased Top, Cut Glass...$3 75   Each.

NUT OR FRUIT BOWL, "JEWEL CUT."
No. 134   As illustrated, 12 inch. Oval................$35 00

NUT OR FRUIT BOWL, "ACCOMAC CUT."
No. 138   As illustrated, 7 inch, Oval.....................$22 50

SOLID SILVER MOUNTED CUT GLASS WARE.

Pungents and Salts Bottles. Sterling Silver Mountings, Guaranteed 925-1000 Fine. Finest Rich Cut Glass.
LIST PRICES EACH.

No. 2660............$5 00
Cut Glass, Sterling Sil-
ver, Chased Top.

$55
1-50-1

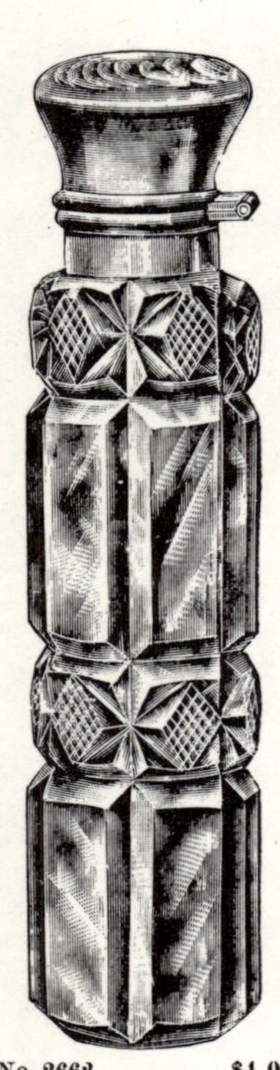

No. 2662............$4 08
Cut Glass, Sterling Sil-
ver, Chased Top.

$45
1-50-2

No. 2664............$2 25
Cut Glass, Sterling Sil-
ver, Chased Top.

$40
1-50-3

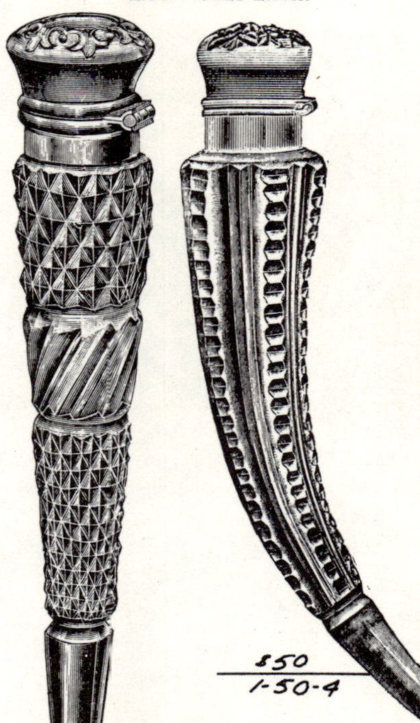

$50
1-50-4

No. 2666............$2 50
Cut Glass, Sterling Sil-
ver, Chased Top.

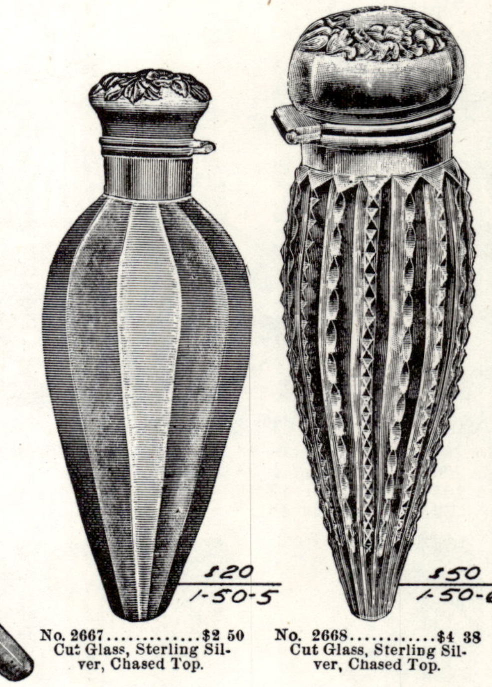

$20
1-50-5

No. 2667............$2 50
Cut Glass, Sterling Sil-
ver, Chased Top.

$50
1-50-6

No. 2668............$4 38
Cut Glass, Sterling Sil-
ver, Chased Top.

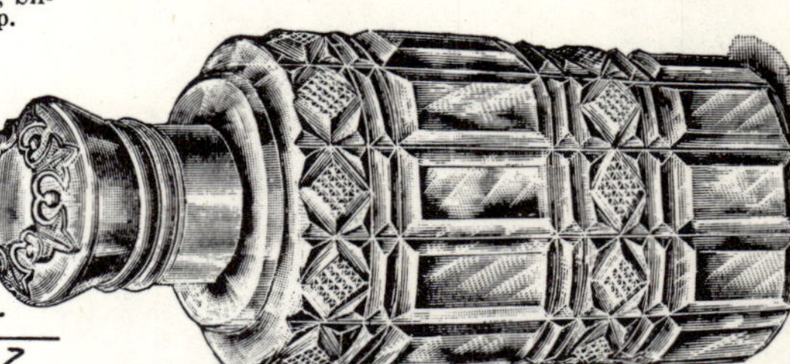

$35
1-50-7

No. 2679   Cut Glass, Sterling Silver, Chased Top................$2 83

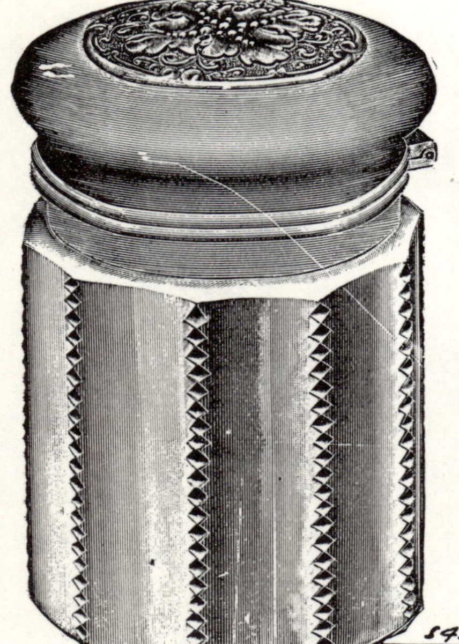

$45
1-50-8

No. 2672.........................$5 95
Cut Glass, Sterling Silver, Chased Top.

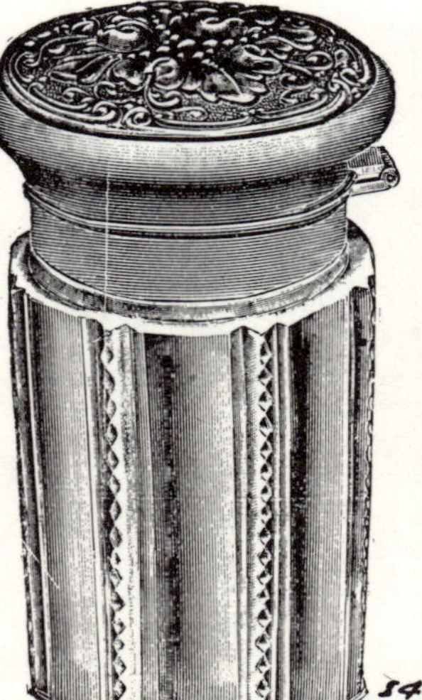

$40
1-50-9

No. 2673.........................$4 38
Cut Glass, Sterling Silver, Chased Top.

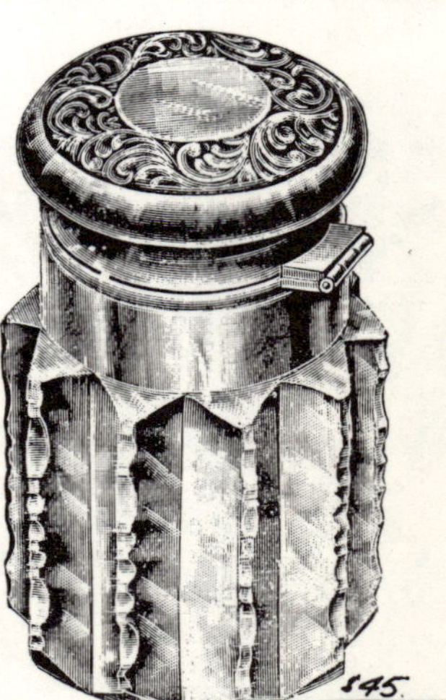

$45
1-50-10

No. 2674............$5 00
Cut Glass, Sterling Silver,
Chased Top.

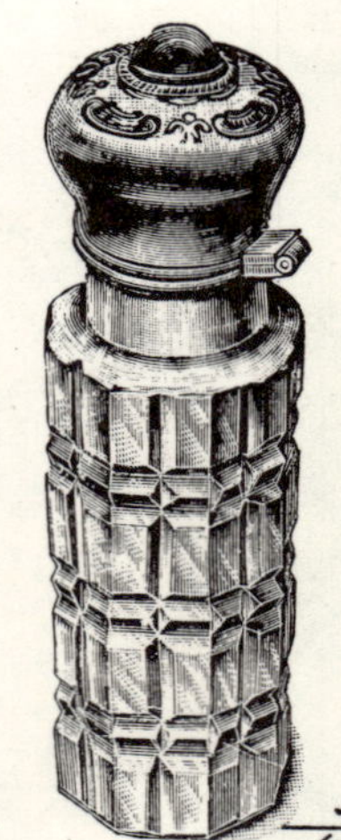

$55
1-50-11

No. 2678............$3 75
Cut Glass, Gilt Top, Ame-
thyst Inlaid.

50

**Ink Wells, Mucilage Bottles,
Fine.**   **Guaranteed Sterling 925-1000**

INK WELL.

$25
1-51-1

No. 2681 . . . . $2 25
Cut Glass, Sterling Silver Chased Top.

$95
1-51-2   INK WELL.

No. 2680 . . . . $5 00
Cut Glass, Sterling Silver Chased Top.

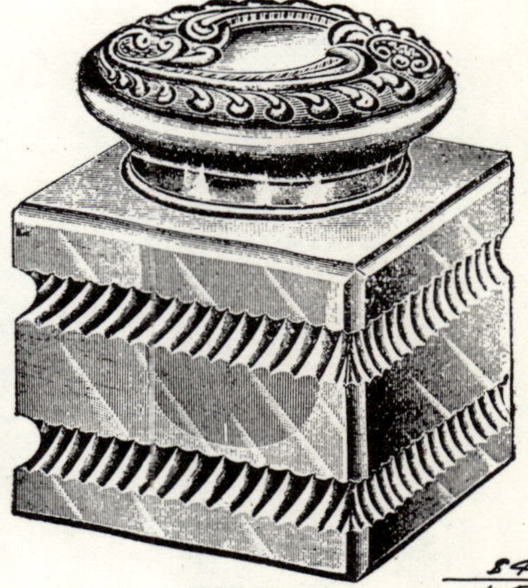

INK WELL. $40
1-51-3

No. 2683 . . . . $3 75
Cut Glass, Sterling Silver Chased Top.

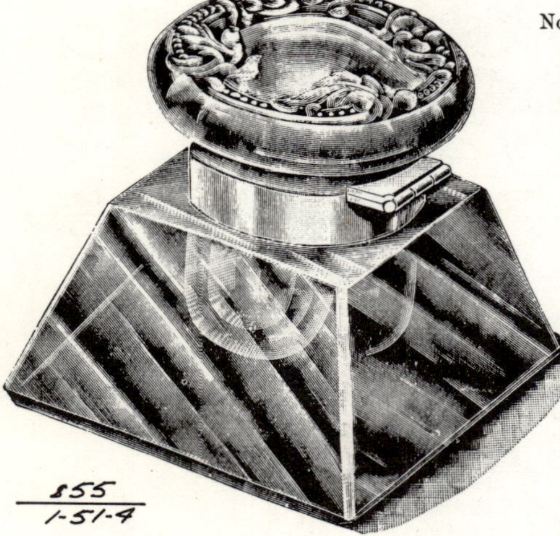

$55
1-51-4

INK WELL.

No. 2686 . . . . $6 88
Cut Glass, Sterling Silver Chased Top.

INK STAND. $55
1-51-5

No. 2684 . . . . $5 63
Cut Glass, Sterling Silver Bead Top.

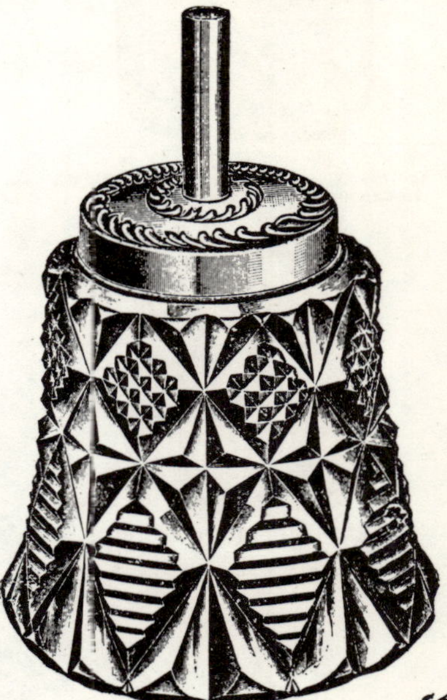

MUCILAGE BOTTLE. $50
1-51-6

No. 2687 . . . . $3 75
Cut Glass, Sterling Silver Chased Top.

VASELINE OR OINTMENT BOX.
No 2702 . . . . $2 83
Fine Cut Glass, Sterling Silver Top.

$30
1-51-7

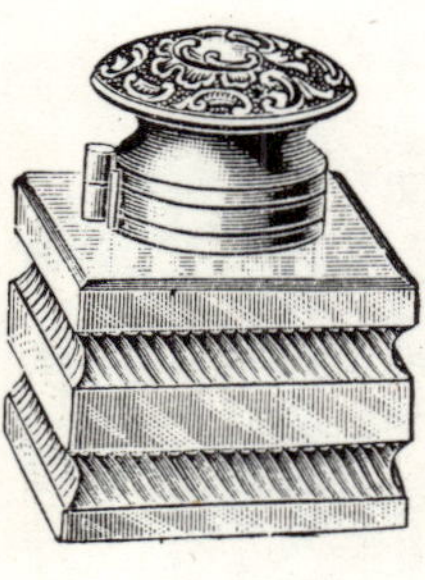

INK STAND.
Chased, Cut Glass Well . . $2 88
Quadruple Plate.
Meriden Britannia Co.

$30
1-51-8

INK STAND.
No. 102 Chased, Cut Glass Well . . $3 13
Quadruple Plate.
Meriden Britannia Co.

$35
1-51-9

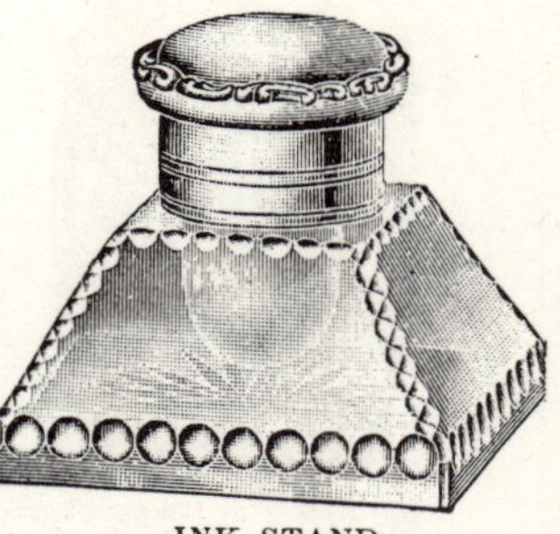

INK STAND.
No. 122 Plain, Cut Glass Well $3 75
Quadruple Plate.
Meriden Britannia Co.

$30
1-51-10

FLASK.
52 Cut Glass, Capacity 2 oz. **$5 63**
Removable Gold Lined Metal Cup.

$60
1-51-1

MUSTARD.
61 Cut Glass..............**$3 13**
Quadruple Plate.
Meriden Britannia Co.

$50
1-51-2

$75
1-51-3

No. FLASK.
2816 4 Inches High....**$5 95**
Cut Glass, Sterling Silver
Top.

SALT SETS.
171 Cut Glass, Per Set..$5 00

$60
1-51-4

VASELINE OR OINTMENT BOX.
No. 2704.....................$0 83
Cut Glass, Sterling Chased Top.

$20
1-51-9

$40
1-51-10

VASELINE OR OINTMENT BOX.
No. 2712...............................$2 83
Fine Cut Glass, Sterling, Gilt Chased Top,
Amethyst inlaid.

No. 288 Cut Glass, Chased Top..........$5 63
Capacity 5 oz.
Quadruple Plate.
Meriden Britannia Co.

$75
1-51-5

No. 276 Cut Glass, Chased Top....$5 63
Capacity 5 oz.
Quadruple Plate.
Meriden Britannia Co.

$75
1-51-6

$40
1-51-7

VASELINE OR OINTMENT BOX.
No. 2705.......................$2 83
Rich Cut Glass, Sterling Silver Chased Top.

$30
1-51-8

VASELINE OR OINTMENT BOX.
No. 2707....................$0 95
Cut Glass, Sterling Silver Chased Top.

Solid Silver Mounted Cut Glass Ware.

Sterling Silver Mountings. Guaranteed Sterling 925-1000 fine. Salts, Syrup Cups, Cologne Bottles, etc. Finest Rich Cut Glass. List Prices Each.

SALT OR PEPPER.
No. 2643.....................$2 20
Cut Glass, Sterling Silver Chased Top.

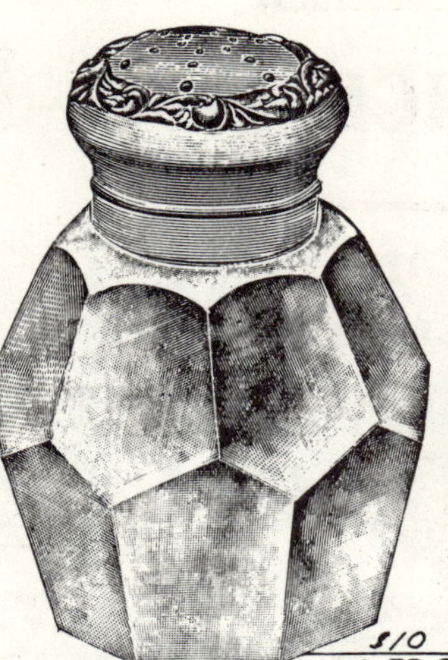

SALT OR PEPPER.
No. 2644.....................$1 58
Cut Glass, Sterling Silver Chased Top.

SALT OR PEPPER.
No. 2645.....................$2 20
Cut Glass, Sterling Silver Chased Top.

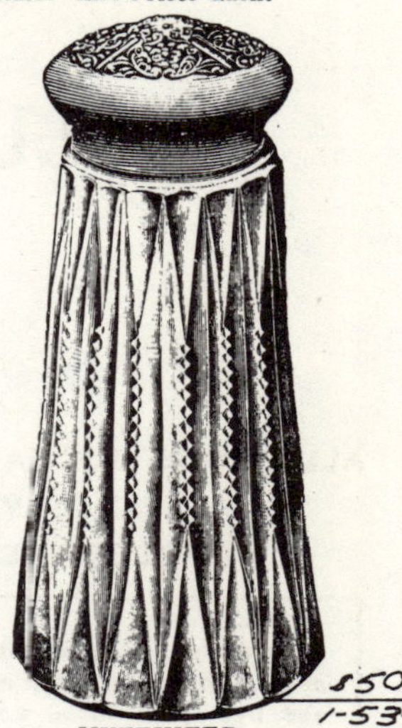

MUFFINEER.
No. 2646.....................$6 88
Cut Glass, Sterling Silver Chased Top.

SUGAR SHAKER.
No. 2647.....................$10 63
Cut Glass, Sterling Silver Chased Top.

SYRUP CUP.
No. 2648.....................$17 50
Cut Glass, Sterling Silver Chased Top.

MUSTARD POT AND SPOON.
No. 2649.....................$10 63
Cut Glass Sterling Silver Chased Top,
Chased Spoon.

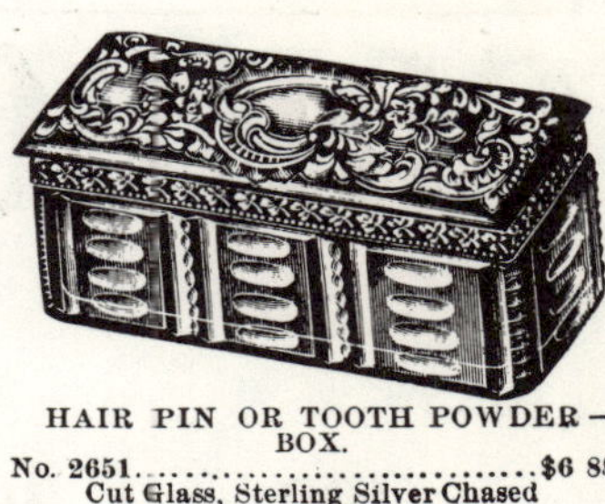

**HAIR PIN OR TOOTH POWDER
BOX.**
No. 2651.....................$6 88
Cut Glass, Sterling Silver Chased
Cover.

TOOTH POWDER BOX.
No. 2650.....................$5 63
Cut Glass, Sterling Silver Chased Top,
Gold lined.   Illustration half size.

COLOGNE BOTTLE.
No. 2652.....................$5 63
Cut Glass, Sterling Silver
Chased Top.
Illustration half size.

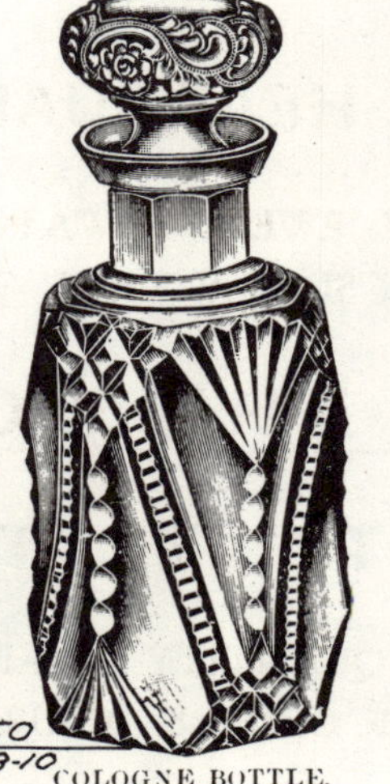

COLOGNE BOTTLE.
No. 2654.....................$8 75
Cut Glass, Sterling Silver
Chased Stopper.

**TOOTH BRUSH
BOTTLE.**
No. 2657.....................$3 75
Cut Glass, Sterling Sil-
ver Chased Top.

COLOGNE BOTTLE.
No. 2659.....................$15 00
Cut Glass, Sterling Silver
Chased Stopper.

Finest Rich American Cut Glass.   First Quality.   Absolutely Guaranteed.   All the Latest Patterns.

Murray Pattern

$65 / 1-55-1

No. 4555. Goblet.
Per doz.............$18 65

$65 / 1-55-2

No. 4556. Champagne.
Per doz...........$15 50

$65 / 1-55-3

No. 4557. Claret.
Per doz.......$13 45

$60 / 1-55-4

No. 4558. Wine.
Per doz.......$12 45

$60 / 1-55-5

No. 4559. Sherry.
Per doz...$12 45

$55 / 1-55-6

No. 4560. Cordial
Per doz... $11.40

$25 / 1-55-7

No. 4561.Whisk'y
Per doz....$9.30

$45 / 1-55-8

No. 4562. Lemonade glass.
Per doz.............$10 35

$25 / 1-55-9

No. 4563. Finger bowl. Doz.$12 45

$18 / 1-55-10

No. 4564. 459 Tumbler.
Per doz.............$6 70

$15 / 1-55-11

No. 4565. Knox Tumbler.
Per doz.............$4 65

$22 / 1-55-12

No. 4566. 458 Tumbler.
Per doz.............$9 30

$70 / 1-55-13

No. 4567. Comport, 6¼ in. Each......$4 15

$70 / 1-55-14

No. 4569. Carafe. Each.................$2 35

4¾ $35 / 1-55-15

5¼ $40 / 1-55-16

Knife rest.
No. 4570. 4¾ inch.
Each $1 00
No. 4571. 5¼ inch.
Each..........$1 15

$80 / 1-55-17

No. 4572½. Carafe. Each.........$2 85

$170 / 1-55-20

No. 4568. Decanter. Murray, 1 quart. Each............$4 15

$120 / 1-55-18

No. 4572. 553 Pitcher, 3 pints. Each.....$4 40

$145 / 1-55-19

No. 4573. 528 Pitcher, 3 pints. Each.........$5 20

Finest Rich American Cut Glass.

FIRST QUALITY.   ABSOLUTELY GUARANTEED.   ALL THE LATEST CUTTINGS.   PRICES EACH.

Albany Sugar.
No. C4537 .... $1 45

Albany Cream.
No. C4538 .... $1 45

Warren Oil.
No. C4530 .... $1 40

914 Catsup Bottle.
No. C4546. Cutting No. 3, $2 70

Lenox Sugar.
No. C4539 .... $1 55

Lenox Cream.
No. C4540 .... $1 55

Barclay Oil.
No. C4531 .... $1 95

608 Sugar.
No. C4041. Cutting No. 129 .... $1 80

628 Cream.
No. C4542. Cutting No. 129 .. $1 80

Diadem Cologne.

No. C4547.	6-oz	$4 15
No. C4548.	9-oz	4 65
No. C4549.	18-oz	5 70
No. C4550.	24-oz	7 00

Revere Celery.
No. C4543. 11½-inch $2 35

Barclay Celery.
No. C4544. 11½-inch $2 85

Lexington Vase.

No. C4532.	8-inch	$1 80
No. C4533.	10-inch	2 35
No. C4534.	12-inch	3 10
No. C4535.	14-inch	4 15
No. C4536.	16-inch	5 45

Milton Ice Cream Tray.
No. C4545. 12x8-inch $5 70

Fulton Vase.

No. C4551.	8-inch	$2 60
No. C4552.	10-inch	3 35
No. C4553.	12-inch	4 15

Finest Rich American Deep Cut Glass.

FIRST QUALITY, ABSOLUTELY GUARANTEED.
ALL THE LATEST PATTERNS.
PRICES EACH.

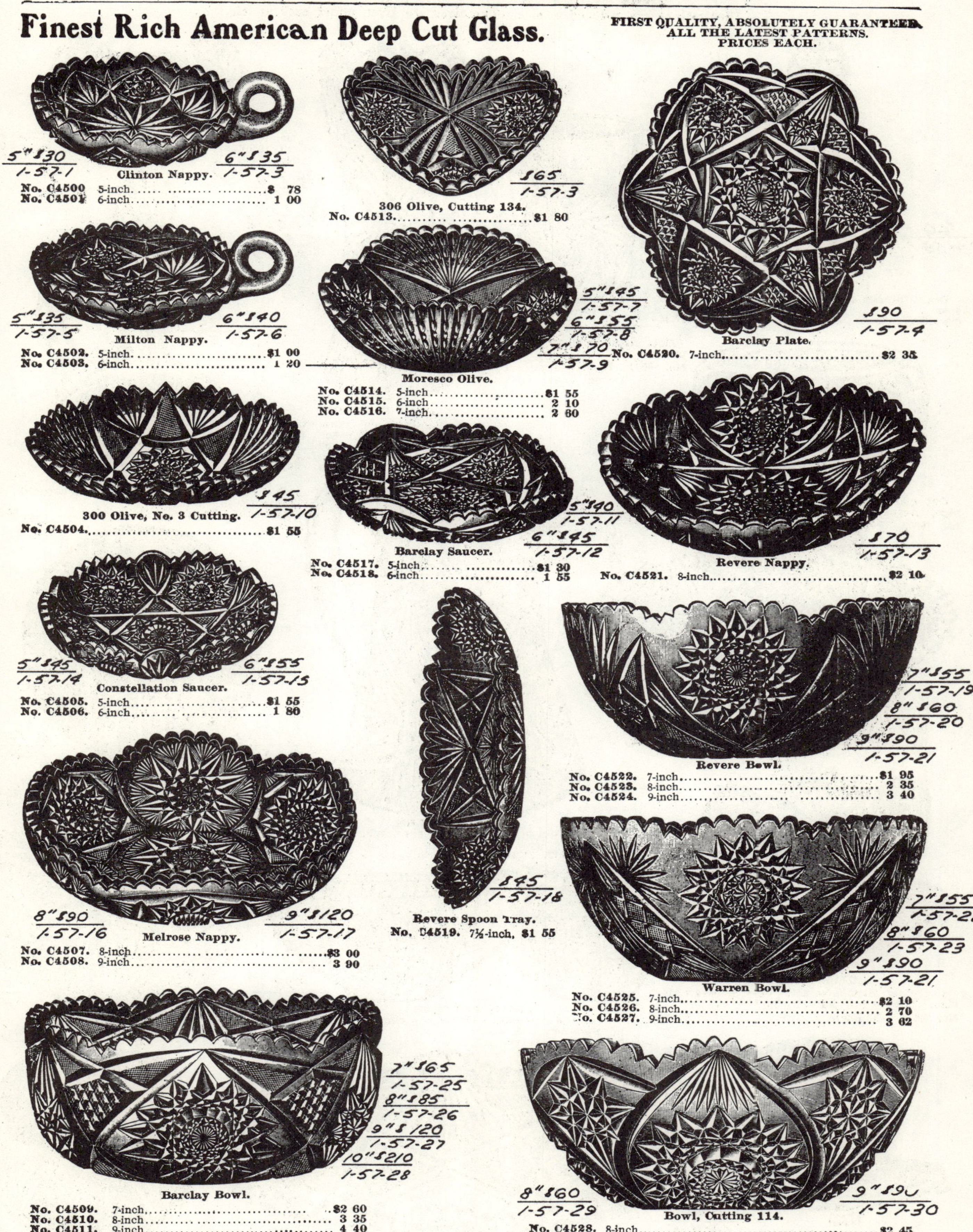

Clinton Nappy.

| No. C4500. | 5-inch | $ 78 |
| No. C4501. | 6-inch | 1 00 |

Milton Nappy.

| No. C4502. | 5-inch | $1 00 |
| No. C4503. | 6-inch | 1 20 |

300 Olive, No. 3 Cutting.

No. C4504. ..... $1 55

Constellation Saucer.

| No. C4505. | 5-inch | $1 55 |
| No. C4506. | 6-inch | 1 80 |

Melrose Nappy.

| No. C4507. | 8-inch | $3 00 |
| No. C4508. | 9-inch | 3 90 |

Barclay Bowl.

No. C4509.	7-inch	$2 60
No. C4510.	8-inch	3 35
No. C4511.	9-inch	4 40
No. C4512.	10-inch	7 25

306 Olive, Cutting 134.

No. C4513. ..... $1 80

Moresco Olive.

No. C4514.	5-inch	$1 55
No. C4515.	6-inch	2 10
No. C4516.	7-inch	2 60

Barclay Saucer.

| No. C4517. | 5-inch | $1 30 |
| No. C4518. | 6-inch | 1 55 |

Revere Spoon Tray.
No. C4519. 7½-inch, $1 55

Barclay Plate.

No. C4520. 7-inch $2 35

Revere Nappy.

No. C4521. 8-inch $2 10

Revere Bowl.

No. C4522.	7-inch	$1 95
No. C4523.	8-inch	2 35
No. C4524.	9-inch	3 40

Warren Bowl.

No. C4525.	7-inch	$2 10
No. C4526.	8-inch	2 70
No. C4527.	9-inch	3 62

Bowl, Cutting 114.

| No. C4528. | 8-inch | $2 45 |
| No. C4529. | 9-inch | 3 50 |

Very Fine Quality Cut Glassware

Illustrations are reduced in size. The sizes are given under each article.

LOTUS PATTERN

Beautiful cut glass cologne bottle, capacity, 4 oz.
No. 16600. Each............................$7.34

LOTUS PATTERN

Cut glass tumblers, capacity ½ pint.
No. 16601. Each..............$ 2.68
Dozen 36.00

LOTUS PATTERN

Beautiful cut glass knife rest.
No. 16606. 3⅜ in. long......................$1.34
No. 16607. 3⅞ in. long.......................2.00
No. 16608. 4¼ in. long ..-......................2.68

LOTUS PATTERN

Very elabtorate cut glass vase.
No. 16602. 8 in. high, each..$ 9.34
No. 16603. 10 in. high, each.. 12.68
No. 16604. 12 in. high, each.. 20.68
No. 16605. 14 in. high, each.. 29.34

LOTUS PATTERN

Very beautiful cut glass cruet; capacity, ½ pint; 6½ in. high.
No. 16610. Each $6.68

LOTUS PATTERN

Cut glass oval salt dip dish. Beautiful design. Actual size.
No. 16609. Per dozen......................$7.34

LOTUS PATTERN

Very beautiful cut glass spoon tray, 7¾ in. long by 3¼ in. wide.
No. 16611. Each $4.40

LOTUS PATTERN

Very elaborate cut glass saucer or nappy.
No. 16613. 5 in., each.................$2.68
No. 16614 6 in., each 3.34

LOTUS PATTERN

Beautiful design water pitcher; capacity three pints.
No. 16612. Each $10.68

LOTUS PATTERN

Cut glass Mayonaise set. Very elaborate design. Bowl 4 in.; plate 4½ in.
No. 16615. Complete $10.68

LOTUS PATTERN

Beautiful cut glass sugar and cream set.; 3¼ in. diameter; 3 in. high.
No. 16616. Per set $7.34

LOTUS PATTERN

Very fine cut glass berry or fruit bowl.
No. 16617. 8 in., each $8.00

LOTUS PATTERN

Very fine cut glass violet ball and plateau. Ball 3½ in.; plateau 5 in.
No. 16618. Complete $7.34

LOTUS PATTERN

Elaborate pattern cut glass celery tray; 11½ in. long and 4½ in. wide.
No. 16619. Each $6.68

LOTUS PATTERN

Very beautiful cut glass pun box.
No. 16620. 4½ in., each $9.34

Finest Quality Cut Glass. Beautiful New Designs

PRICES EACH AND PER DOZEN.

TILSON PATTERN.

Very elaborate pattern puff box. Size 5 in.
No. 16700. Price $6.00

7" $75 / 1-59-2
8" $85 / 1-59-3
9" $95 / 1-59-4
10" $125 / 1-59-5

GOLF PATTERN.

Very fine cut glass bowl.
No. 16701. 7 in., price ....$ 7.34
No. 16702. 8 in., price 9.34
No. 16703. 9 in., price 12.00
No. 16704. 10 in., price 20.68

5" $40 / 1-59-6
6" $45 / 1-59-7

RYE PATTERN

Beautiful cut glass saucer.
No. 16705. 5 in., price $3.34
No. 16706. 6 in., price 4.00

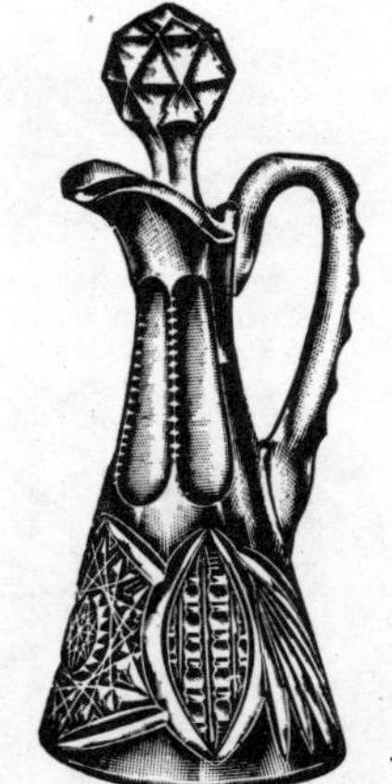

$75 / 1-59-8

CROWN PATTERN.

Very beautiful cut glass cruet; capacity, ½ pint.
No. 16707. Price $4.68

7" $95 / 1-59-9
8" $125 / 1-59-10
9" $150 / 1-59-11
10" $170 / 1-59-12

CROWN PATTERN.

Very elaborate cut glass bowl.
No. 16708. 7 in., price ....$ 6.68
No. 16709. 8 in., price 8.00
No. 16710. 9 in., price 10.68
No. 16711. 10 in., price 20.00

$65 / 1-59-13

ITHACA PATTERN.

Beautiful cut glass goblet.
No. 16712. Each ....$ 3.34
Dozen 34.00

ITHACA PATTERN $50 / 1-59-14

Beautiful pattern wine glasses.
No. 16713. Each ....$ 2.54
Dozen 24.00

$95 / 1-59-15

GOLF PATTERN

Sugar and cream set. Very elaborate design.
No. 16714. Per set $9.34

LATONIA PATTERN $35 / 1-59-16

Cut glass tooth pick holder.
No. 16715. Each $3.34

$55 / 1-59-17

ROSE PATTERN

Beautiful cut glass comport. Size 4¾ by 4¾.
No. 16716. Each $4.40

$150 / 1-59-18

LARERTES PATTERN

Beautiful cut glass sugar and cream set.
No. 16717. Per set $14.00

$16 / 1-59-19

ROME PATTERN

Cut glass tumblers.
No. 16718. Each ....$ 1.34
Dozen 14.00

Finest Quality Cut Glass
Beautiful Designs.   Highly Polished.

1911

5" $25
1-60-1
6" $35
1-60-2

DON PATTERN
Beautiful cut glass Saucer.
No. 16800.   5-inch, price $4.40
No. 16801.   6-inch, price 5.34

6" $60
1-60-3
7" $70
1-60-4
8" $85
1-60-5
9" $105
1-60-6
10" $130
1-60-7

HEBE PATTERN
Very beautiful design Sandwich Plate.
No. 16802.   6-inch, price .... $ 5.34
No. 16803.   7-inch, price 6.68
No. 16804.   8-inch, price 8.68
No. 16805.   9-inch, price 10.00
No. 16806.   10-inch, price 12.00

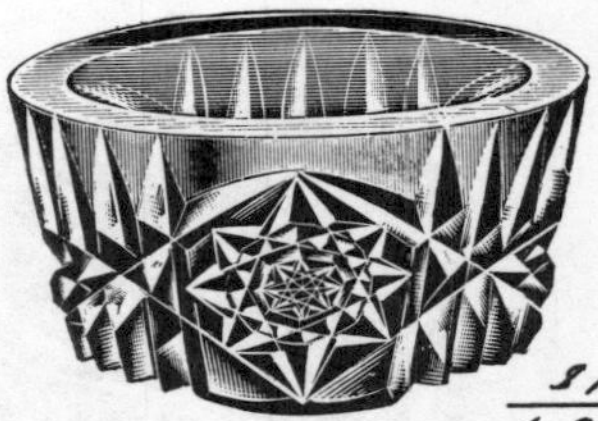

$12
1-60-8

VELMA PATTERN
Beautiful cut glass Open Salt Dish.
No. 16807.   Each .... $ 1.74
Dozen 18.68

$65
1-60-9

MURRAY PATTERN
Very elaborate design cut glass Olive Dish.
No. 16812.   7½-inch, price $4.40

7" $50
1-60-10
8" $60
1-60-11
9" $70
1-60-12
10" $90
1-60-13

CROWN PATTERN
Very elaborate pattern Nappy Dish.
No. 16808.   7-inch, price .... $ 5.34
No. 16809.   8-inch, price 7.34
No. 16810.   9-inch, price 8.68
No. 16811.   10-inch, price 12.68

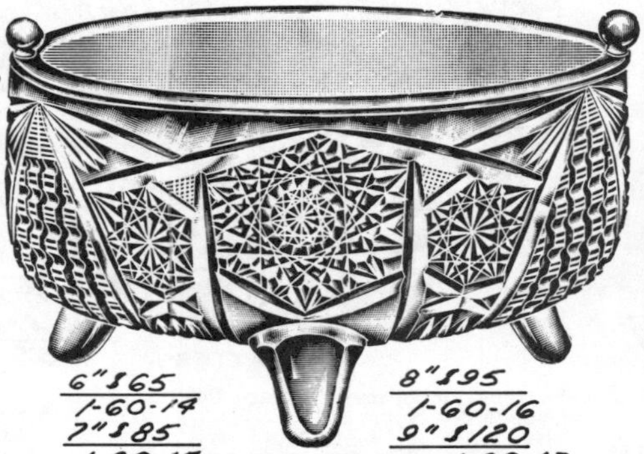

6" $65
1-60-14
7" $85
1-60-15
8" $95
1-60-16
9" $120
1-60-17

CROWN PATTERN
Very fine cut glass Fern Dish.   Has separate silver lining and stands on square legs.
No. 16814.   6-inch, price .... $ 8.68
No. 16815.   7-inch, price 10.68
No. 16816.   8-inch, price 12.00
No. 16817.   9-inch, price 18.68

$85
1-60-18

HUNTER PATTERN
Very elaborate cut glass Bowl.
No. 16818.   8-inch, price $7.34

$50
1-60-29

CROWN PATTERN
Very beautiful cut glass Spoon Tray.   Size 8 by 4 inches.
No. 16813.   Each $4.68

6" $65
1-60-19
8" $75
1-60-20
10" $85
1-60-21
12" $95
1-60-22

CLEO PATTERN
Very elaborate cut glass Vase.
No. 16819.   6-inch, price .... $ 6.68
No. 16820.   8-inch, price 8.68
No. 16821.   10-inch, price 12.68
No. 16822.   12-inch, price 20.68
No. 16823.   14-inch, price 30.68

$16 EA
1-60-24
$80
1-60-23

ROME PATTERN
Beautiful pattern Water Set, consisting of:
One No. 16824   1 qt. Rome pattern Carafe.. $7.34
Six No. 16825   7 oz. Rome pattern Tumblers 7.34
One No. 16826   14 in. Plain pattern Plateau.. 18.68

6" $50
1-60-24
8" $60
1-60-25
10" $70
1-60-26
12" $80
1-60-27
14" $90
1-60-28

PALM PATTERN
Beautiful pattern cut glass Vase.
No. 16827.   6-inch, price .... $ 4.68
No. 16828.   8-inch, price 5.34
No. 16829.   10-inch, price 7.34
No. 16830.   12-inch, price 9.34
No. 16831.   14-inch, price 12.68

Very Fine Quality Cut Glassware

Illustrations are reduced in size. The sizes are given under each article.

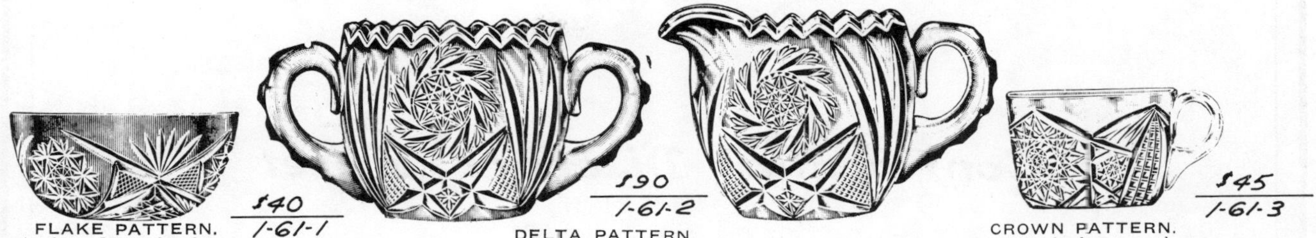

FLAKE PATTERN.
Beautiful cut glass finger bowl.
No. 16900. Price, each.....................$ 2.68
, per doz...........................26.00

$40
1-61-1

DELTA PATTERN.
Sugar and Cream Set. Very elaborate design.
No. 16901. Price, per set...................$6.68

$90
1-61-2

CROWN PATTERN.
Beautiful pattern cut glass punch cup.
No. 16902. Each.......................$ 2.40
Dozen 23.34

$45
1-61-3

SAVOY PATTERN.
glass Syrup Jug with fine silver plated
ver. Capacity, ½ pint.
16903. Price...........................$8.00

$100
1-61-4

MAPLE PATTERN.
Beautiful cut glass Sugar and Cream Set.
No. 16904. Price, per set..................$6.00

$80
1-61-5

HERMES PATTERN.
Very beautiful cut glass Cruet.
No. 16905. Each............................$4.40

$75
1-61-6

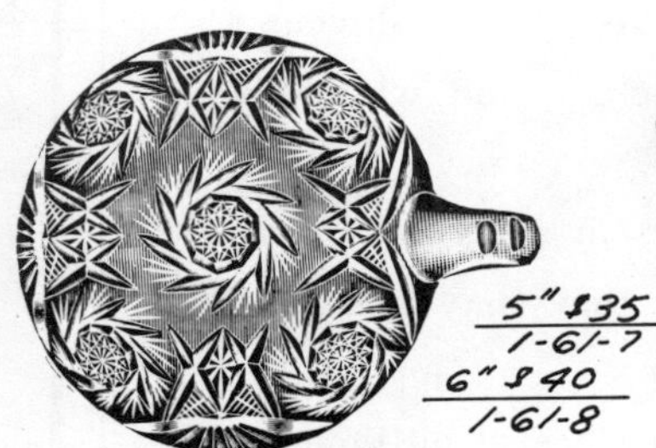

GOLF PATTERN.
ry beautiful cut glass Nappy with handle.
16906. 5-inch, price $4.68
16907. 6-inch, price 5.34

5" *$35*
1-61-7

6" *$40*
1-61-8

CROWN PATTERN.
Beautiful cut glass Celery Tray. Size, 11x5
inches.
No. 16908. Price...........................$7.34

$70
1-61-9

CUBA PATTERN.
Cut glass Saucer. Beautiful design.
No. 16909. 5-inch, price...................$2.68

$40
1-61-10

We handle only first quality Cut Glass beautifully cut and polished.	We guarantee each piece of Cut Glass to be perfectly cut and without a flaw.

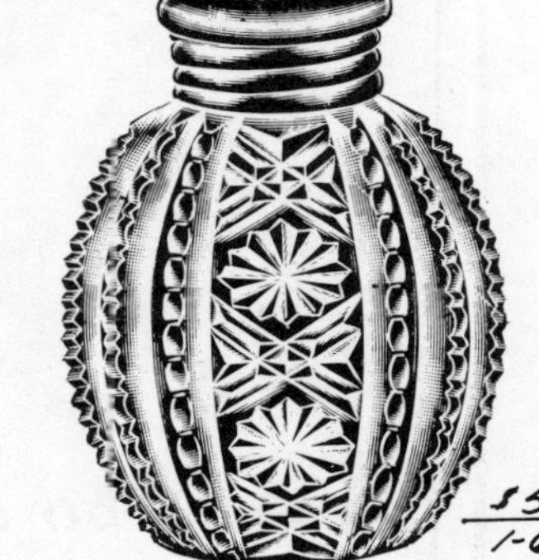

Beautiful cut glass Salt and Pepper Shaker.
No. 16910. Price, per pair..................$4.68

$45 PR
1-61-11

LIBERTY PATTERN.
Very beautiful cut glass Water Set, consisting
of
One No. 16911. 3-pt. Liberty pattern, Jug..$8.68
Six No. 16912. ½-pt. Texas pattern Tum-
blers 8.00
One No. 16913. 14-in. Plateau 5.34
No. 16914. Set complete..................20.00

$120
1-61-13

$16 EA
1-61-12

Elaborate cut glass Salt and Pepper Shaker.
No. 16915. Per pair........................$2.68

$50 PR
1-61-14

Confidential Discount Sheet

—FOR—

CATALOGUE No. 87, 1903.

SPECIAL NOTICE.

Prices on all goods listed in this catalogue subject to

A Discount of 6 Per Cent.

for cash with order, C. O. D. bills and all bills paid within ten days.

This change of discount applies to this catalogue only and has no effect on the discounts of our other catalogues. Those who have not done business with us before, and who want credit, will save time by giving Chicago reference or that of their bank.

The price lists of watch cases and movements in this catalogue is in accordance with those issued by the various watch companies and is subject to any change they may make; all former watch prices withdrawn.

Compare our prices with those of other houses and you will find they are at all times as low or lower than those of any legitimate Jewelry House in the United States. Don't be deceived by houses giving big discounts; compare the **net prices** of goods. These are the ones that count. It is not how big a discount you get, but what the goods actually cost that should interest you.

Your orders, no matter how small, will always receive the most careful and courteous attention and will be filled and shipped promptly. We take pleasure in referring you to The First National Bank of Chicago, Dun or Bradstreet's Commercial Agencies or to any General Agent of any Express Company in Chicago as to our business standing and responsibility.

M. BAZZETT & CO.

145 State Street
CHICAGO, ILL.

DO NOT CUT UP OR DESTROY THIS CATALOGUE.

Finest Quality American Cut Glass.

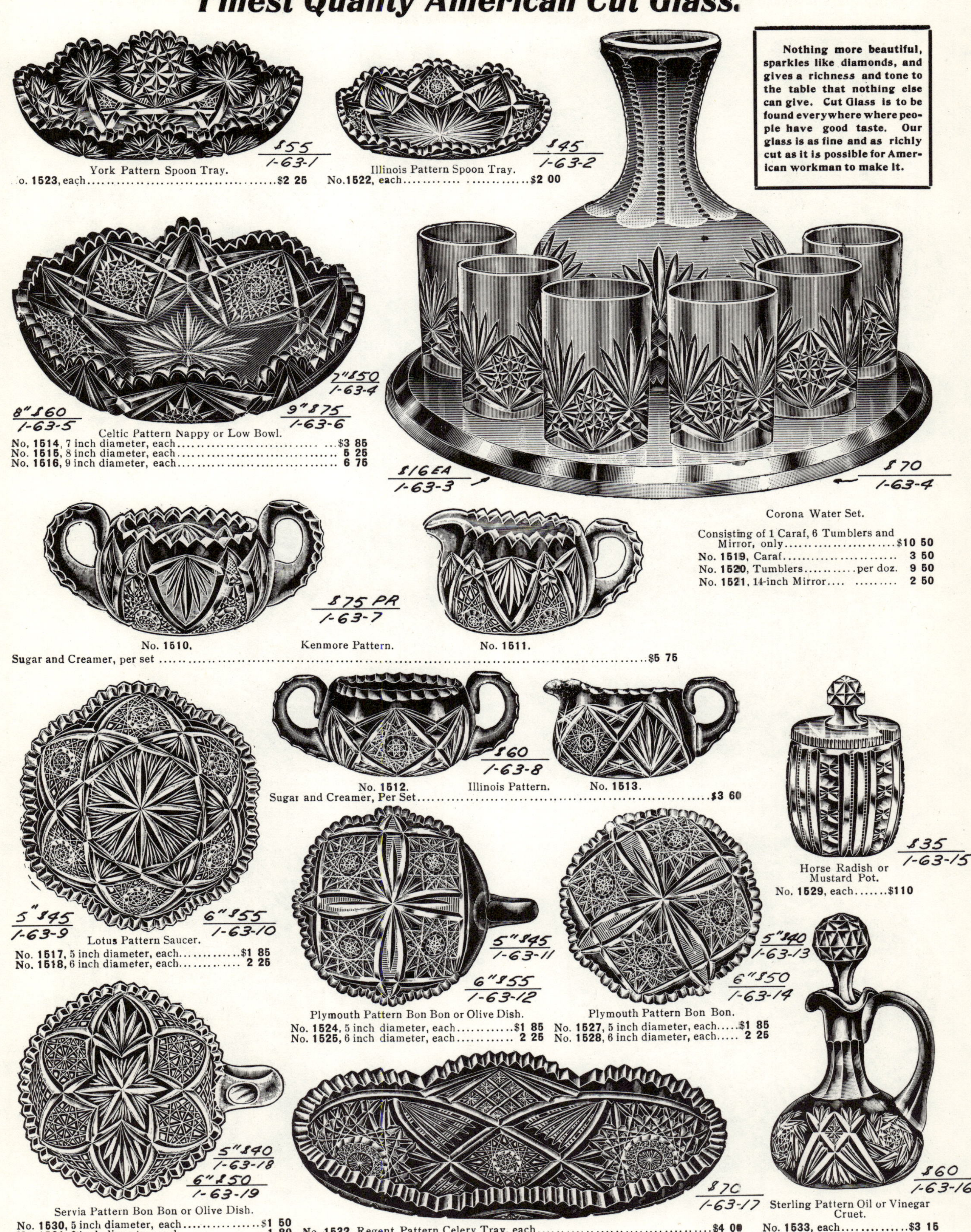

York Pattern Spoon Tray.
$55
1-63-1
o. 1523, each...................$2 25

Illinois Pattern Spoon Tray.
$45
1-63-2
No.1522, each...............$2 00

Celtic Pattern Nappy or Low Bowl.
8" $60
1-63-5
2" $50
1-63-4
9" $75
1-63-6
No. 1514, 7 inch diameter, each.....................$3 85
No. 1515, 8 inch diameter, each.......................... 5 25
No. 1516, 9 inch diameter, each.......................... 6 75

$16 EA
1-63-3

$70
1-63-4

Corona Water Set.
Consisting of 1 Caraf, 6 Tumblers and Mirror, only......................$10 50
No. 1519, Caraf......................... 3 50
No. 1520, Tumblers..........per doz. 9 50
No. 1521, 14-inch Mirror.... .... 2 50

No. 1510.
Kenmore Pattern.
No. 1511.
$75 PR
1-63-7
Sugar and Creamer, per set $5 75

No. 1512.
Illinois Pattern.
No. 1513.
$60
1-63-8
Sugar and Creamer, Per Set...............................$3 60

Lotus Pattern Saucer.
5" $45
1-63-9
6" $55
1-63-10
No. 1517, 5 inch diameter, each............$1 85
No. 1518, 6 inch diameter, each............ 2 25

Plymouth Pattern Bon Bon or Olive Dish.
5" $45
1-63-11
6" $55
1-63-12
No. 1524, 5 inch diameter, each............$1 85
No. 1525, 6 inch diameter, each............ 2 25

Plymouth Pattern Bon Bon.
5" $40
1-63-13
6" $50
1-63-14
No. 1527, 5 inch diameter, each.....$1 85
No. 1528, 6 inch diameter, each..... 2 25

Horse Radish or Mustard Pot.
$35
1-63-15
No. 1529, each.......$110

Servia Pattern Bon Bon or Olive Dish.
5" $40
1-63-18
6" $50
1-63-19
No. 1530, 5 inch diameter, each.................$1 50
No. 1531, 6 inch diameter, each................. 1 80

$70
1-63-17
No. 1532, Regent Pattern Celery Tray, each...................................$4 00

Sterling Pattern Oil or Vinegar Cruet.
$60
1-63-16
No. 1533, each.................$3 15

Rich American Cut Glass.

Our Glass is all Cut from the Finest Selected Crystal Blanks and is a Work of Art and Beauty.   It has a Richness of Cutting and a Brilliancy Unsurpassed.

No. 1501, per doz..$11 00
York pattern, full sized tumbler.

No. 1502, per dozen....$15 00
Starling pattern, full sized tumbler.

No. 1503, each...................$4 00
Starling pattern, square water caraf.

No. 1500, each.....................$3 25
Very beautifully cut caraf or water bottle, York pattern.

No. 1504, each.........................$3 00
Kenmore pattern whipped cream bowl.

No. 1505, each...................$0 75
Prism cut knife rest.

York Pattern, Deep Bowl.

No. 1506, 8 inches in diameter. each.........................$4 75
No. 1506, 9 inches in diameter, each...........................6 50

Aurora Pattern, Deep Bowl.

No. 1507, 8 inches in diameter, each............................$ 7 75
No. 1507, 9 inches in diameter, each............................10 00
Very richly cut.

Lyric Pattern. Deep Bowl.

No. 1508, 8 inches in diameter, each..................$4 75
No. 1508, 9 inches in diameter, each..................7 25

Liberty Pattern, Deep Bowl.

No. 1509, 7 inches in diameter, each...................................$4 00
No. 1509, 8 inches in diameter, each....................................5 00

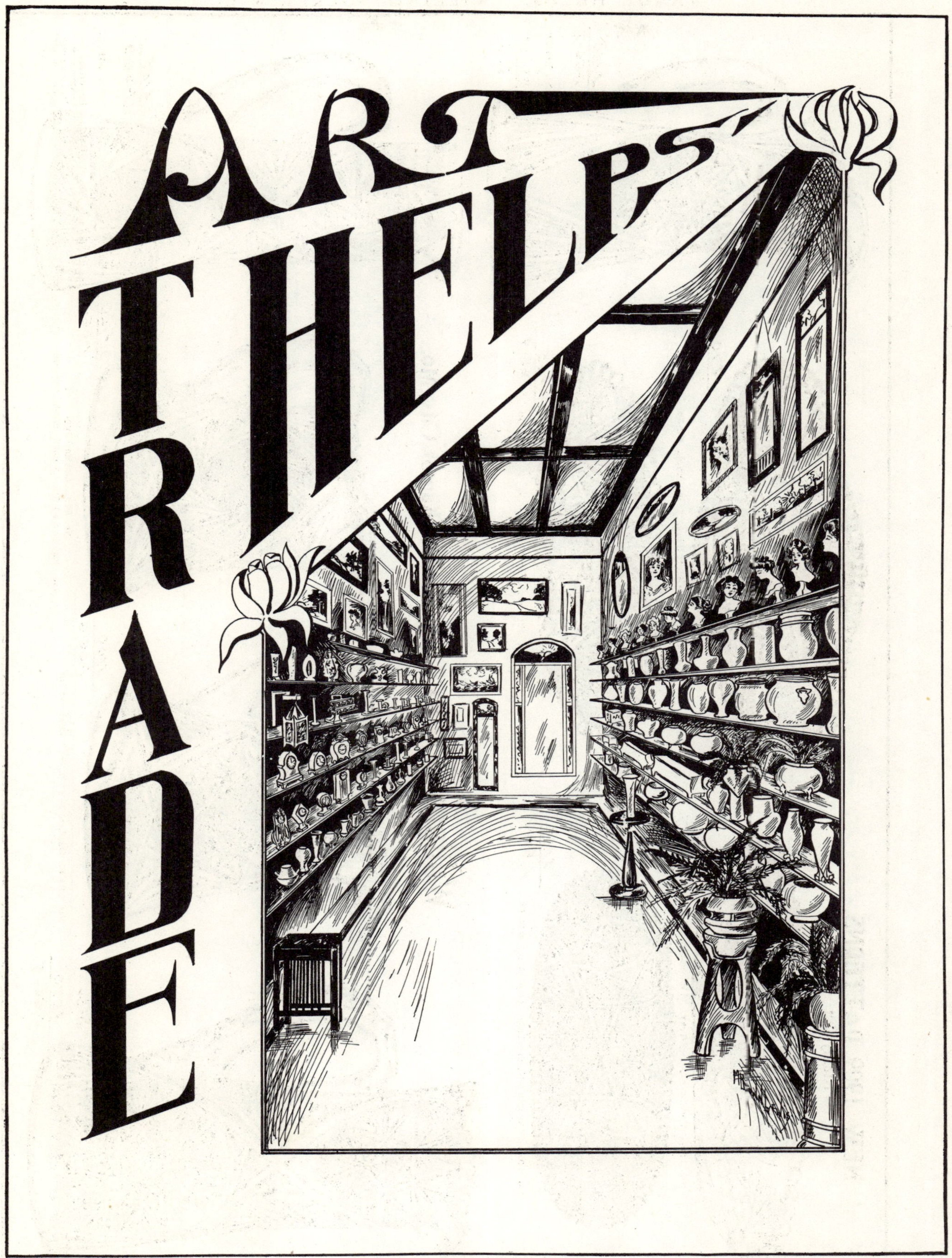
ART
THELPS
TRADE

NEW 1909 PATTERNS.
Richly Cut.

William Volker & Co., Kansas City, Mo.

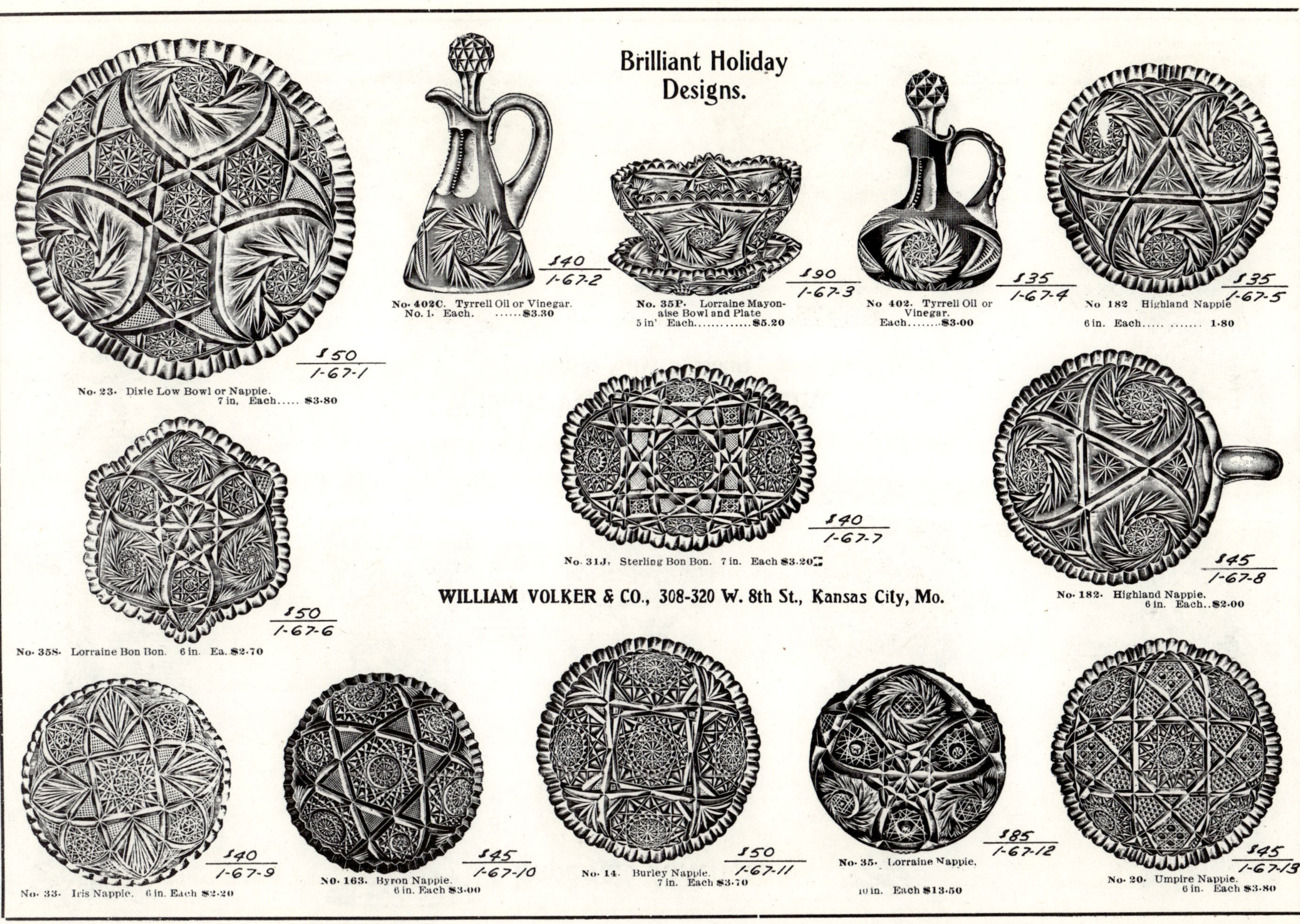
Brilliant Holiday Designs.

WILLIAM VOLKER & CO., 308-320 W. 8th St., Kansas City, Mo.

No. 23. Dixie Low Bowl or Nappie. 7 in. Each..... $3.80 $50 1-67-1

No. 402C. Tyrrell Oil or Vinegar. No. 1. Each. $3.30 $40 1-67-2

No. 35P. Lorraine Mayonaise Bowl and Plate 5 in' Each.............$5.20 $90 1-67-3

No 402. Tyrrell Oil or Vinegar. Each.......$3.00 $35 1-67-4

No 182 Highland Nappie 6 in. Each..... .... 1.80 $35 1-67-5

No. 358. Lorraine Bon Bon. 6 in. Ea. $2.70 $50 1-67-6

No. 31J. Sterling Bon Bon. 7 in. Each $3.20 $40 1-67-7

No. 182. Highland Nappie. 6 in. Each..$2.00 $45 1-67-8

No. 33. Iris Nappie. 6 in. Each $2.20 $40 1-67-9

No. 163. Byron Nappie. 6 in. Each $3.00 $45 1-67-10

No. 14. Burley Nappie. 7 in. Each $3.70 $50 1-67-11

No. 35. Lorraine Nappie. 10 in. Each $13.50 $85 1-67-12

No. 20. Umpire Nappie. 6 in. Each $3.80 $45 1-67-13

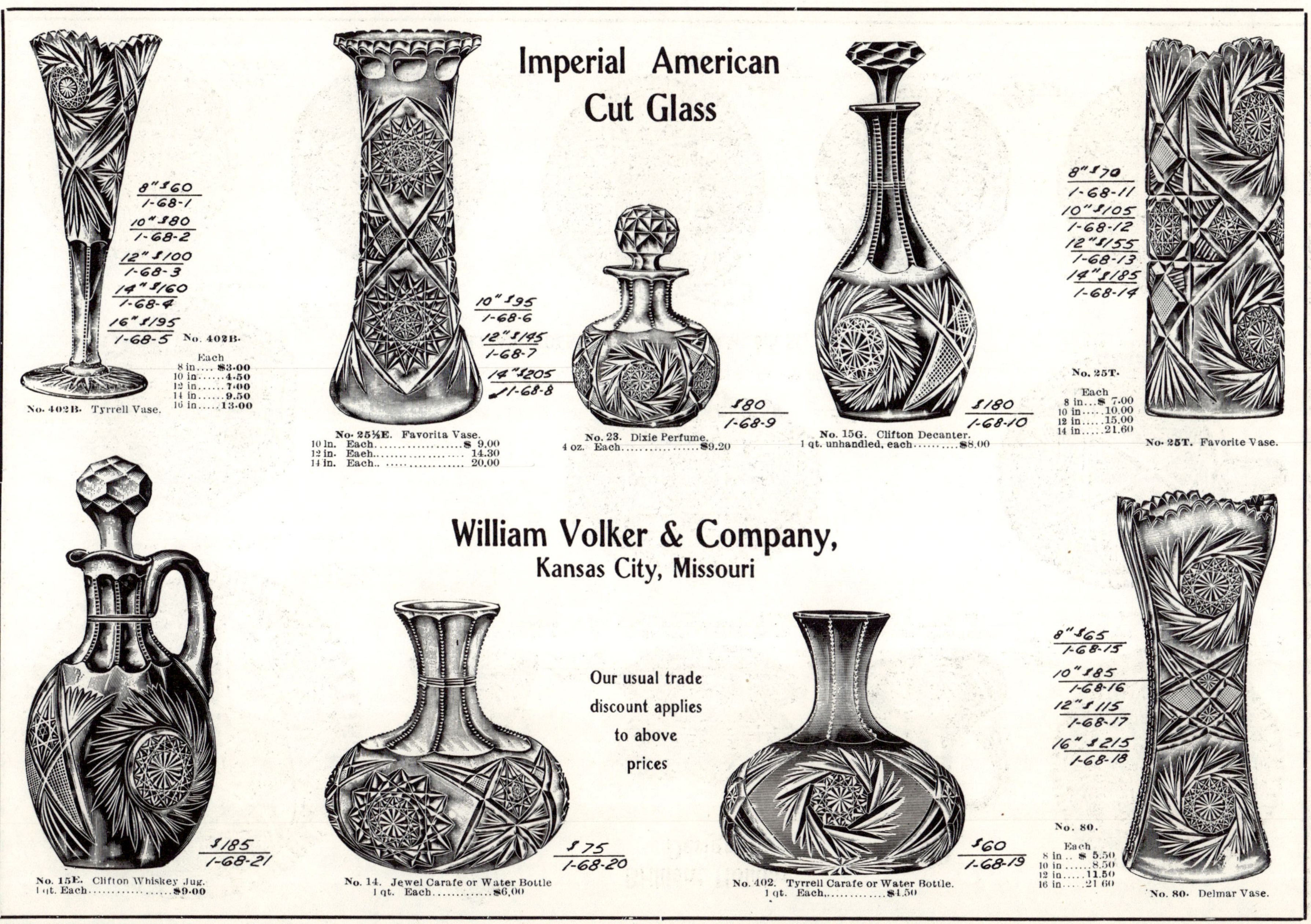
Imperial American
Cut Glass

William Volker & Company,
Kansas City, Missouri

Our usual trade
discount applies
to above
prices

8" $60 / 1-68-1
10" $80 / 1-68-2
12" $100 / 1-68-3
14" $160 / 1-68-4
16" $195 / 1-68-5
No. 402B.
Each
8 in.... $3.00
10 in..... 4.50
12 in..... 7.00
14 in..... 9.50
16 in..... 13.00
No. 402B. Tyrrell Vase.

10" $95 / 1-68-6
12" $145 / 1-68-7
14" $205 / 1-68-8
No. 25½E. Favorita Vase.
10 in. Each.............. $ 9.00
12 in. Each.............. 14.30
14 in. Each.............. 20.00

No. 23. Dixie Perfume.
4 oz. Each................$9.20
$80 / 1-68-9

No. 15G. Clifton Decanter.
1 qt. unhandled, each........$8.00
$180 / 1-68-10

8" $70 / 1-68-11
10" $105 / 1-68-12
12" $155 / 1-68-13
14" $185 / 1-68-14
No. 25T.
Each
8 in.... $ 7.00
10 in.... 10.00
12 in.... 15.00
14 in.... 21.60
No. 25T. Favorite Vase.

$185 / 1-68-21
No. 15E. Clifton Whiskey Jug.
1 qt. Each..............$9.00

$75 / 1-68-20
No. 14. Jewel Carafe or Water Bottle
1 qt. Each...........$6.00

$60 / 1-68-19
No. 402. Tyrrell Carafe or Water Bottle.
1 qt. Each.............$4.50

8" $65 / 1-68-15
10" $85 / 1-68-16
12" $115 / 1-68-17
16" $215 / 1-68-18
No. 80.
Each
8 in.... $ 5.50
10 in.... 8.50
12 in.... 11.50
16 in.... 21.60
No. 80. Delmar Vase.

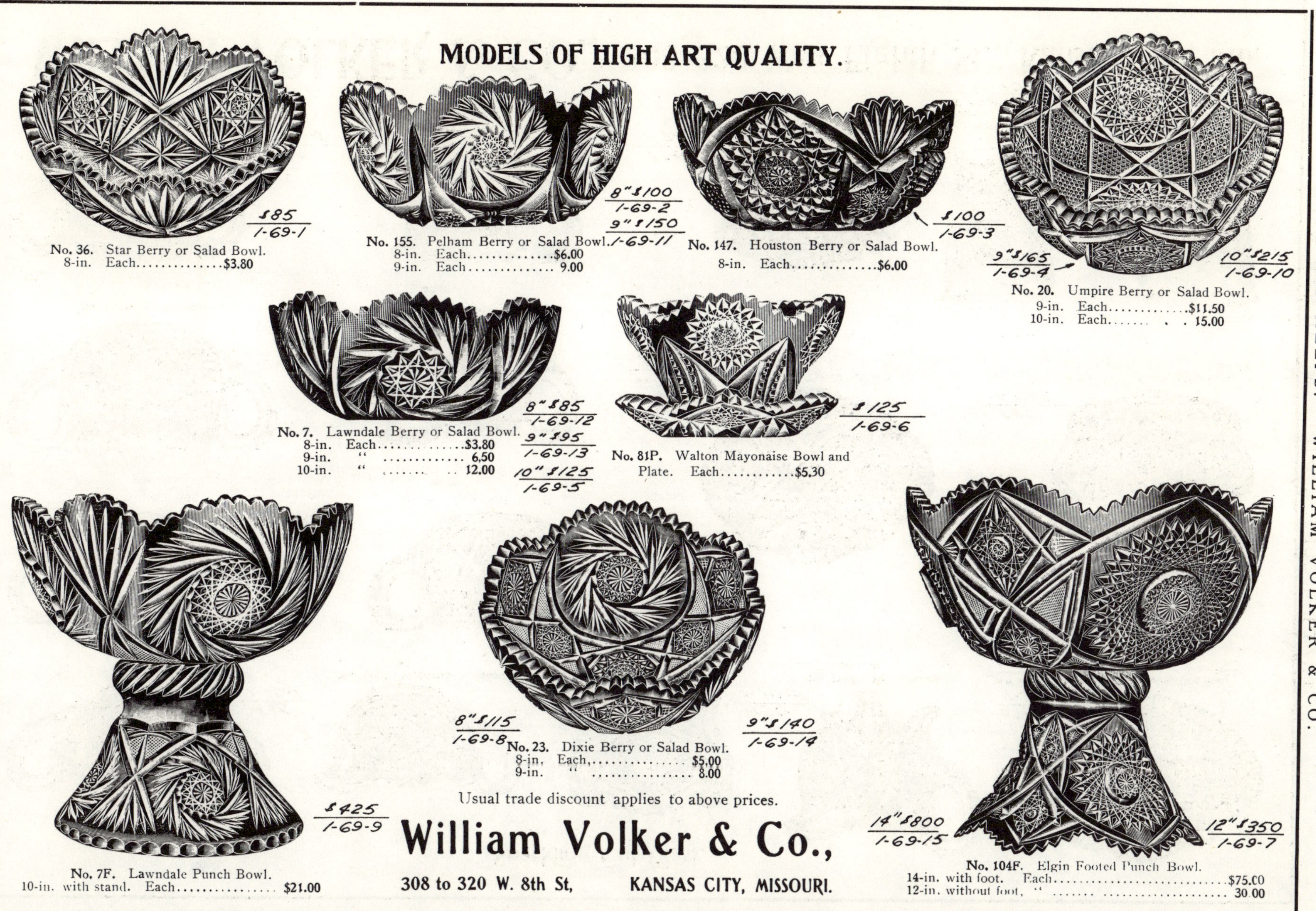
MODELS OF HIGH ART QUALITY.

No. 36.   Star Berry or Salad Bowl.
8-in.   Each.............$3.80
$85
1-69-1

No. 155.   Pelham Berry or Salad Bowl.
8-in.   Each.............$6.00
9-in.   Each.............9.00
8"$100
1-69-2
9"$150
1-69-11

No. 147.   Houston Berry or Salad Bowl.
8-in.   Each.............$6.00
$100
1-69-3

No. 20.   Umpire Berry or Salad Bowl.
9-in.   Each.............$11.50
10-in.   Each....... . 15.00
9"$165
1-69-4
10"$215
1-69-10

No. 7.   Lawndale Berry or Salad Bowl.
8-in.   Each.............$3.80
9-in.   " 6.50
10-in.   " $2.00
8"$85
1-69-12
9"$95
1-69-13
10"$125
1-69-5

No. 81P.   Walton Mayonaise Bowl and
Plate.   Each.............$5.30
$125
1-69-6

No. 7F.   Lawndale Punch Bowl.
10-in. with stand.   Each.............$21.00
$425
1-69-9

No. 23.   Dixie Berry or Salad Bowl.
8-in.   Each,.............$5.00
9-in.   " 8.00
8"$115
1-69-8
9"$140
1-69-14

Usual trade discount applies to above prices.

William Volker & Co.,
308 to 320 W. 8th St,   KANSAS CITY, MISSOURI.

No. 104F.   Elgin Footed Punch Bowl.
14-in. with foot.   Each.............$75.00
12-in. without foot,   " 30.00
14"$800
1-69-15
12"$350
1-69-7

Sparkling Cut Glass.

WILLIAM VOLKER & CO., 308-320 West Eighth St., Kansas City, Mo.

Jewelry
Diamonds
Watches
Clocks
Cut Glass
Tableware
Novelties

MARSHALL FIELD & COMPANY
Chicago

1911 - 12   NO. 178 

Berry or Salad Bowls

AMERICAN CUT GLASS

8" $40
1-72-1

70062—Each 3.20
8 inch
70116—Each 5.00
9 inch

9" $55
1-72-3

8" $40
1-72-2

70068—Each 3.50
8 inch
70121—Each 5.50
9 inch

9" $60
1-72-4

70098—Each 4.50
8 inch

$50
1-72-5

8" $50
1-72-6

70095—Each 4.25
8 inch
70149—Each 6.50
9 inch

9" $70
1-72-7

70112—Each 5.00
8 inch

$55
1-72-8

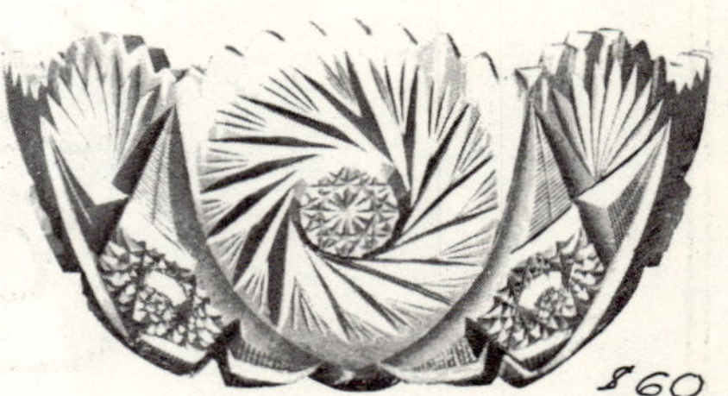

70123—Each 5.50
8 inch

$60
1-72-9

$65
1-72-10

70130—Each 6.00
8 inch

8" $70
1-72-11

70151—Each 6.70
8 inch
70208—Each 9.00
9 inch

9" $100
1-72-12

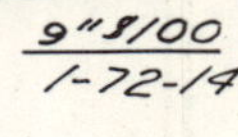

8" $75
1-72-13

70186—Each 7.00
8 inch
20254—Each 9.00
9 inch

9" $100
1-72-14

$85
1-72-15

70173—Each 7.50
8 inch

8" $110
1-72-16

70182—Each 8.00
8 inch
70223—Each 10.00
9 inch

9" $140
1-72-17

70198—Each 8.70
8 inch

$90
1-72-18

8" $100
1-72-19

70206—Each 9.00
8 inch
70262—Each 12.50
9 inch

9" $125
1-72-20

70207—Each 9.00
8 inch

$75
1-72-21

70213—Each 9.50
8 inch

$110
1-72-22

Berry, Fruit or Salad Bowls

AMERICAN CUT GLASS

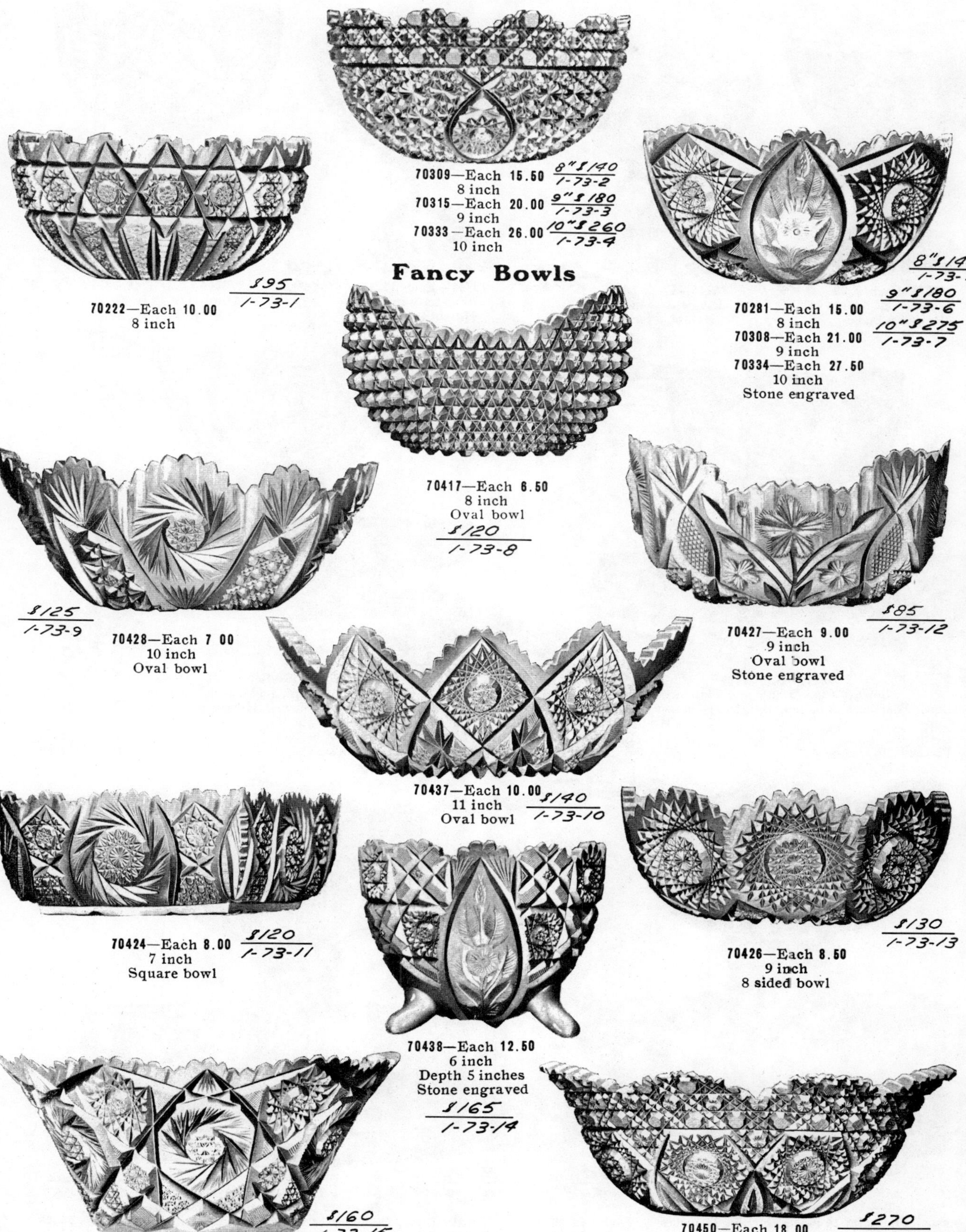

70309—Each 15.50
8 inch
8" $140
1-73-2

70315—Each 20.00
9 inch
9" $180
1-73-3

70333—Each 26.00
10 inch
10" $260
1-73-4

70222—Each 10.00
8 inch
$95
1-73-1

70281—Each 15.00
8 inch
8" $140
1-73-5

70308—Each 21.00
9 inch
9" $180
1-73-6

70334—Each 27.50
10 inch
Stone engraved
10" $275
1-73-7

Fancy Bowls

70417—Each 6.50
8 inch
Oval bowl
$120
1-73-8

70428—Each 7 00
10 inch
Oval bowl
$125
1-73-9

70427—Each 9.00
9 inch
Oval bowl
Stone engraved
$85
1-73-12

70437—Each 10.00
11 inch
Oval bowl
$140
1-73-10

70424—Each 8.00
7 inch
Square bowl
$120
1-73-11

70426—Each 8.50
9 inch
8 sided bowl
$130
1-73-13

70438—Each 12.50
6 inch
Depth 5 inches
Stone engraved
$165
1-73-14

70439—Each 13.00
10 inch
$160
1-73-15

70450—Each 18.00
11 inch
Oval bowl
$270
1-73-16

Footed Bowls and Punch Sets

AMERICAN CUT GLASS

70702—Each 8.00
Diameter 9 inches
Height 9 inches

70715—Each 11.00
Diameter 8 inches
Height 8 inches

70733—Each 15.00
Diameter 9 inches
Height 9 inches

70800—Each 48.00
Diameter 12 inches
Height 12¾ inches

79312—Set 36.00
Bowl, 6 Cups, Ladle and Plateaux

70751—Bowl, Diameter 10 inches, Height 9½ inches	Each	19.00
74991—Cups	Dozen	12.00
76700—Ladle	Each	6.00
74025—Plateaux 16 inches	Each	6.20

79316—Set 60.00
Bowl, 12 Cups, Ladle and Plateaux

70762—Bowl, Diameter 10 inches, Height 10 inches	Each	22.00
75023—Cups	Dozen	19.00
76700—Ladle	Each	6.00
79055—Plateaux 16 inches	Each	12.00

79314—Set 96.00
Bowl, 12 Cups, Ladle and Plateaux

70812—Bowl, Diameter 14 inches, Height 14 inches	Each	60.00
75041—Cups	Dozen	21.00
76701—Ladle	Each	13.00
79098—Plateaux	Each	9.00

79317—Set 134.00
Bowl, 12 Cups, Ladle and Plateaux

70824—Bowl, Diameter 12 inches, Height 12 inches	Each	70.00
75050—Cups	Dozen	36.00
76701—Ladle	Each	13.00
79095—Plateaux 18 inches	Each	16.00

Compotes

AMERICAN CUT GLASS

70531—Each 2.30
Height 4½ inches
Diameter 4½ inches
$45 / 1-75-1

70540—Each 2.50
Height 5 inches
Diameter 5 inches
Satin Flashes
$50 / 1-75-2

70567—Each 3.00
Height 5 inches
Diameter 5 inches
5" $55 / 1-75-3

70614—Each 4.50
Height 6 inches
Diameter 6 inches
6" $60 / 1-75-4

70613—Each 4.25
Height 5½ inches
Diameter 6½ inches
$60 / 1-75-5

70501—Each 1.50
Height 5¼ inches
Diameter 4¾ inches
Satin Engraving
$15 / 1-75-16

70630—Each 5.00
Height 7½ inches
Diameter 6 inches
$65 / 1-75-7

70642—Each 5.50
Height 8 inches
Diameter 6 inches
$70 / 1-75-8

70643—Each 5.50
Height 6¼ inches
Diameter 4½ inches
Square
$60 / 1-75-9

70662—Each 6.50
Height 9 inches
Diameter 6 inches
Satin Flashes
$80 / 1-75-10

70677—Each 7.00
Height 9½ inches
Diameter 6 inches
$80 / 1-75-11

70663—Each 6.50
Height 6 inches
Diameter 6 inches
$75 / 1-75-12

70680—Each 7.50
Height 3 inches
Diameter 7 inches
Satin Flowers
$85 / 1-75-13

70707—Each 8.50
Height 7½ inches
Diameter 6½ inches
$95 / 1-75-14

70711—Each 10.00
Height 9¾ inches
Diameter 7 inches
$110 / 1-75-15

70726—Each 13.00
Height 9¾ inches
Diameter 7 inches
Satin Flowers
$140 / 1-75-16

70732—Each 15.00
Height 7¼ inches
Diameter 8 inches
Satin Flowers
$160 / 1-75-17

Saucers and Nappies

AMERICAN CUT GLASS

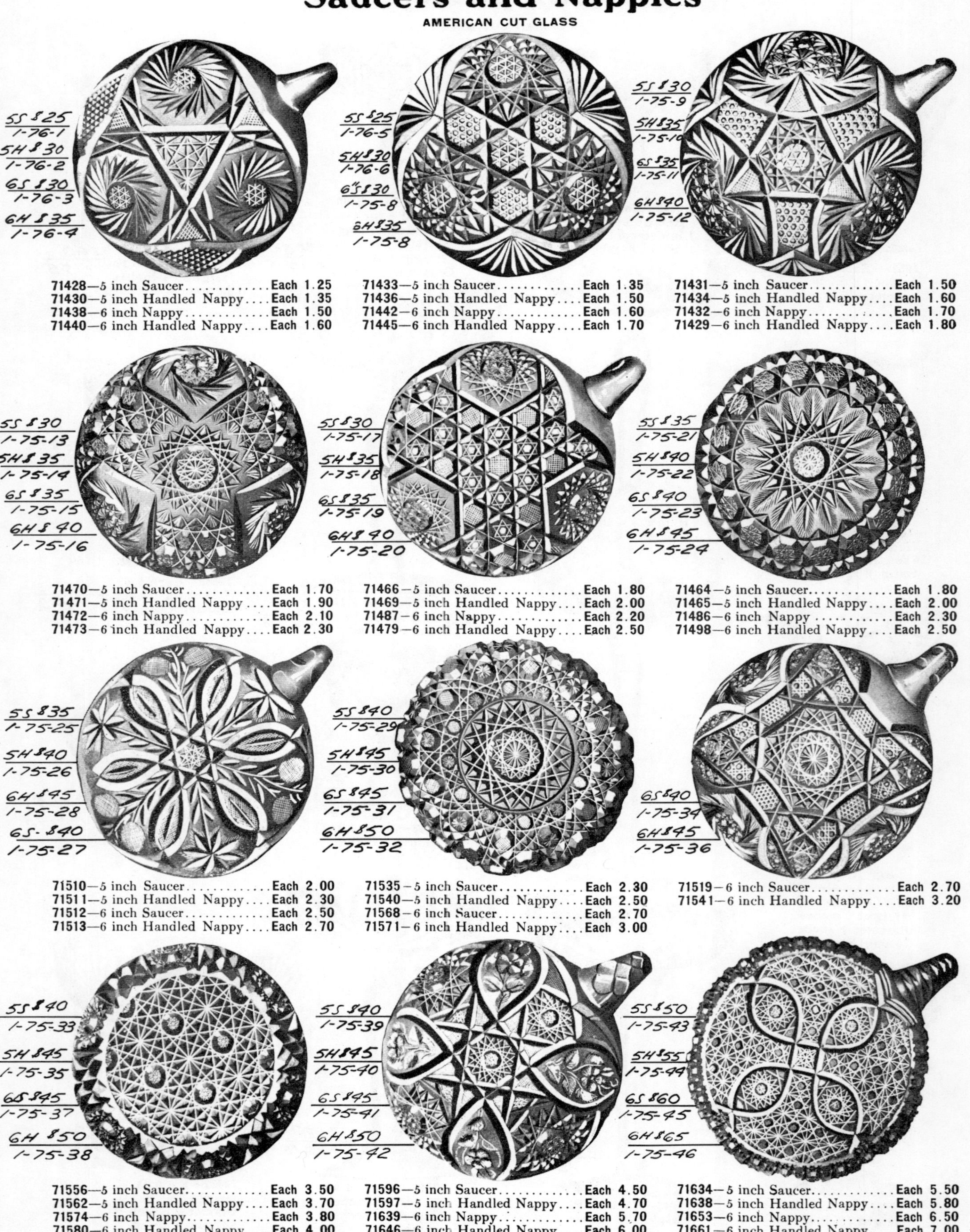

71428—5 inch Saucer............Each 1.25
71430—5 inch Handled Nappy....Each 1.35
71438—6 inch Nappy............Each 1.50
71440—6 inch Handled Nappy....Each 1.60

71433—5 inch Saucer............Each 1.35
71436—5 inch Handled Nappy....Each 1.50
71442—6 inch Nappy............Each 1.60
71445—6 inch Handled Nappy....Each 1.70

71431—5 inch Saucer............Each 1.50
71434—5 inch Handled Nappy....Each 1.60
71432—6 inch Nappy............Each 1.70
71429—6 inch Handled Nappy....Each 1.80

71470—5 inch Saucer............Each 1.70
71471—5 inch Handled Nappy....Each 1.90
71472—6 inch Nappy............Each 2.10
71473—6 inch Handled Nappy....Each 2.30

71466—5 inch Saucer............Each 1.80
71469—5 inch Handled Nappy....Each 2.00
71487—6 inch Nappy............Each 2.20
71479—6 inch Handled Nappy....Each 2.50

71464—5 inch Saucer............Each 1.80
71465—5 inch Handled Nappy....Each 2.00
71486—6 inch Nappy............Each 2.30
71498—6 inch Handled Nappy....Each 2.50

71510—5 inch Saucer............Each 2.00
71511—5 inch Handled Nappy....Each 2.30
71512—6 inch Saucer............Each 2.50
71513—6 inch Handled Nappy....Each 2.70

71535—5 inch Saucer............Each 2.30
71540—5 inch Handled Nappy....Each 2.50
71568—6 inch Saucer............Each 2.70
71571—6 inch Handled Nappy....Each 3.00

71519—6 inch Saucer............Each 2.70
71541—6 inch Handled Nappy....Each 3.20

71556—5 inch Saucer............Each 3.50
71562—5 inch Handled Nappy....Each 3.70
71574—6 inch Nappy............Each 3.80
71580—6 inch Handled Nappy....Each 4.00

71596—5 inch Saucer............Each 4.50
71597—5 inch Handled Nappy....Each 4.70
71639—6 inch Nappy............Each 5.70
71646—6 inch Handled Nappy....Each 6.00

71634—5 inch Saucer............Each 5.50
71638—5 inch Handled Nappy....Each 5.80
71653—6 inch Nappy............Each 6.50
71661—6 inch Handled Nappy....Each 7.00

Large Nappies Deep Dishes

AMERICAN CUT GLASS

71488—7 inch Each 2.30
71489—8 inch Each 3.50

7" $50 — 1-77-1
8" $55 — 1-77-2

71507—7 inch Each 2.50
71563—8 inch Each 3 70

7" $50 — 1-77-3
8" $55 — 1-77-4

71524—7 inch Each 3.00
71573—8 inch Each 4.00
71635—9 inch Each 5.50

7" $55 — 1-77-5
8" $60 — 1-77-6
9" $90 — 1-77-7

71546—7 inch Each 3.50

$75 — 1-77-8

71581—7 inch Each 4.00
71633—8 inch Each 5 50
71663—9 inch Each 7 00

7" $75 — 1-77-9
8" $100 — 1-77-10
9" $140 — 1-77-11

71636—8 inch Each 5.70
71681—9 inch Each 8.00

8" $100 — 1-77-12
9" $140 — 1-77-13

71649—7 inch Each 6.00
71659—8 inch Each 7.50
71699—9 inch Each 9.00

7" $90 — 1-77-14
8" $100 — 1-77-15
9" $110 — 1-77-16

71662—7 inch Each 7.00
71715—8 inch Each 9.50
71759—9 inch Each 14.50
71777—10 inch Each 21.00
Satin Flowers

7" $140 — 1-77-17
8" $120 — 1-77-18
9" $150 — 1-77-19
10" $230 — 1-77-20

71714—7 inch Each 9.50
71744—8 inch Each 13.50
71755—9 inch Each 16.50
71766—10 inch Each 20.00

7" $100 — 1-77-21
8" $130 — 1-77-22
9" $180 — 1-77-23
10" $220 — 1-77-24

Almond, Olive and Bon-Bon Dishes

AMERICAN CUT GLASS

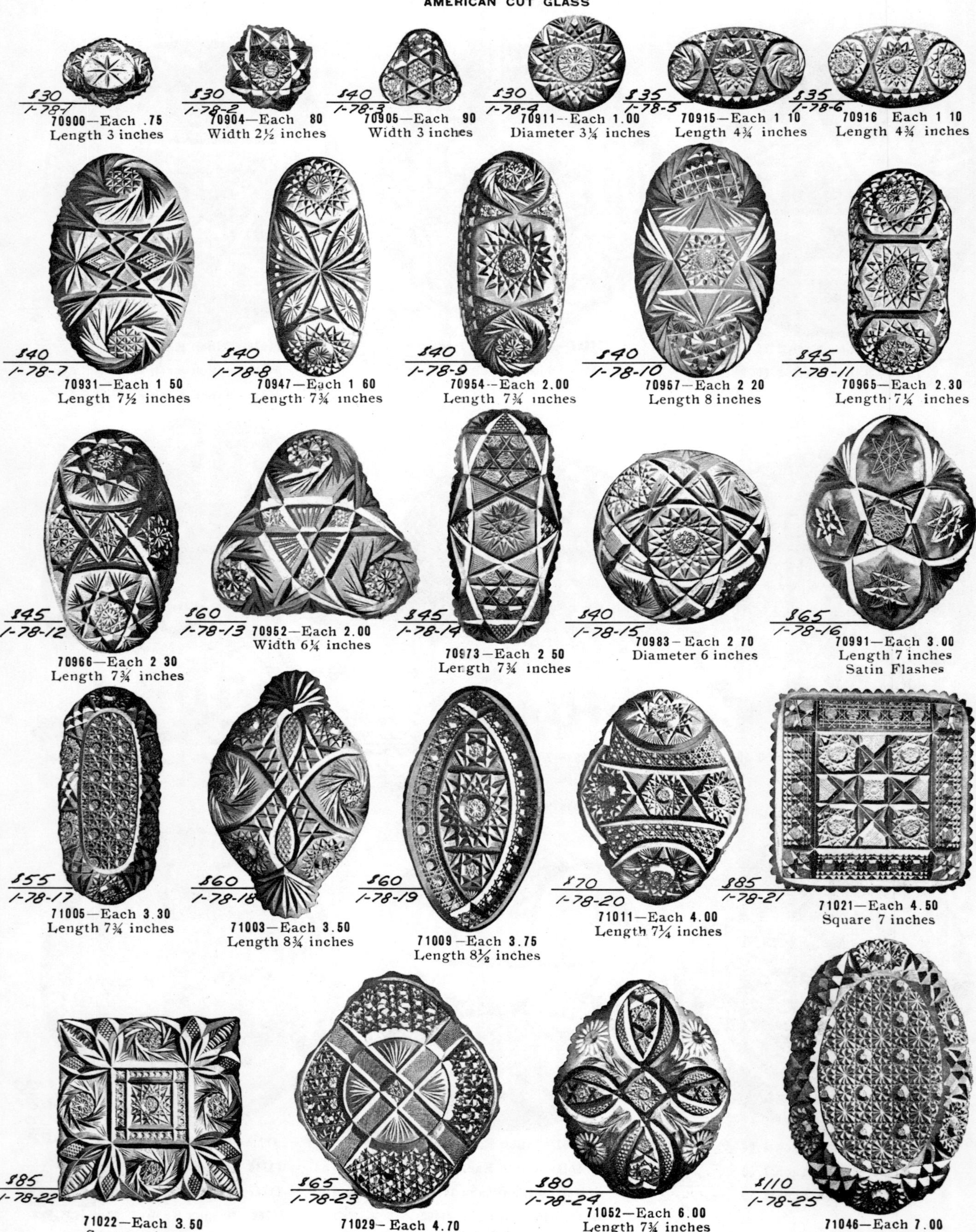

$30
1-78-1
70900—Each .75
Length 3 inches

$30
1-78-2
70904—Each 80
Width 2½ inches

$40
1-78-3
70905—Each 90
Width 3 inches

$30
1-78-4
70911—Each 1.00
Diameter 3¼ inches

$35
1-78-5
70915—Each 1 10
Length 4¾ inches

$35
1-78-6
70916 Each 1 10
Length 4¾ inches

$40
1-78-7
70931—Each 1 50
Length 7½ inches

$40
1-78-8
70947—Each 1 60
Length 7¾ inches

$40
1-78-9
70954—Each 2.00
Length 7¾ inches

$40
1-78-10
70957—Each 2 20
Length 8 inches

$45
1-78-11
70965—Each 2.30
Length 7¼ inches

$45
1-78-12
70966—Each 2 30
Length 7¾ inches

$60
1-78-13
70952—Each 2.00
Width 6¼ inches

$45
1-78-14
70973—Each 2 50
Length 7¾ inches

$40
1-78-15
70983—Each 2 70
Diameter 6 inches

$65
1-78-16
70991—Each 3.00
Length 7 inches
Satin Flashes

$55
1-78-17
71005—Each 3.30
Length 7¾ inches

$60
1-78-18
71003—Each 3.50
Length 8¾ inches

$60
1-78-19
71009—Each 3.75
Length 8½ inches

$70
1-78-20
71011—Each 4.00
Length 7¼ inches

$85
1-78-21
71021—Each 4.50
Square 7 inches

$85
1-78-22
71022—Each 3.50
Square 6 inches

$65
1-78-23
71029—Each 4.70
Length 8 inches

$80
1-78-24
71052—Each 6.00
Length 7¾ inches
Satin Flowers

$110
1-78-25
71046—Each 7.00
9½ Inches

78

Handled Nappies and Relish Dishes

AMERICAN CUT GLASS

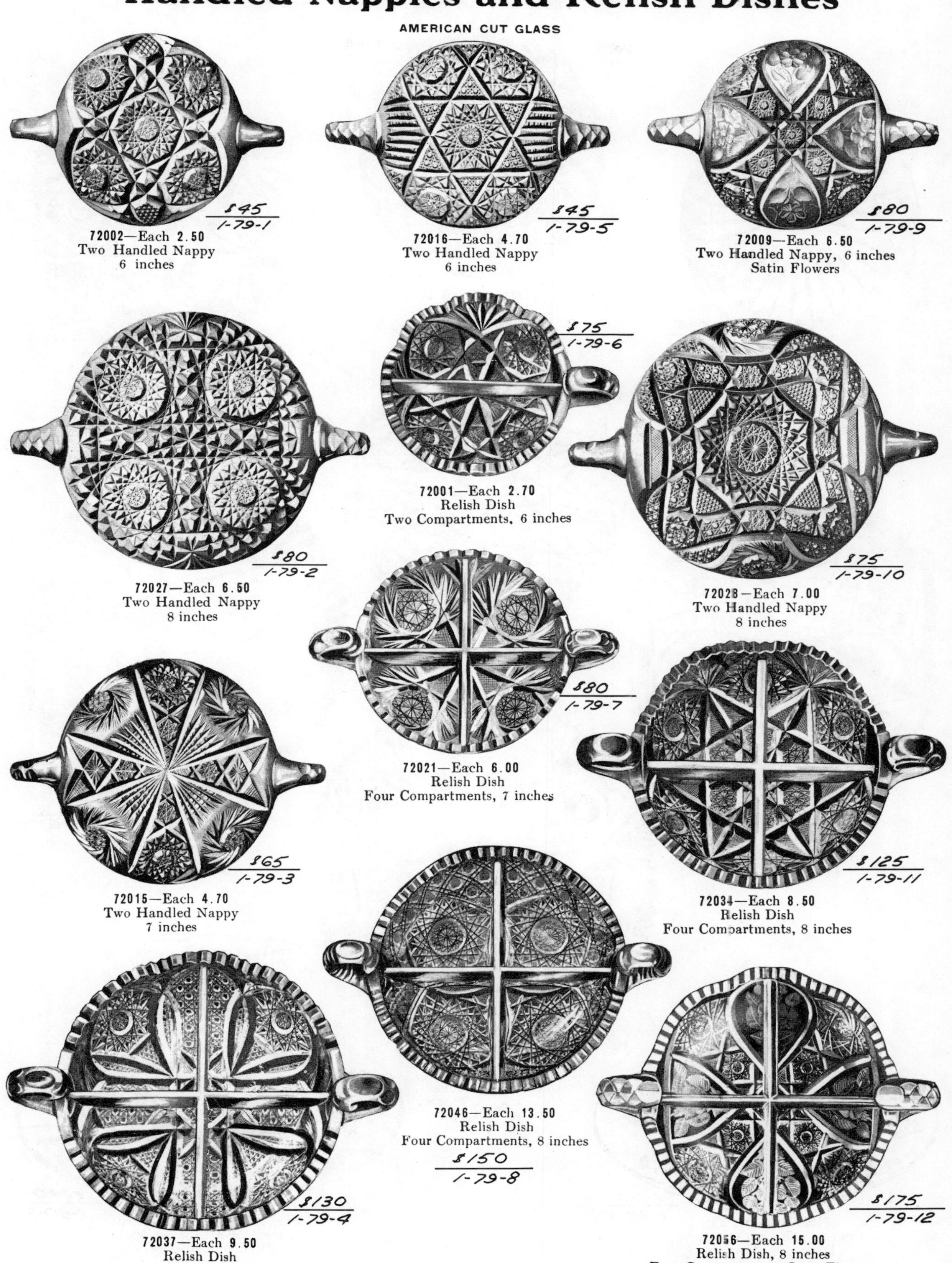

72002—Each 2.50
Two Handled Nappy
6 inches

72016—Each 4.70
Two Handled Nappy
6 inches

72009—Each 6.50
Two Handled Nappy, 6 inches
Satin Flowers

72027—Each 6.50
Two Handled Nappy
8 inches

72001—Each 2.70
Relish Dish
Two Compartments, 6 inches

72028—Each 7.00
Two Handled Nappy
8 inches

72015—Each 4.70
Two Handled Nappy
7 inches

72021—Each 6.00
Relish Dish
Four Compartments, 7 inches

72034—Each 8.50
Relish Dish
Four Compartments, 8 inches

72037—Each 9.50
Relish Dish
Four Compartments, 9 inches

72046—Each 13.50
Relish Dish
Four Compartments, 8 inches

72056—Each 15.00
Relish Dish, 8 inches
Four Compartments, Satin Flowers

Sandwich, Cake, Cheese and Cracker Plates

AMERICAN CUT GLASS

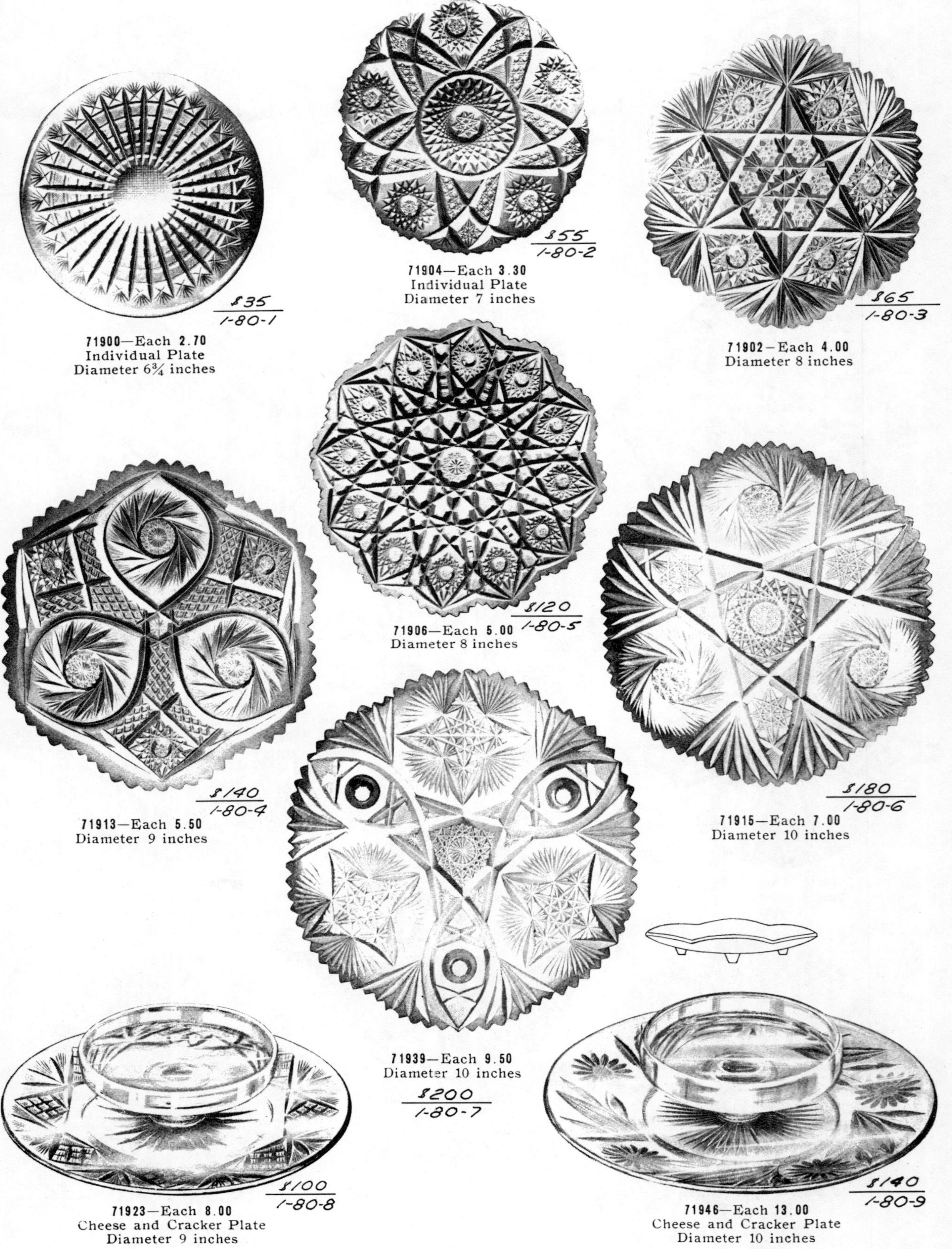

71900—Each 2.70
Individual Plate
Diameter 6¾ inches

71904—Each 3.30
Individual Plate
Diameter 7 inches

71902—Each 4.00
Diameter 8 inches

71906—Each 5.00
Diameter 8 inches

71913—Each 5.50
Diameter 9 inches

71915—Each 7.00
Diameter 10 inches

71939—Each 9.50
Diameter 10 inches

71923—Each 8.00
Cheese and Cracker Plate
Diameter 9 inches

71946—Each 13.00
Cheese and Cracker Plate
Diameter 10 inches

Ice Cream and Bread Trays
AMERICAN CUT GLASS

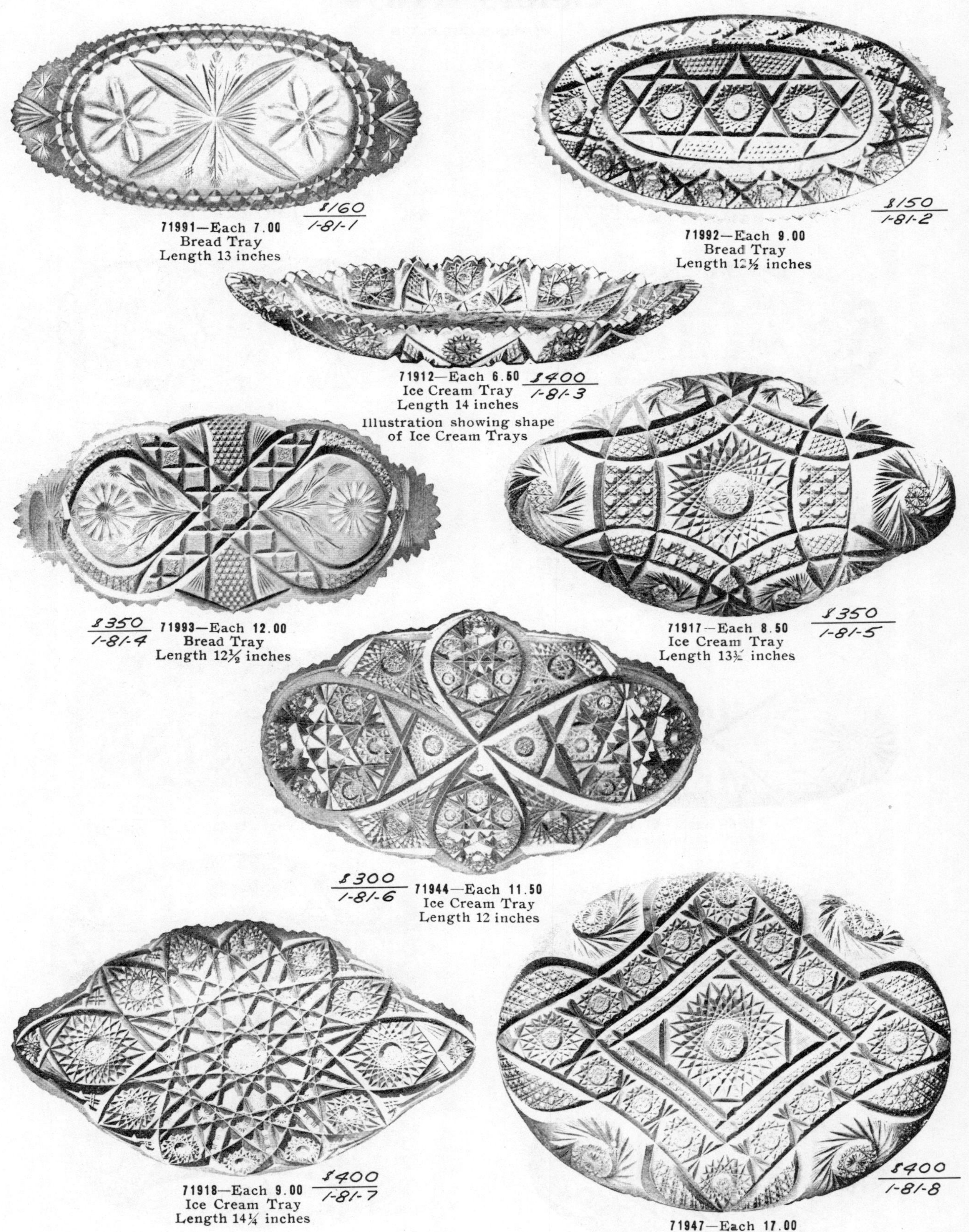

71991—Each 7.00
Bread Tray
Length 13 inches

$160
1-81-1

71992—Each 9.00
Bread Tray
Length 12½ inches

$150
1-81-2

71912—Each 6.50
Ice Cream Tray
Length 14 inches
Illustration showing shape
of Ice Cream Trays

$400
1-81-3

$350
1-81-4
71993—Each 12.00
Bread Tray
Length 12½ inches

71917—Each 8.50
Ice Cream Tray
Length 13½ inches

$350
1-81-5

$300
1-81-6
71944—Each 11.50
Ice Cream Tray
Length 12 inches

71918—Each 9.00
Ice Cream Tray
Length 14¼ inches

$400
1-81-7

71947—Each 17.00
Ice Cream Tray
Length 14 inches

$400
1-81-8

Celery Trays

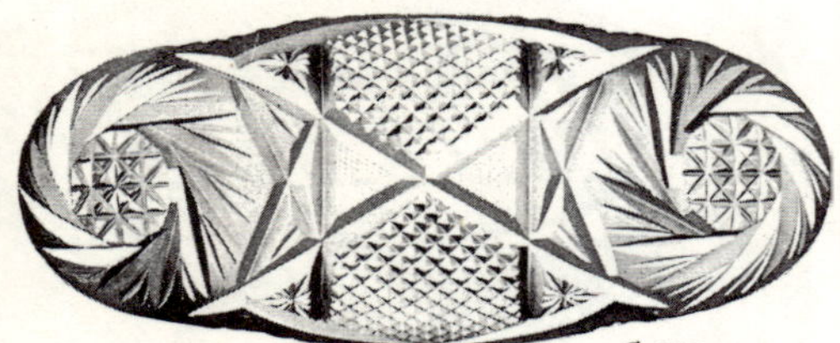

71209—Each 2.80
Length 11 inches
$50
1-82-1

71215—Each 3.30
Length 11 inches
$60
1-82-7

71228—Each 3.70
Length 10¾ inches
$60
1-82-2

71240—Each 4.50
Length 11½ inches
$65
1-82-8

71276—Each 6.70
Length 11½ inches
$105
1-82-3

71275—Each 5.50
Length 11¾ inches
$85
1-82-9

71279—Each 7.50
Length 12 inches
$75
1-82-4

71282—Each 7.70
Length 11 inches
$90
1-82-10

71281—Each 8.00
Length 11½ inches
$90
1-82-5

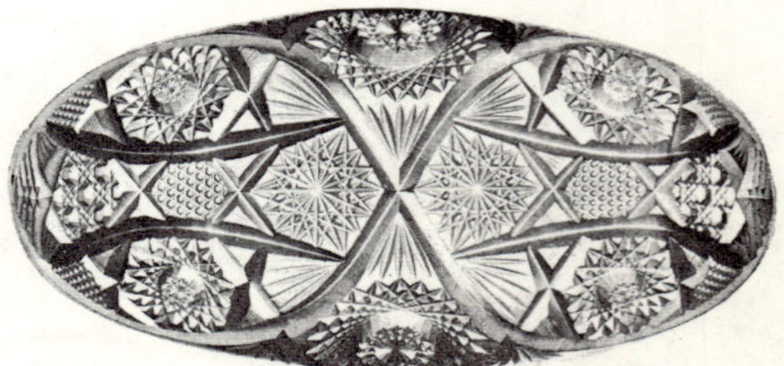

71291—Each 8.50
Length 12 inches
$130
1-82-11

71292—Each 9.50
Length 12 inches
$150
1-82-6

71313—Each 12.50
Length 11½ inches
Engraved flowers
$160
1-82-12

Mayonnaise or Whipped Cream Sets

AMERICAN CUT GLASS

76004—Each 2.00
$50
1-83-1
Bowl
Diameter 6 inches

76003—Each 2.00
$50
1-83-2
Bowl
Diameter 6 inches

76008—Set 4.00
$110
1-83-3
Bowl and Plate
Diameter of Bowl 5 inches
Diameter of Plate 6 inches

76017—Set 4.50
$125
1-83-4
Bowl and Plate
Diameter of Bowl 6 inches
Diameter of Plate 6½ inches

76013—Set 5.00
$110
1-83-5
Bowl and Plate
Diameter of Bowl 5¼ inches
Diameter of Plate 5½ inches

76019—Set 4.70
$120
1-83-6
Bowl and Plate
Diameter of Bowl 6 inches
Diameter of Plate 7 inches

76030—Set 6.00
$130
1-83-7
Bowl and Plate
Diameter of Bowl 5½ inches
Diameter of Plate 7 inches

76023—Set 7.00
$130
1-83-8
Bowl and Plate
Diameter of Bowl 5 inches
Diameter of Plate 7 inches

76031—Set 7.00
$130
1-83-9
Bowl and Plate
Square shape
Width of Bowl 4½ inches
Width of Plate 6 inches

76032—Set 8.50
$140
1-83-10
Bowl and Plate
Oval shape
Length of Bowl 6¼ inches
Length of Plate 7½ inches

76033—Set 9.00
$140
1-83-11
Bowl and Plate
Diameter of Bowl 6 inches
Diameter of Plate 7¼ inches

76036—Set 14.00
$180
1-83-12
Mayonnaise Set
Diameter of Bowl 6 inches
Diameter of Plate 7 inches
Engraved Flowers

76045—Set 16.00
$180
1-83-13
Bowl and Plate
Diameter of Bowl 6¼ inches
Diameter of Plate 7 inches

Sugar and Cream Sets

73726—Per Set 2.70 *$50* *1-84-1*
Diameter of Sugar   3 inches
Diameter of Creamer 3 inches

73728—Per Set 2.80 *$50* *1-84-2*
Diameter of Sugar   3 inches
Diameter of Creamer 3 inches

73721—Per Set 3.00 *$60* *1-84-3*
Diameter of Sugar   4 inches
Diameter of Creamer 3½ inches
Engraved

73730—Per Set 3.50 *$55* *1-84-4*
Diameter of Sugar   3½ inches
Diameter of Creamer 3¼ inches

73770—Per Set 4.50 *$60* *1-84-5*
Diameter of Sugar   3½ inches
Diameter of Creamer 3½ inches

73791—Per Set 5.00 *$60* *1-84-6*
Diameter of Sugar   4½ inches
Diameter of Creamer 3½ inches

73812—Per Set 5.50 *$65* *1-84-7*
Diameter of Sugar   4 inches
Diameter of Creamer 3¾ inches

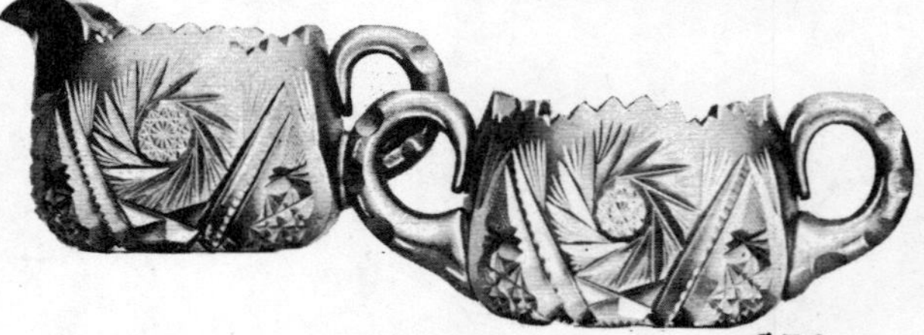

73816—Per Set 6.50 *$70* *1-84-8*
Diameter of Sugar   4¼ inches
Diameter of Creamer 4¼ inches

73843—Per Set 7.00 *$75* *1-84-9*
Diameter of Sugar   4 inches
Diameter of Creamer 3½ inches

73846—Per Set 7.50 *$125* *1-84-10*
Diameter of Sugar   3½ inches
Diameter of Creamer 3 inches

73865—Per Set 8.00 *$125* *1-84-11*
Diameter of Sugar   4 inches
Diameter of Creamer 4 inches
Engraved

73873—Per Set 8.00 *$120* *1-84-12*
Diameter of Sugar   3¼ inches
Diameter of Creamer 4 inches

Sugar and Cream Sets, Tea Bell, Syrup and Milk Pitcher

8130
1-85-1

73932—Per Set 8.50
Diameter of Sugar 4 inches
Diameter of Cream 3⅛ inches

8150
1-85-2

73888—Per Set 9.50
Diameter of Sugar 3¼ inches
Diameter of Cream 3¼ inches

8175
1-85-3

73902—Per Set 10.00
Diameter of Sugar 4 inches
Diameter of Cream 3¼ inches

8175
1-85-4

73951—Per Set 13.00
Diameter of Sugar 4¼ inches
Diameter of Cream 4 inches

8175
1-85-5

73952—Per Set 13.00
Diameter of Sugar 3⅛ inches
Diameter of Cream 3½ inches

8210
1-85-6

73991—Per Set 17.00
Diameter of Sugar 4¼ inches
Diameter of Cream 4 inches

855
1-85-7

75803—Each 4.70
Syrup, Silver Plated Top
Height 5¾ inches

8125
1-85-8

74303—Each 3.30
Tea Bell, Height 5½ inches

8125
1-85-9

74304—Each 3.50
Tea Bell, Height 5¾ inches

875
1-85-10

74405—Each 3.50
Milk pitcher ½ pint
Height 5 inches

Cut Glass Table Articles

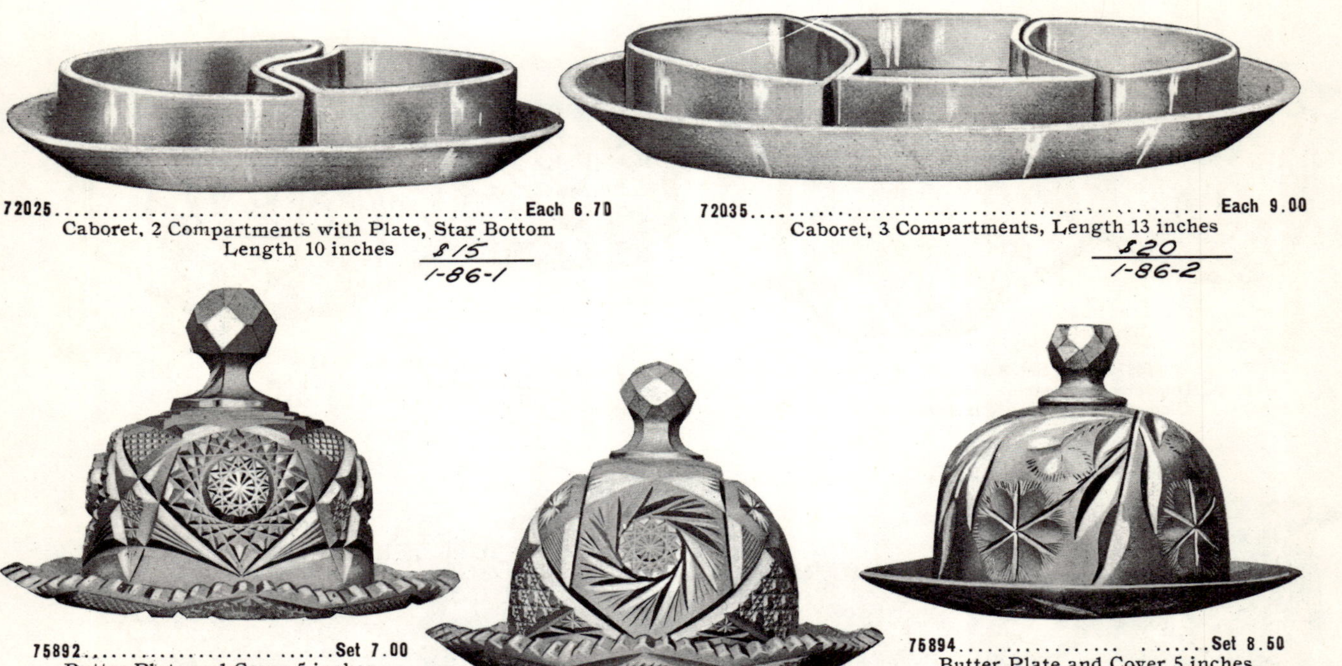

72025.............................Each 6.70
Caboret, 2 Compartments with Plate, Star Bottom
Length 10 inches *$15*
1-86-1

72035.............................Each 9.00
Caboret, 3 Compartments, Length 13 inches
$20
1-86-2

75892.....................Set 7.00
Butter Plate and Cover 5 inches *$300*
Diameter of Plate 8 inches
1-86-3

75893......................Set 7.50
Butter Plate and Cover 5 inches
Diameter of Plate 8 inches
$325
1-86-4

75894.......................Set 8.50
Butter Plate and Cover 5 inches
Diameter of Plate 8 inches *$300*
1-86-5

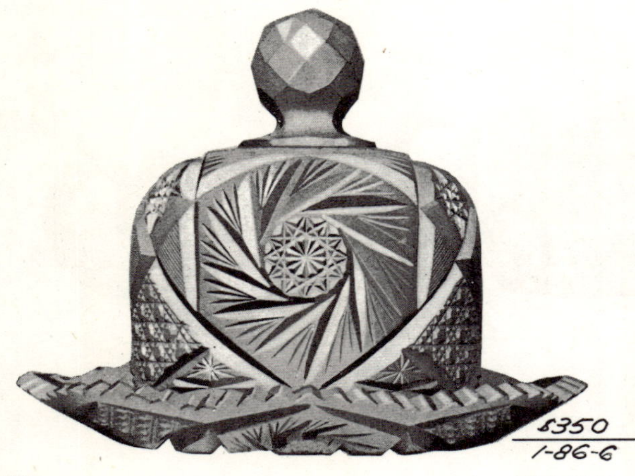

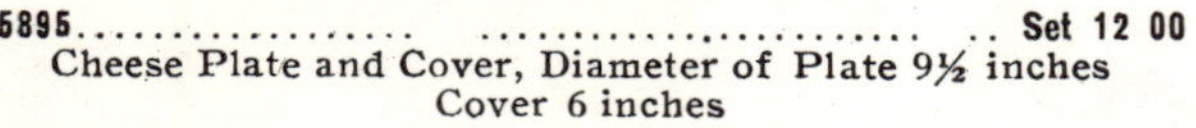

$350
1-86-6

75895.............................Set 12 00
Cheese Plate and Cover, Diameter of Plate 9½ inches
Cover 6 inches

$100
1-86-7

75947.............................Set 10.00
2 Oil Bottles, 1 Pan, Salt and Pepper, One 10 inch Tray
75944.............................Each 4.50
Tray Star Bottom, Length 10 inches, Width 6½ inches

$170
1-86-8

74161.........................Each 4.70
Ice Tub, Diameter 6 inches

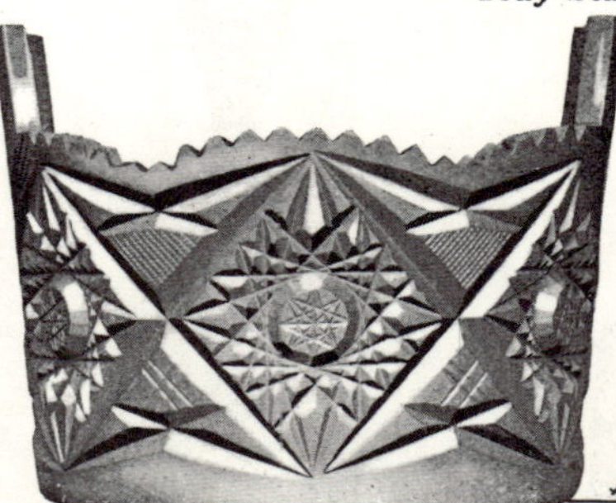

$195
1-86-9

74160.........................Each 5.50
Ice Tub, Diameter 7 inches

$250
1-86-10

74162.........................Set 8.50
Ice Tub and Plate
Diameter of Ice Tub 6 inches
Diameter of Plate   8 inches

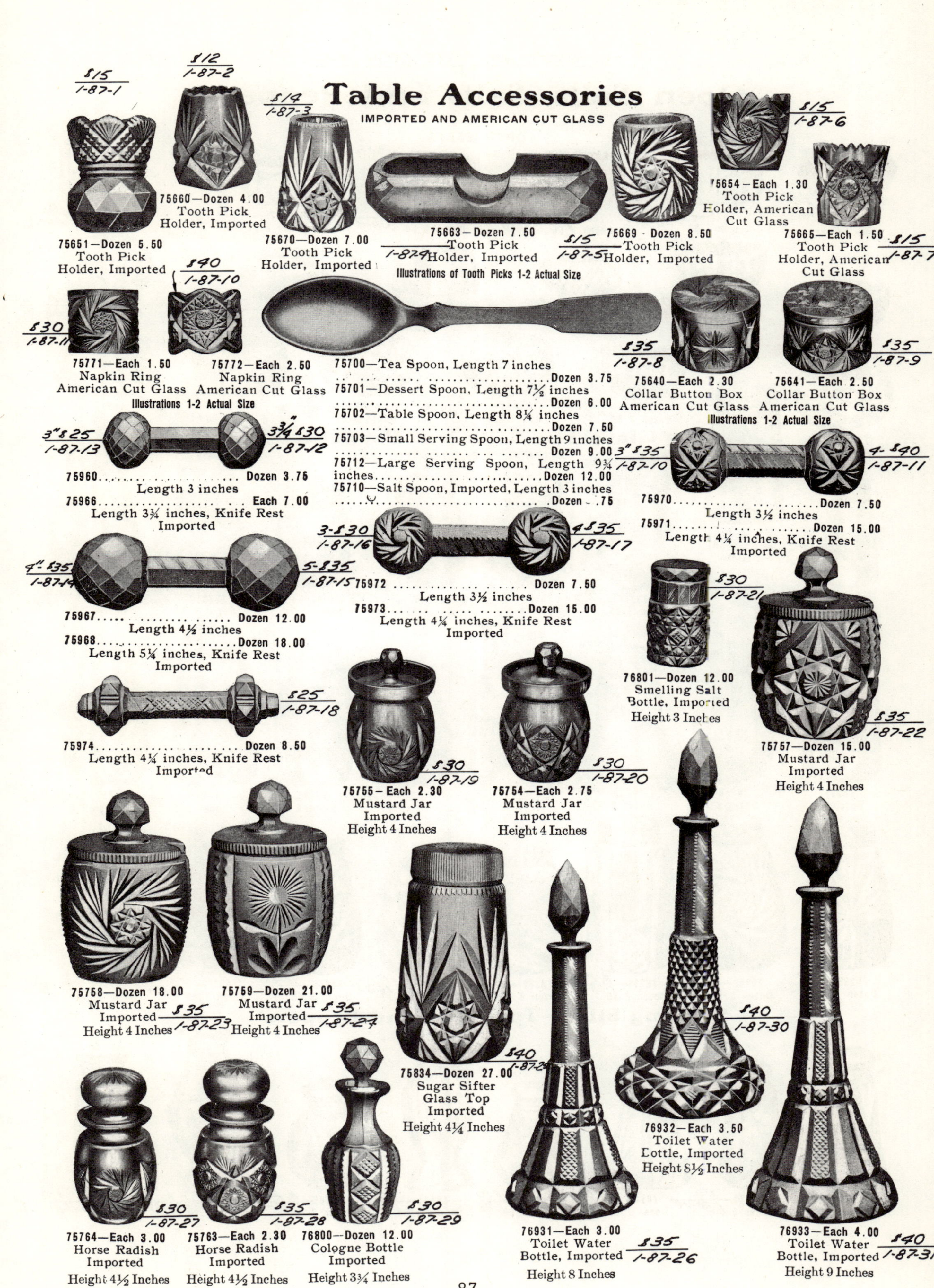

Table Accessories

IMPORTED AND AMERICAN CUT GLASS

75660—Dozen 4.00
Tooth Pick
Holder, Imported

75651—Dozen 5.50
Tooth Pick
Holder, Imported

75670—Dozen 7.00
Tooth Pick
Holder, Imported

75663—Dozen 7.50
Tooth Pick
Holder, Imported
Illustrations of Tooth Picks 1-2 Actual Size

75669 · Dozen 8.50
Tooth Pick
Holder, Imported

75654—Each 1.30
Tooth Pick
Holder, American
Cut Glass

75665—Each 1.50
Tooth Pick
Holder, American
Cut Glass

75771—Each 1.50
Napkin Ring
American Cut Glass

75772—Each 2.50
Napkin Ring
American Cut Glass
Illustrations 1-2 Actual Size

75700—Tea Spoon, Length 7 inches
....Dozen 3.75
75701—Dessert Spoon, Length 7½ inches
....Dozen 6.00
75702—Table Spoon, Length 8¼ inches
....Dozen 7.50
75703—Small Serving Spoon, Length 9 inches
....Dozen 9.00
75712—Large Serving Spoon, Length 9¾
inches...Dozen 12.00
75710—Salt Spoon, Imported, Length 3 inches
....Dozen .75

75640—Each 2.30
Collar Button Box
American Cut Glass

75641—Each 2.50
Collar Button Box
American Cut Glass
Illustrations 1-2 Actual Size

75960...Dozen 3.75
Length 3 inches
75966...Each 7.00
Length 3¾ inches, Knife Rest
Imported

75970...Dozen 7.50
Length 3½ inches
75971...Dozen 15.00
Length 4¼ inches, Knife Rest
Imported

75967...Dozen 12.00
Length 4½ inches
75968...Dozen 18.00
Length 5¼ inches, Knife Rest
Imported

75972...Dozen 7.50
Length 3½ inches
75973...Dozen 15.00
Length 4¼ inches, Knife Rest
Imported

75974...Dozen 8.50
Length 4¼ inches, Knife Rest
Imported

76801—Dozen 12.00
Smelling Salt
Bottle, Imported
Height 3 Inches

75757—Dozen 15.00
Mustard Jar
Imported
Height 4 Inches

75755—Each 2.30
Mustard Jar
Imported
Height 4 Inches

75754—Each 2.75
Mustard Jar
Imported
Height 4 Inches

75758—Dozen 18.00
Mustard Jar
Imported
Height 4 Inches

75759—Dozen 21.00
Mustard Jar
Imported
Height 4 Inches

75834—Dozen 27.00
Sugar Sifter
Glass Top
Imported
Height 4¼ Inches

76932—Each 3.50
Toilet Water
Bottle, Imported
Height 8½ Inches

75764—Each 3.00
Horse Radish
Imported
Height 4½ Inches

75763—Each 2.30
Horse Radish
Imported
Height 4½ Inches

76800—Dozen 12.00
Cologne Bottle
Imported
Height 3¾ Inches

76931—Each 3.00
Toilet Water
Bottle, Imported
Height 8 Inches

76933—Each 4.00
Toilet Water
Bottle, Imported
Height 9 Inches

Open Salts, Salts and Peppers

OPEN SALTS

76520 — $8
Dozen 1.25 1-88-1
Small Size

76521 — $9
Dozen 1.50 1-88-2

76540 — $10
Dozen 2.50 1-88-3

76541 — $10
Dozen 2.50 1-88-4

76542 — $10
Dozen 2.70 1-88-5

76557 — $10
Dozen 2.70 1-88-6

76562 — $10
Dozen 3.30 1-88-11

76560 — $10
Dozen 3.30 1-88-10

76543 — $6
Dozen 3.50 1-88-9

76551 — $6
Dozen 3.50 1-88-8

76559 — $12
Dozen 3.50 1-88-7

76550 — $10
Dozen 3.00 1-88-12

76566 — $10
Dozen 3.50 1-88-13

76567 — $10
Dozen 3.50 1-88-14

76569 — $10
Dozen 3.50 1-88-15

76576 — $10
Dozen 4.00 1-88-16

76577 — $9
Dozen 4.00 1-88-17

76564 — $10
Dozen 3.50 1-88-18

Glass Top Salts and Peppers

EXTRA TOPS $1.50 DOZEN

76140-1 — $5
Dozen 3.30 1-88-20
2 inch

76174 — $5
Dozen 4.00 1-88-19

76182 — $6
Dozen 4.00 1-88-21

76185 — $6
Dozen 4.00 1-88-22

76186 — $8
Dozen 4.00 1-88-23

76446 — $6
Dozen 4.25 1-88-24

76231 — $8
Dozen 6.00 1-88-25

76241 — $8
Dozen 6.00 1-88-26

76257 — $8
Dozen 6.00 1-88-27

76258 — $8
Dozen 6.00 1-88-28

76267 — $6
Dozen 6.00 1-88-29

76284 — $6
Dozen 7.00 1-88-30

76259 — $8
Dozen 7.00 1-88-31

76233 — $8
Dozen 7.00 1-88-32

76278 — $10
Dozen 7.50 1-88-33

76256 — $10
Dozen 7.00 1-88-34

76283 — $12
Dozen 7.50 1-88-35

76340 — $12
Dozen 8.00 1-88-36

76264 — $12
Dozen 8.00 1-88-37

76282 — $10
Dozen 8.00 1-88-38

76341 — $12
Dozen 8.50 1-88-39

76279 — $12
Dozen 8.50 1-88-40

76277 — $12
Dozen 8.50 1-88-41

76285 — $9
Dozen 8.50 1-88-42

Sterling Silver Top Salts and Peppers

76343 — $9
Dozen 4.00 1-88-43

76321 — $10
Dozen 6.00 1-88-44

76344 — $10
Dozen 7.50 1-88-45

76371 — $10
Dozen 8.50 1-88-46

76381 — $12
Dozen 8.50 1-88-47

76380 — $12
Dozen 9.00 1-88-48

76392 — $7
Dozen 9.00 1-88-49

76397 — $12
Dozen 12.00 1-88-50

Oil and Vinegar Bottles
American Cut Glass

73416—Each 1.30
Height 7 inches
Imported

73430—Each 1.70
Height 8 inches
Imported

73451—Each 2.00
Height 7 inches
Imported

73480—Each 2.50
Height 6½ inches
Imported

73505—Each 2.70
Height 7 inches

73491—Each 2.90
Height 7 inches

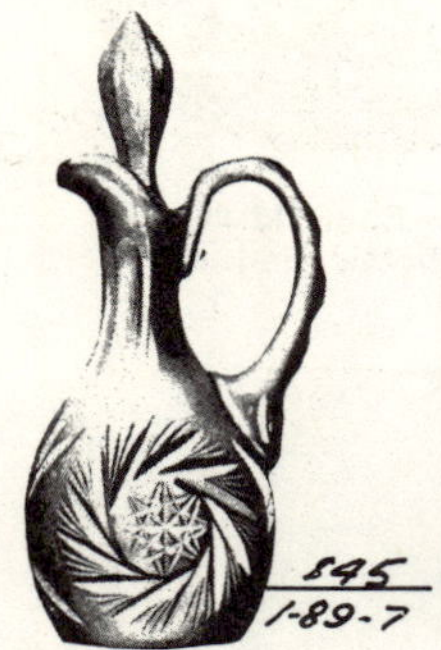

73508—Each 3.20
Height 8 inches

73510—Each 3.30
Height 6 inches
American
Stone engraved

73501—Each 3.20
Height 7¾ inches
Imported

73514—Each 3.50
Height 8 inches

73511—Each 3.60
Height 7 inches

73525—Each 3.75
Height 7 inches

73554—Each 4.00
Height 8 inches
American
Stone engraved

73532—Each 4.00
Height 7 inches

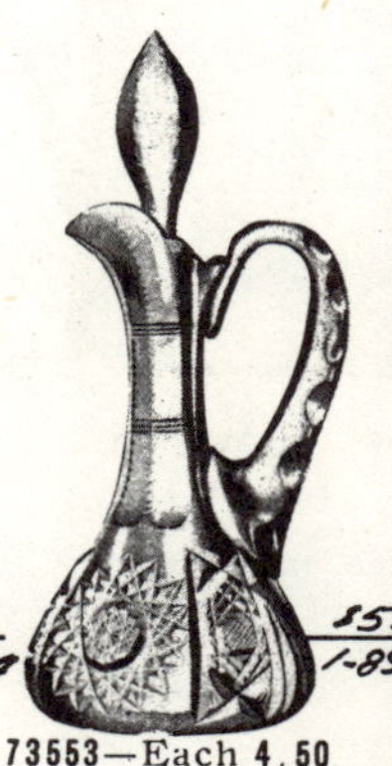

73553—Each 4.50
Height 8 inches

73572—Each 5.00
Height 7 inches
Satin flowers

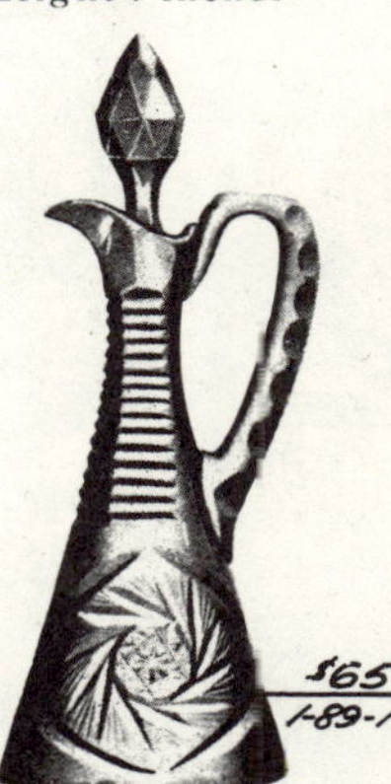

73580—Each 5.50
Height 9½ inches

73581—Each 5.50
Height 9 inches

73602—Each 6.00
Height 7 inches
Satin flowers

73611—Each 6.50
Height 9 inches

73495—Pair 3.50
Double Oil Bottles
Height 7 inches
Imported

73513—Pair 4.00
Double Oil Bottles
Height 7¾ inches
Imported

75790—Set 5.50
Condiment Set
Length of tray 5¾ inches
Height of bottle 6½ inches
Imported

Water Bottles, Water Sets and Jugs

AMERICAN CUT GLASS

72230—Each 3.50
Water bottle, 1 quart

72234—Each 4.00
Water bottle, 1 quart

72275—Each 6.50
Water bottle, 1 quart

72300—Each 10.00
Water bottle, 1 quart

72345—Set 4.00
Guest or sick room
water set, 1 pint

72341—Set 8.00
Guest or sick room
water set, 1 pint

72401—Each 1.40
3 pints
Star Design
Star on Bottom

72403—Each 1.40
3 pints
Star Design

72414—Each 4.70
2½ pints

72427—Each 5.30
3 pints

72451—Each 7.00
3 pints

72455—Each 7.50
3 pints

Water, Ice Tea and Lemonade Jugs

AMERICAN CUT GLASS

72471—Each 8.00 — $85 — 1-91-1
4 pints
Height 10 inches

72472—Each 8.50 — $90 — 1-91-2
4 pints
Height 10½ inches

72473—Each 9.00 — $95 — 1-91-3
4 pints
Height 10½ inches

72485—Each 9.50 — $100 — 1-91-4
3 pints
Height 11 inches

72501—Each 10.00 — $105 — 1-91-5
4 pints
Height 10½ inches

72499—Each 10.50 — $110 — 1-91-6
3 pints
Height 11 inches

72512—Each 12.00 — $100 — 1-91-7
4 pints
Height 10¼ inches

72540—Each 15.00 — $160 — 1-91-8
4 pints
Height 10 inches

72536—Each 17.00 — $175 — 1-91-9
4 pints
Height 10¾ inches

72539—Each 17.00 — $220 — 1-91-10
4 pints
Height 12¼ inches

72563—Each 21.00 — $250 — 1-91-11
4 pints
Height 11 inches

72567—Each 26.00 — $275 — 1-91-12
4 pints
Height 12½ inches

Tumblers

AMERICAN CUT GLASS

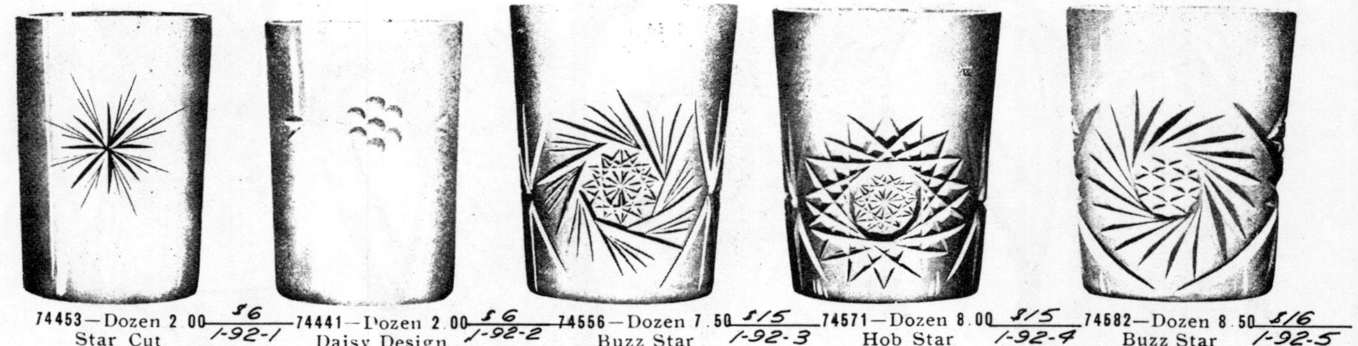

74453—Dozen 2.00 *$6* / *1-92-1* — Star Cut 74441—Dozen 2.00 *$6* / *1-92-2* — Daisy Design 74556—Dozen 7.50 *$15* / *1-92-3* — Buzz Star 74571—Dozen 8.00 *$15* / *1-92-4* — Hob Star 74582—Dozen 8.50 *$16* / *1-92-5* — Buzz Star

Barrel lots, packed 20 dozen in barrel, either
74456 or 74445................Dozen 1.45

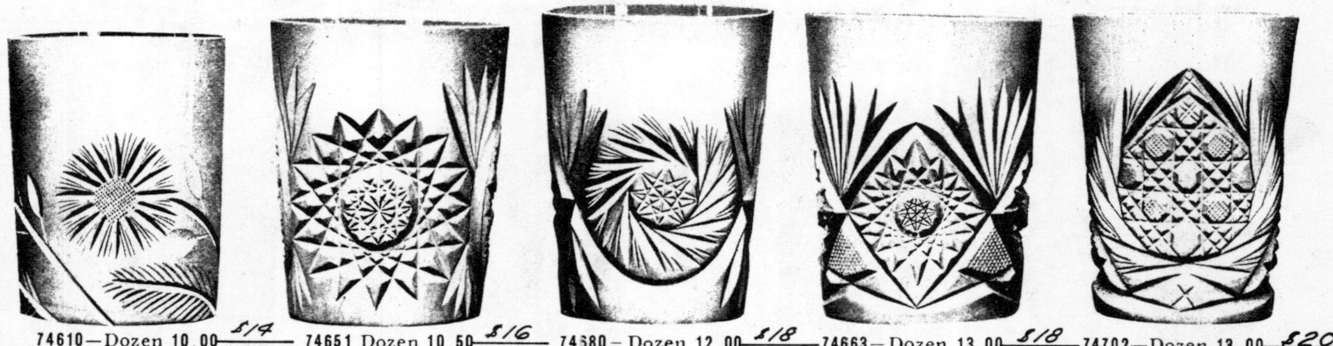

74610—Dozen 10.00 *$14* / *1-92-6* — Floral Design 74651—Dozen 10.50 *$16* / *1-92-7* — Hob Star 74680—Dozen 12.00 *$18* / *1-92-8* — Buzz Star 74663—Dozen 13.00 *$18* / *1-92-9* — Hob Star 74702—Dozen 13.00 *$20* / *1-92-10* — Wreath Design

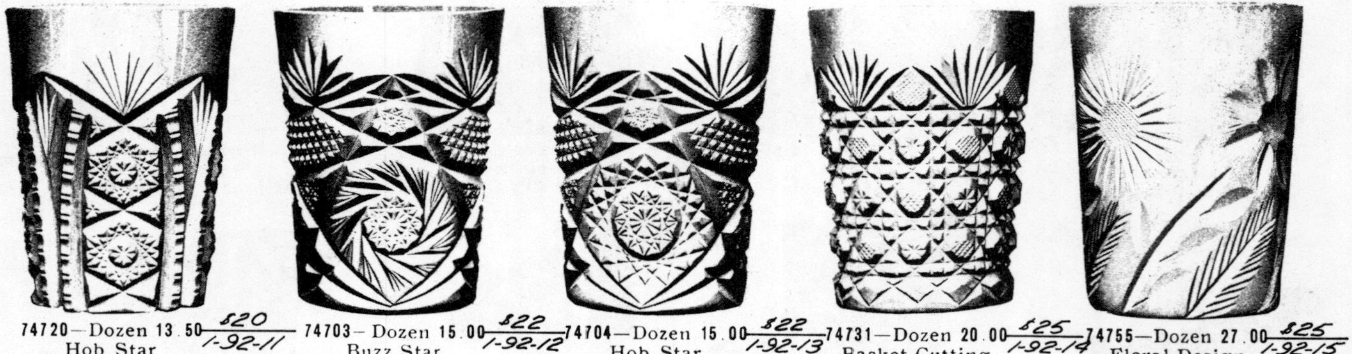

74720—Dozen 13.50 *$20* / *1-92-11* — Hob Star 74703—Dozen 15.00 *$22* / *1-92-12* — Buzz Star 74704—Dozen 15.00 *$22* / *1-92-13* — Hob Star 74731—Dozen 20.00 *$25* / *1-92-14* — Basket Cutting 74755—Dozen 27.00 *$25* / *1-92-15* — Floral Design

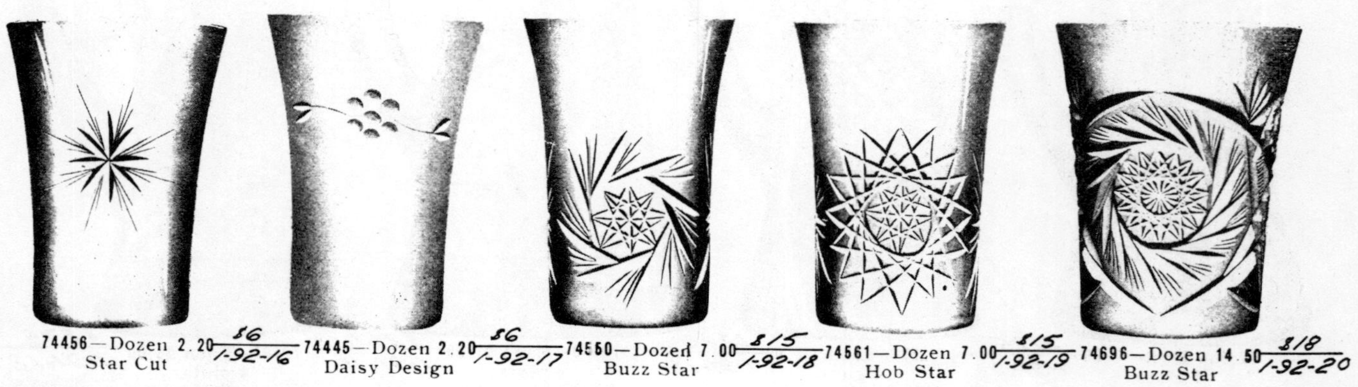

74456—Dozen 2.20 *$6* / *1-92-16* — Star Cut 74445—Dozen 2.20 *$6* / *1-92-17* — Daisy Design 74550—Dozed 7.00 *$15* / *1-92-18* — Buzz Star 74561—Dozen 7.00 *$15* / *1-92-19* — Hob Star 74696—Dozen 14.50 *$18* / *1-92-20* — Buzz Star

Barrel lots, packed 20 dozen in barrel, either
74453 or 74441................Dozen 1 60

Water Sets

J 815
1-93-1   79230—Set 4.00   G 86
1-93-2
3 pint water jug, ½ dozen tumblers,
12 inch plateau, nickel plated mounting

J 875
1-93-3   79231—Set 9.30   G 815
1-93-4
2½ pint water jug, ½ dozen tumblers,
12 inch plateau, nickel plated mounting

8 850
1-93-5   79248—Set 9.00   T 815
1-93-6
Water bottle, ½ dozen tumblers,
12 inch plateau

J 875
1-93-7   79239—Set 10.50   T 815
1-93-8
3 pint water jug, ½ dozen tumblers,
12 inch plateau, nickel plated mounting

J 885
1-93-9   79188—Set 15.50   T 814
1-93-10
3 pint water jug, ½ dozen tumblers,
14 inch plateau, silver plated mounting

J 890
1-93-11   79233—Set 18.00   T 818
1-93-12
4 pint water jug, ½ dozen tumblers,
14 inch plateau, silver plated mounting

J 895
1-93-13   79234—Set 20.50   T 818
1-93-14
4 pint water jug, ½ dozen tumblers,
14 inch plateau, silver plated mounting

J 8200
1-93-15   79174—Set 21.50   T 820
1-93-16
4 pint water jug, ½ dozen tumblers,
14 inch plateau, silver plated mounting

J 8125
1-93-17   79235—Set 22.50   T 818
1-93-18
4 pint water jug, ½ dozen tumblers,
15½ inch mirror bottom serving tray,
silver plated mounting

J 8105
1-93-19   79236—Set 25.00   T 822
1-93-20
4 pint water jug, ½ dozen tumblers,
14 inch plateau. silver plated mounting

J 8250
1-93-21   79237—Set 30.00   T 822
1-93-22
4 pint water jug, ½ dozen tumblers,
15½ inch plateau silver plated mounting

J 8275
1-93-23   79238—Set 37.00   T 825
1-93-24
4 pint water jug. ½ dozen tumblers.
14 inch plateau, silver plated mounting

Wine and Whiskey Decanters

AMERICAN CUT GLASS

73200—Each 1.50
Individual Bottle
and Tumbler
Imported

$50
1-94-2

$40
1-94-1
73202—Each 2.50
1 Pint Cordial
Imported

$70
1-94-3 **73201**—Each 3.00
1 Pint Cordial
Imported

$80
1-94-4
73224—Each 4.00
1 Quart Imported

$160
1-94-5 **73252**—Each 8.50
1 Quart
No Handle

$205
1-94-6 **73253**—Each 9.50
1 Quart Handled
Wine

$160
1-94-7 **73254**—Each 8.50
1 Quart
No Handle

$205
1-94-8 **73255**—Each 9.50
1 Quart Handled
Wine

$160
1-94-9
73259—Each 9.00
1 Quart Wine

$210
1-94-10 **73261**—Each 12.00
1 Quart Wine

$250
1-94-11
73257—Each 15.00
No Handle
1 Quart Wine

$300
1-94-12
73258—Each 16.50
Handled
1 Quart Wine

$180
1-94-13
73267—Each 10.00
1 Quart Whiskey

$180
1-94-14
73262—Each 10.00
1 Quart Whiskey

$210
1-94-15 **73263**—Each 12.00
1 Quart Whiskey

$250
1-94-16 **73296**—Each 10.00
1 Quart Whiskey

$275
1-94-17
73295—Each 13.00
1 Quart Whiskey
Engraved Flowers

$300
1-94-18
73289—Each 15.00
1 Quart Whiskey

$300
1-94-19
73293—Each 15.50
1 Quart Whiskey

Wine and Whiskey Sets

AMERICAN CUT GLASS

D 8160 1-95-1   G 850 1-95-2

79449—Wine.................Set 21.00
1 Quart Decanter, ½ dozen Glasses
Plateaux 12 inches, Nickel Rim

D 8160 1-95-5   G 850 1-95-6

79453—Wine.................Set 22.50
Quart Decanter, ½ dozen Glasses
11 inch Tray, Nickel, Tile Bottom

79452—Wine.................Set 27.00
D 8205 Quart Decanter, ½ dozen Glasses G 850
1-95-3   13½ inch Plateau, Silver Plated Rim   1-95-4

B 8180 1-95-11   T 820 1-95-12

79448—Whiskey.................Set 14.50
Quart Bottle, ½ dozen Tumblers
12 inch Plateau, Nickel Rim

79451—Wine.................Set 40.00
D 8250 Quart Decanter, ½ dozen Glasses G 865
1-95-9   12 inch Plateau, Silver Plated   1-95-10

79450—Wine.................Set 27.00
D 8210 Quart Decanter, ½ dozen Glasses G 850
1-95-7   12 inch Silver Plated Plateau   1-95-8

J 8250 1-95-13   T 820 1-95-14

79447—Whiskey.................Set 18.00
Whiskey Jug, ½ dozen Tumblers
12 inch Plateau, Silver Plated

B 8300 1-95-15   T 830 1-95-16

79445—Whiskey.................Set 23.50
Quart Bottle, ½ dozen Tumblers
15 inch Tray, Nickel Rim, Tile Bottom

B 8275 1-95-17   T 822 1-95-18

79446—Whiskey.................Set 30.00
Quart Bottle, ½ dozen Tumblers
13½ inch Tray, Silver Plated
Mirror Bottom

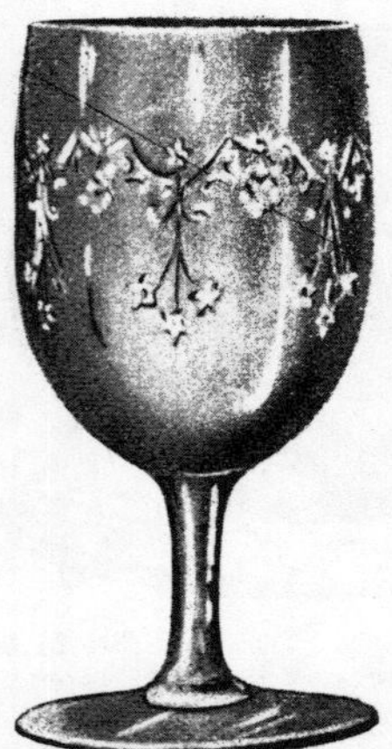

75100—Dozen 4.80
Goblet
75150—Dozen 4.80
Saucer Champagne
75200—Dozen 4.40
Claret
75300—Dozen 2.80
Whiskey
75350—Dozen 3.00
High Ball
75400—Dozen 3.20
Ice Tea Tumbler
75250—Dozen 7.50
Finger Bowl
Needle Etched

75101—Dozen 5.00
Goblet
75151—Dozen 5.00
Saucer Champagne
75201—Dozen 4.50
Claret
75251—Dozen 7.50
Finger Bowl
75451—Dozen 18.50
Grape Fruit with lining
Iridescent optic

75113—Dozen 4.00
Goblet
75164—Dozen 4.00
Saucer Champagne
75217—Dozen 3.70
Claret
75218—Dozen 3.50
Wine
75258—Dozen 6.00
Finger Bowl
75312—Dozen 2.70
Whiskey
Star cut

75102—Dozen 8.25
Goblet
75152—Dozen 8.25
Saucer Champagne
75202—Dozen 7.75
Claret
75302—Dozen 5.50
Whiskey
75352—Dozen 5.50
High Ball
75402—Dozen 6.50
Ice Tea
75452—Dozen 22.50
Grape Fruit
75252—Dozen 11.00
Finger Bowl
Laurel wreath, cut band

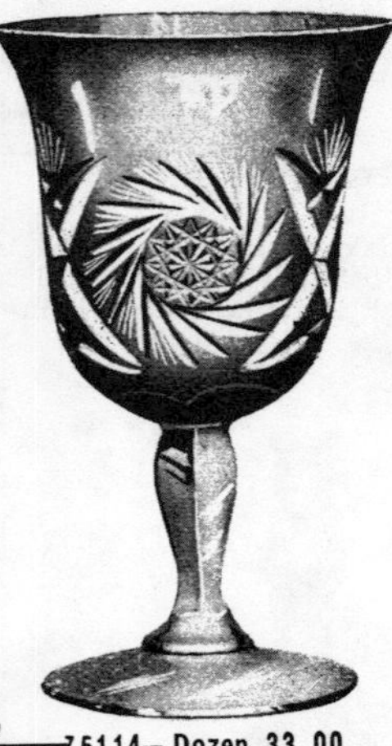

$60 / 1-96-1 — 75114—Dozen 33.00
Goblet
$55 / 1-96-7 — 75165—Dozen 33.00
Saucer Champagne
$45 / 1-96-2 — 75209—Dozen 24.50
Wine
$45 / 1-96-8 — 75219—Dozen 27.00
Claret
$45 / 1-96-3 — 75220—Dozen 27.00
Cocktail
$45 / 1-96-9 — 75221—Dozen 24.50
Sherry
$45 / 1-96-4 — 75223—Dozen 23.00
Cordial
$30 / 1-96-10 — 75259—Dozen 20.00
Finger Bowl
$30 / 1-96-5 — 75313—Dozen 11.00
Whiskey
$30 / 1-96-11 — 75358—Dozen 15.00
High Ball
$75 / 1-96-6 — 75166—Dozen 36.00
Hollow Stem Champagne
American cut glass

$55 / 1-96-15 — 75103—Dozen 31.00
Goblet
$50 / 1-96-12 — 75153—Dozen 31.00
Saucer Champagne
$50 / 1-96-16 — 75203—Dozen 26.00
Claret
$30 / 1-96-13 — 75303—Dozen 8.50
Whiskey
$35 / 1-96-17 — 75353—Dozen 17.00
High Ball
$30 / 1-96-14 — 75403—Dozen 18.50
Ice Tea
$30 / 1-96-18 — 75253—Dozen 26.00
Finger Bowl
We can furnish finger bowl plate at 26.00 dozen; delivery two weeks time. Buzz star, American cut glass

$60 / 1-96-23 — 75104—Dozen 32.00
Goblet
$55 / 1-96-19 — 75154—Dozen 32.00
Saucer Champagne
$45 / 1-96-24 — 75204—Dozen 27.00
Claret
$30 / 1-96-20 — 75304—Dozen 9.00
Whiskey
$35 / 1-96-24 — 75354—Dozen 18.00
High Ball
$30 / 1-96-21 — 75404—Dozen 19.50
Ice Tea Tumbler
$75 / 1-96-26 — 75454—Dozen 55.00
Grape Fruit
$30 / 1-96-22 — 75254—Dozen 27.00
Finger Bowl
We can furnish finger bowl plate at 27.00 dozen; delivery two weeks time. Hob star pattern. American cut glass.

$75 / 1-96-30 — 75105—Dozen 53.50
Goblet
$70 / 1-96-27 — 75155—Dozen 53.50
Saucer Champagne
$65 / 1-96-31 — 75205—Dozen 44.00
Claret
$30 / 1-96-28 — 75305—Dozen 19.50
Whiskey
$35 / 1-96-32 — 75355—Dozen 25.50
High Ball
75255—Dozen 50.00
Finger Bowl
$35 / 1-96-29 — Hob star pattern
American cut glass

Sherbets, Ice Cream Cups and Grape Fruits

74903—Dozen 4.00 $7 / 1-97-1
Star Cut

74902—Dozen 3.70 $7 / 1-97-2
Daisy Design

74991—Dozen 12.00 $30 / 1-97-3
Buzz Star

74992—Dozen 12.00 $30 / 1-97-4
Hob Star

74301—Dozen 3.30 $5 / 1-97-5
Star Cut

74900—Dozen 3.30 $5 / 1-97-6
Daisy Design

74980—Dozen 9.50 $5 / 1-97-7
Wreath Design

75023—Dozen 21.00 $30 / 1-97-8
Buzz Star

75164—Dozen 4.00 $5 / 1-97-9
Star Cut

75041—Dozen 21.00 $30 / 1-97-10
Hob Star

74930—Dozen 5.00 $5 / 1-97-11
Etched

75151—Dozen 5.00 $5 / 1-97-12
Iridescent Glass

75451—Dozen 18.50 $10 / 1-97-13
Grape Fruit Iridescent Glass

75153—Dozen 31.00 $40 / 1-97-14
Buzz Star

75154—Dozen 32.00 $40 / 1-97-15
Hob Star

75455—Dozen 23.00 $10 / 1-97-16
Grape Fruit Etched

Vases

72755—Each 2.70
8 inch
72795—Each 4.50
10 inch
72833—Each 6.50
12 inch

8"$65 / 1-98-1
10"$75 / 1-98-2
12"$95 / 1-98-3

72796—Each 4.70
10 inch
72822—Each 6.00
12 inch
Satin Flowers

10"$75 / 1-98-4
12"$95 / 1-98-5

72804—Each 5.00
10 inch
72843—Each 7.00
12 inch

10"$85 / 1-98-6
12"$110 / 1-98-7

72815—Each 5 50
10 inch
72844—Each 7.00
12 inch
72886—Each 9.00
14 inch
Satin Flowers

10"$80 / 1-98-8
12"$100 / 1-98-9
14"$130 / 1-98-10

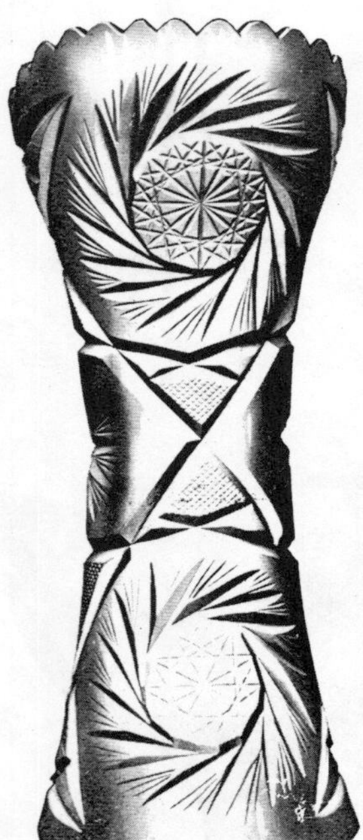

72789—Each 4.50
8 inch
72834—Each 6.50
10 inch
72895—Each 9.50
12 inch
72922—Each 13.50
14 inch

8"$80 / 1-98-11
10"$100 / 1-98-12
12"$130 / 1-98-13
14"$150 / 1-98-14

72902—Each 10.00
10 inch

$130 / 1-98-15

72832—Each 6.50
8 inch
72884—Each 9.00
10 inch
72921—Each 12.00
12 inch
72948—Each 15.50
14 inch

8"$90 / 1-98-16
10"$120 / 1-98-17
12"$140 / 1-98-18
14"$170 / 1-98-19

72914—Each 13.50
12 inch
72968—Each 19.00
14 inch
73011—Each 27.00
16 inch

12"$150 / 1-98-20
14"$185 / 1-98-21
16"$225 / 1-98-22

Vases

72915—Each 12.00 *$150*
1-99-1
12 inch

10"*$130*
1-99-2
13"*$150*
1-99-3
15"*$200*
1-99-4
18"*$330*
1-99-5

72909—Each 11.00
10 inch
72957—Each 17.00
13 inch
72988—Each 21.00
15 inch
73039—Each 35.00
18 inch

72931—Each 12.00 *$130*
1-99-6
10 inch
Satin Flowers

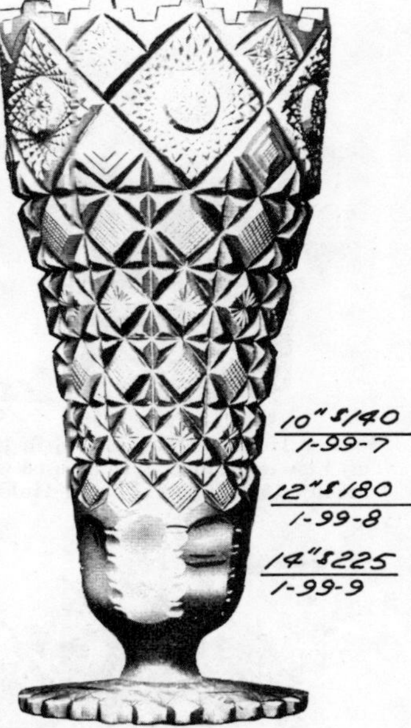

10"*$140*
1-99-7
12"*$180*
1-99-8
14"*$225*
1-99-9

72949—Each 14.00
10½ inch
72965—Each 18.00
12 inch
72989—Each 21.00
14 inch

72966—Each 19.00 *$160*
1-99-10
14 inch
Satin Flowers

72905—Each 14.00 *$140*
1-99-11
10 inch
72969—Each 19.00 *$65*
1-99-12
12 inch

72971—Each 20.00 *$225*
1-99-13
12 inch

10"*$110*
1-99-14
12"*$130*
1-99-15
14"*$165*
1-99-16

72943—Each 16.00
10 inch
73004—Each 24.00
12 inch
73021—Each 30.00
14 inch
Satin Flowers

Flower Holders and Fern Dishes

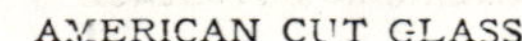

AMERICAN CUT GLASS

75540—2½ inch—Dozen 3.80
75541—3½ inch—Dozen 5.70
75542—4½ inch—Dozen 7.60
Flower Holder can be
used in any size dish

75580—Each 3.30 *$50 1-100-1*
Flower Holder, Diameter 4½ inches
This Flower Holder is to be used with
75540—75541 Glass Flower Holder

72835—Each 6.50 *$75 1-100-2*
Sweet Pea Vase
Width 6 inches
Height 7 inches

75583—6½ inch—Each 3.75
75584— 8 inch—Each 5.00
75585—10 inch—Each 7.00
75586—12 inch—Each 8.50
American Stone Engrave
To be used with Flower Holder No.
75540, Etc. Prices without holder

75572—Each 5.50 *$85 1-100-3*
Fern Dish, 8 inches

79022—Each 3.00
Plateau, 10 inches
Silver Plated Rim

75561—Each 3.50 *$60 1-100-4*
Fern Dish, 6 inches

75563—Each 5.50 *$85 1-100-5*
Fern Dish, 8 inches

79006—Each 1.50
Plateau, 10 inches
Nickel Plated Rim

75575—Each 4.70 *$95 1-1005*
Fern Dish, 6 inches

75574—Each 8.00 *$125 1-100-6*
Fern Dish, 8 inches

75573—Each 11.00 *$125 1-100-7*
Fern Dish only, 6 inches, 8 sided

75565—Each 8.50 *$100 1-100-8*
Round Fern Dish, Diameter 8 inches

79091—Each 7.00
Plateau, 10 inches
Silver Plated Rim

75588—Each 18.00 *$150 1-100-9*
Fern Dish, 9 inches
Satin Flowers

Cologne Bottles, Hair Receivers and Puff Boxes

AMERICAN CUT GLASS

76810—Each 2.20
1 ounce

76812—Each 2 50
4 ounce
76822—Each 3.00
6 ounce

76813—Each 2.70
2 ounce
76829—Each 3.30
4 ounce
76831 Each 3.50
6 ounce

76823—Each 3.00
2 ounce
76832—Each 3.50
4 ounce

76840—Each 3.80
6 ounce

76841—Each 3.50
4 ounce
76883—Each 4.50
6 ounce

76890—Each 6.50
6 ounce

76897—Each 7.50
8 ounce
Satin Flashes

77186—Each 3.70
Hair Receiver
Diameter 4 inches

76930—Each 6.50
Toilet Water Bottle
4 ounce

76928—Each 7.00
Toilet Water Bottle
4 ounce
Satin Flowers

76929—Each 8.00
Toilet Water Bottle
4 ounce
Satin Flowers

77185—Each 5.00
Hair Receiver
Diameter 4½ inches
Satin Flashes

77187—Each 5.00
Hair Receiver
Diameter 3½ inches
Satin Flashes

77011—Each 3.00
Puff Box
Diameter 3½ inches

77090—Each 7.00
Puff Box
Length 7 inches

77041—Each 4.50
Puff Box
Diameter 4½ inches

77072—Each 6.00
Puff Box
Diameter 4⅛ inches

77081—Each 6.50
Puff Box
Diameter 4½ inches

77006—Each 2.70
Puff Box
Diameter 3½ inches

77135—Each 8.00
Puff Box
Diameter 5 inches

77141—Each 10.00
Puff Box
Diameter 6 inches

77139—Each 12.00
Puff Box
Diameter 6 inches

69359......Each 69.00
2 Lights, Cut Glass
Height 22 inches
Diameter of Shade
12 inches

$1500
1-102-1

69342......Each 45.00
1 Light, Cut Glass
Height 19 inches
Diameter of Shade
10 inches

$1200
1-102-2

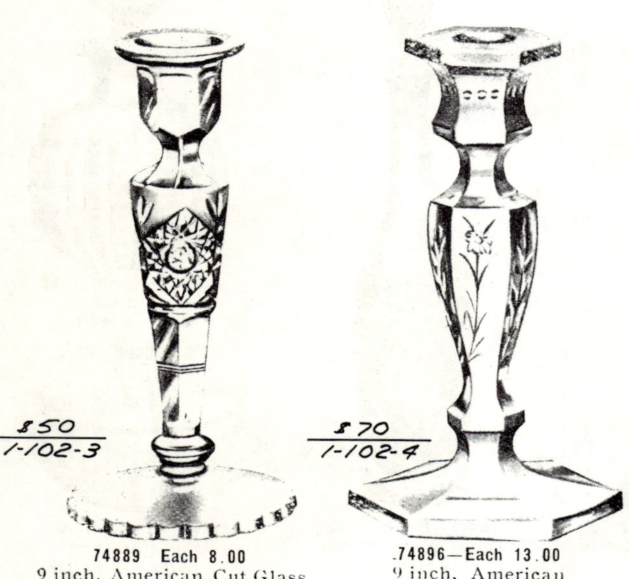

$850
1-102-3

74889 Each 8.00
9 inch, American Cut Glass

$70
1-102-4

74896—Each 13.00
9 inch, American
Stone Engraved Glass

$1400
1-102-5

69362..........................Each 60.00
2 Lights, Cut Glass, Height 21 inches
Diameter of Shade 12 inches

Cut Glass Cigar Jars and Ash Trays

$6
1-102-10
75946—Each 2.00
Ash Tray, Star Bottom
Diameter 4 inches

$225
1-102-6
75864—Each 10.00
Cigar Jar, Height 6 inches
Capacity 25 Cigars

$175
1-102-7
75865 Each 8.50
Cigar Jar, Height 8 inches
Capacity 25 Cigars

$200
1-102-8
75866 Each 13.00
Cigar Jar, Height 9 inches
Capacity 50 Cigars

$6
1-102-9
75945 Each 3.00
Ash Tray, Star Bottom
Diameter 5 inches

FINE, RICH, DEEP-CUT GLASS BOWLS AND NAPPIES.

ILLUSTRATIONS ARE REDUCED SIZE.   PRICES EACH.

N. A. & Co.
1909

DEEP BOWL.

$225 / 103-1   9"$285 / 1-103-2   10"$300 / 1-103-3

No. 2738.	8 inch	$25.00
No. 2739.	9 inch	30.00
No. 2740.	10 inch	37.50

OLIVE DISH.

$80 / 1-103-4

| No. 2741. | 6 inch | $8.45 |

DEEP BOWL.

8"$165 / 1-103-5   9"$200 / 1-103-6   10"$275 / 1-103-7

No. 2742.	8 inch	$17.50
No. 2743.	9 inch	22.50
No. 2744.	10 inch	30.00

DEEP BOWL.

$130 / 3-8 $165 / 03-9 $200 / 103-10   0"$275 / 1-103-11

No. 2746.	7 inch	$13.40
No. 2747.	8 inch	20.00
No. 2748.	9 inch	26.70
No. 2749.	10 inch	33.40

OLIVE DISH.

$40 / 1-103-12

| No. 2745. | 7 inch | $5.00 |

OLIVE DISH.

$35 / 1-103-12

| No. 2750. | 6 inch | $4.38 |

DEEP BOWL.

8"$155 / 1-103-14   9"$175 / 1-103-15   10"$200 / 1-103-16

No. 2751.	8 inch	$14.00
No. 2752.	9 inch	22.70
No. 2753.	10 inch	32.00

OVAL BOWL.

$195 / 1-103-17

| No. 2754. | 10x7 inches | $15.00 |

OLIVE DISH.

$40 / 1-103-18

| No. 2755. | 6 inch | $3.50 |

DEEP BOWL.

7"$165 / 1-103-19   8"$175 / 1-103-20   9"$195 / 1-103-21   10"$215 / 1-103-22

No. 2756.	7 inch	$9.40
No. 2757.	8 inch	12.00
No. 2758.	9 inch	18.70
No. 2759.	10 inch	24.00

DEEP BOWL.

$135 / 03-25 $145 / 103-26   9"$160 / 1-103-27   10"$175 / 1-103-28

No. 2762.	7 inch	$8.00
No. 2763.	8 inch	10.70
No. 2764.	9 inch	14.70
No. 2765.	10 inch	21.40

SAUCER.

5"$45 / 1-103-23   6"$50 / 1-103-24

| No. 2760. | 5 inch | $3.48 |
| No. 2761. | 6 inch | 4.06 |

SAUCER.

5"$45 / 1-103-29   6"$50 / 1-103-30

| No. 2769. | 5 inch | $2.50 |
| No. 2770. | 6 inch | 3.13 |

DEEP BOWL.

8"$115 / 1-103-31   9"$140 / 1-103-32   10"$175 / 1-103-33

No. 2766.	8 inch	$10.70
No. 2767.	9 inch	15.40
No. 2768.	10 inch	20.70

DEEP BOWL.

$140 / 03-34 $175 / 103-35   10"$225 / 1-103-36

No. 2771.	8 inch	$8.75
No. 2772.	9 inch	11.88
No. 2773.	10 inch	16.88

SAUCER.

5"$35 / 1-103-37   6"$40 / 1-103-38

| No. 2774. | 5 inch | $1.88 |
| No. 2775. | 6 inch | 2.39 |

DEEP BOWL.

8"$155 / 1-103-39   9"$180 / 1-103-40

| No. 2776. | 8 inch | $14.38 |
| No. 2777. | 9 inch | 18.13 |

FINE, RICH, DEEP-CUT GLASS BOWLS AND NAPPIES.

ILLUSTRATIONS ARE REDUCED SIZE. PRICES EACH.

N. A. & Co. 1909

DEEP BOWL.

No. 2778.	7 inch	$ 5.40
No. 2779.	8 inch	6.70
No. 2780.	9 inch	10.00
No. 2781.	10 inch	14.00

NAPPY.

| No. 2782. | 6 inch | $3.00 |
| No. 2783. | 7 inch | 5.00 |

ORANGE BOWL.

| No. 2784. | 9½ inch | $11.25 |

BOWL.

| No. 2785. | 8 inch | $9.00 |

SAUCER.

| No. 2786. | 5 inch | $2.14 |
| No. 2787. | 6 inch | 2.44 |

DEEP BOWL.

| No. 2788. | 8 inch | $ 6.80 |
| No. 2789. | 9 inch | 10.80 |

DEEP BOWL.

| No. 2790. | 8 inch | $6.50 |

SAUCER.

| No. 2791. | 5 inch | $2.30 |
| No. 2792. | 6 inch | 2.81 |

DEEP BOWL.

| No. 2793. | 8 inch | $8.00 |

Very New with Silver Finished Star.

DEEP BOWL.

| No. 2794. | 8 inch | $5.00 |

SAUCER.

| No. 2795. | 5 inch | $1.70 |
| No. 2796. | 6 inch | 2.14 |

DEEP BOWL.

| No. 2797. | 8 inch | $5.40 |

DEEP BOWL.

| No. 2798. | 8 inch | $4.25 |

SAUCER.

| No. 2799. | 5 inch | $1.70 |
| No. 2800. | 6 inch | 2.00 |

DEEP BOWL.

| No. 2803. | 7 inch | $4.06 |
| No. 2804. | 8 inch | 5.63 |

FINE, RICH, DEEP-CUT GLASS BOWLS AND NAPPIES.

ILLUSTRATIONS ARE REDUCED SIZE.   PRICES EACH.

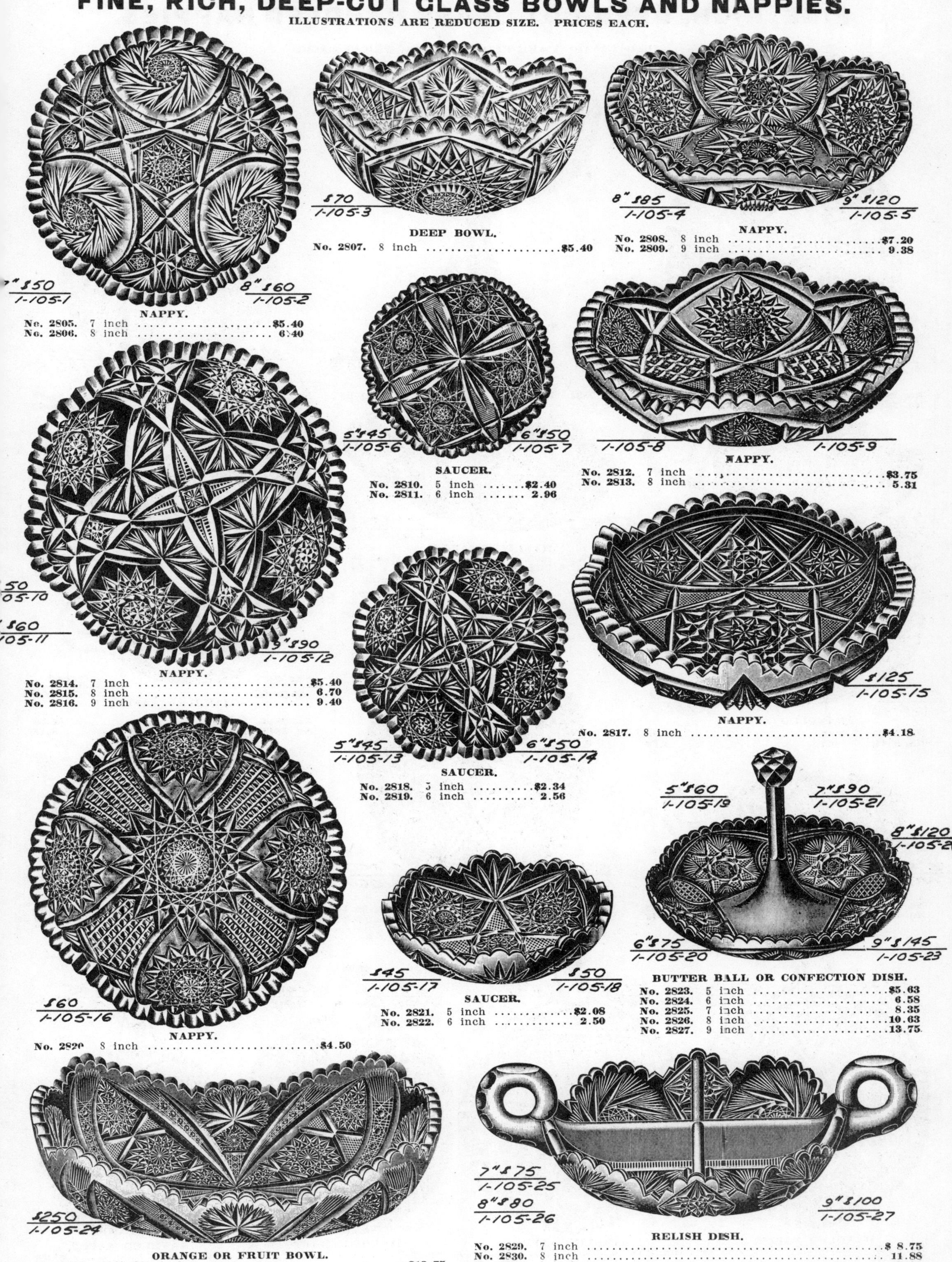

DEEP BOWL.

No. 2807.   8 inch $5.40

NAPPY.

No. 2808.   8 inch $7.20
No. 2809.   9 inch 9.38

NAPPY.

No. 2805.   7 inch $5.40
No. 2806.   8 inch 6.40

SAUCER.

No. 2810.   5 inch $2.40
No. 2811.   6 inch 2.96

NAPPY.

No. 2812.   7 inch $3.75
No. 2813.   8 inch 5.31

NAPPY.

No. 2814.   7 inch $5.40
No. 2815.   8 inch 6.70
No. 2816.   9 inch 9.40

SAUCER.

No. 2818.   5 inch $2.34
No. 2819.   6 inch 2.56

NAPPY.

No. 2817.   8 inch $4.18

BUTTER BALL OR CONFECTION DISH.

No. 2823.   5 inch $5.63
No. 2824.   6 inch 6.58
No. 2825.   7 inch 8.35
No. 2826.   8 inch 10.63
No. 2827.   9 inch 13.75

NAPPY.

No. 2820.   8 inch $4.50

SAUCER.

No. 2821.   5 inch $2.08
No. 2822.   6 inch 2.50

ORANGE OR FRUIT BOWL.

No. 2828.   11½ x 6½ inches $13.75

RELISH DISH.

No. 2829.   7 inch ....$ 8.75
No. 2830.   8 inch 11.88
No. 2831.   9 inch 15.00

FINE, RICH, DEEP-CUT GLASS HANDLED NAPPIES.

ILLUSTRATIONS ARE REDUCED SIZE.   PRICES EACH.

N. A. & Co.
1909

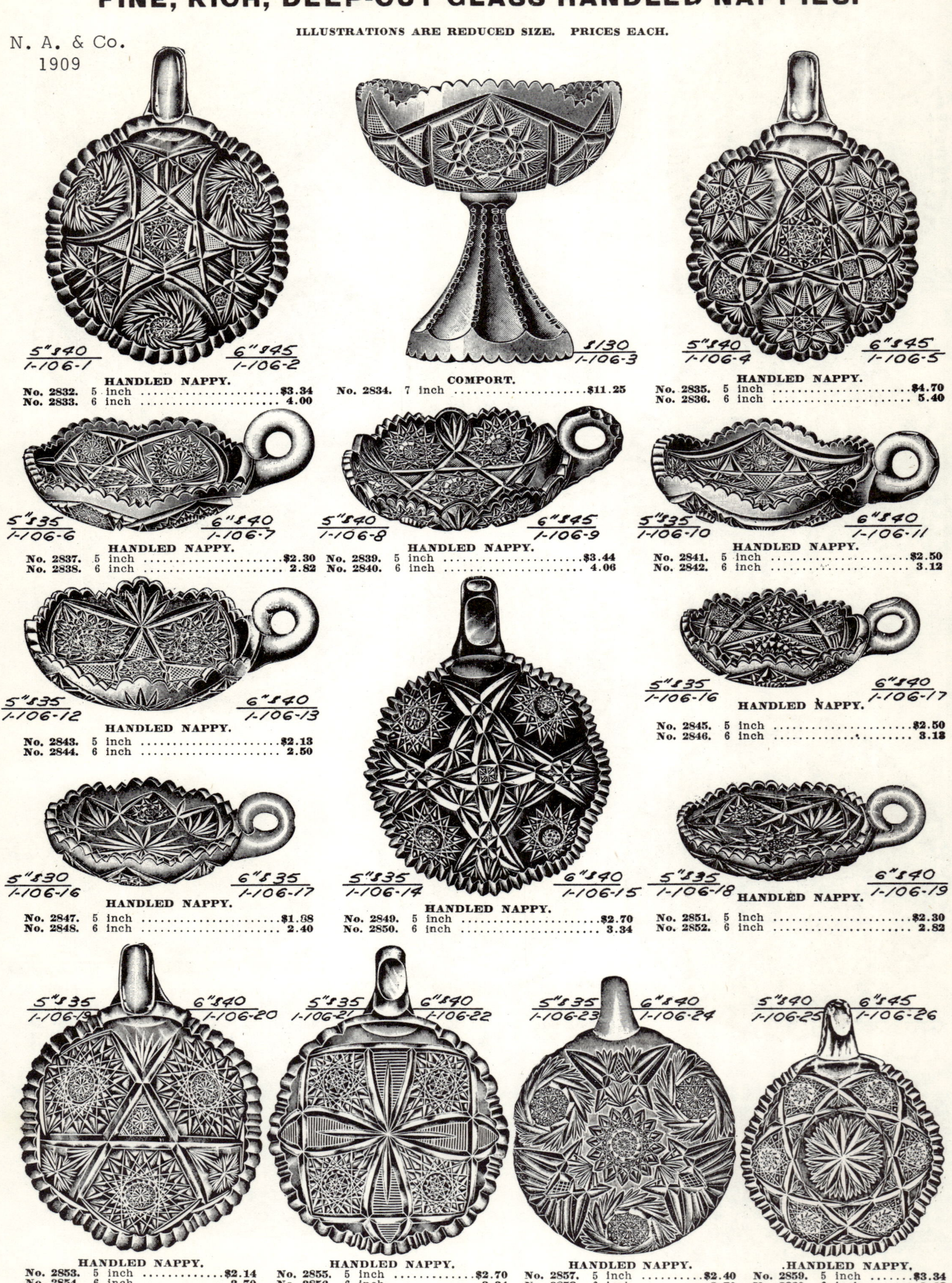

HANDLED NAPPY.
No. 2832. 5 inch $3.34
No. 2833. 6 inch 4.00

COMPORT.
No. 2834. 7 inch $11.25

HANDLED NAPPY.
No. 2835. 5 inch $4.70
No. 2836. 6 inch 5.40

HANDLED NAPPY.
No. 2837. 5 inch $2.30
No. 2838. 6 inch 2.82

No. 2839. 5 inch $3.44
No. 2840. 6 inch 4.06

HANDLED NAPPY.
No. 2841. 5 inch $2.50
No. 2842. 6 inch 3.12

HANDLED NAPPY.
No. 2843. 5 inch $2.13
No. 2844. 6 inch 2.50

HANDLED NAPPY.
No. 2845. 5 inch $2.50
No. 2846. 6 inch 3.13

HANDLED NAPPY.
No. 2847. 5 inch $1.88
No. 2848. 6 inch 2.40

HANDLED NAPPY.
No. 2849. 5 inch $2.70
No. 2850. 6 inch 3.34

HANDLED NAPPY.
No. 2851. 5 inch $2.30
No. 2852. 6 inch 2.82

HANDLED NAPPY.
No. 2853. 5 inch $2.14
No. 2854. 6 inch 2.70

HANDLED NAPPY.
No. 2855. 5 inch $2.70
No. 2856. 6 inch 3.34

HANDLED NAPPY.
No. 2857. 5 inch $2.40
No. 2858. 6 inch 2.70

HANDLED NAPPY.
No. 2859. 5 inch $3.34
No. 2860. 6 inch 3.68

FINE, RICH, DEEP-CUT GLASS SPOON TRAYS, PLATES AND COMPORTS.

N. A. Co.
1909

ILLUSTRATIONS ARE REDUCED SIZE. PRICES EACH.

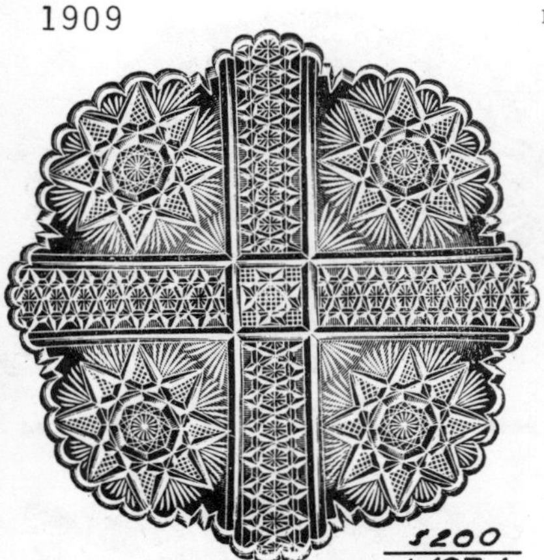

$200
1-107-1

PLATE.
No. 2877. 7 inch $7.50

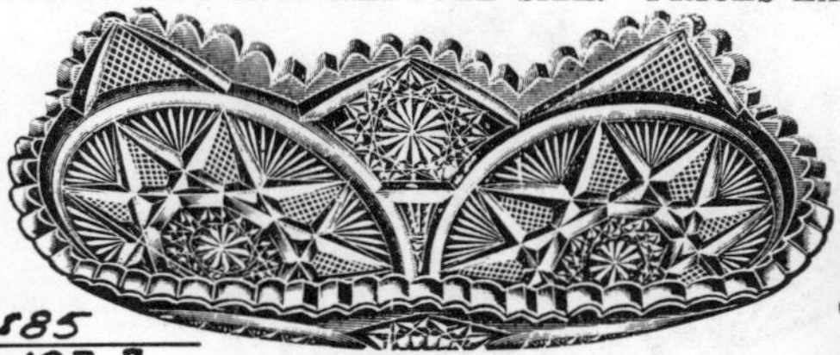

$85
1-107-2

SPOON TRAY.
No. 2876. 8 inch $5.63

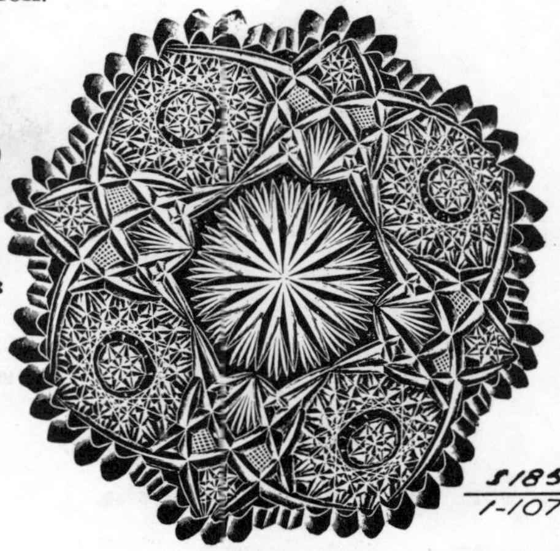

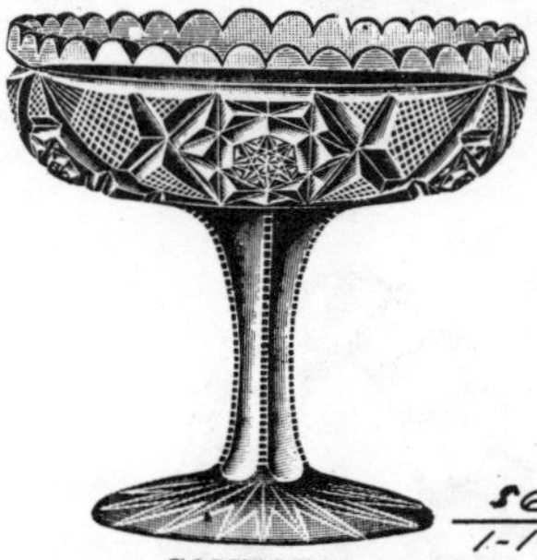

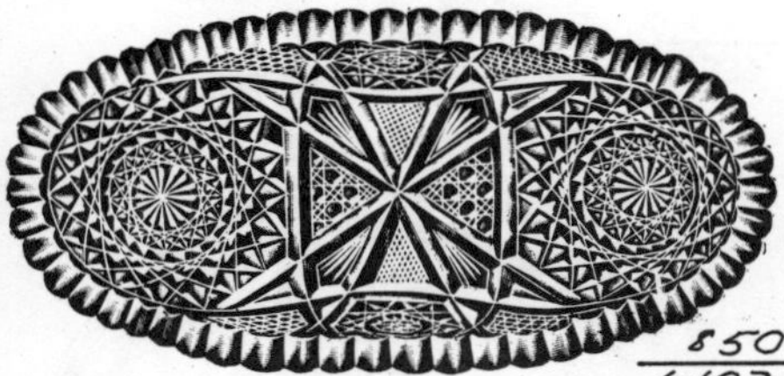

$185
1-107-4

PLATE.
No. 2879. 7 inch $5.40

$60
1-107-3

COMPORT.
No. 2878. 4¾ inch $5.00

$50
1-107-5

SPOON TRAY.
No. 2880. 7 inch $3.90

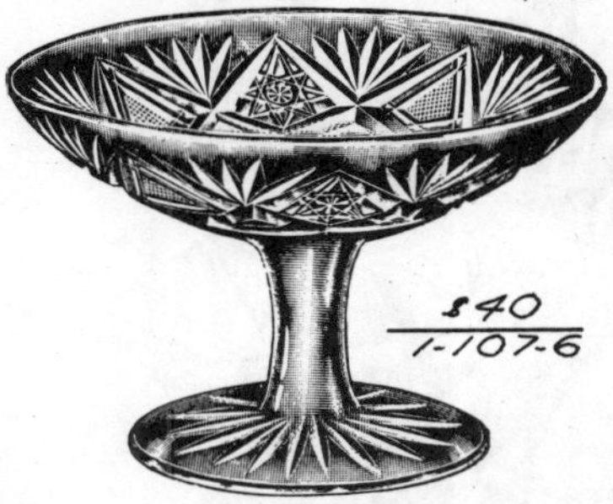

$40
1-107-6

COMPORT.
No. 2882. 3½ inches High....$4.00

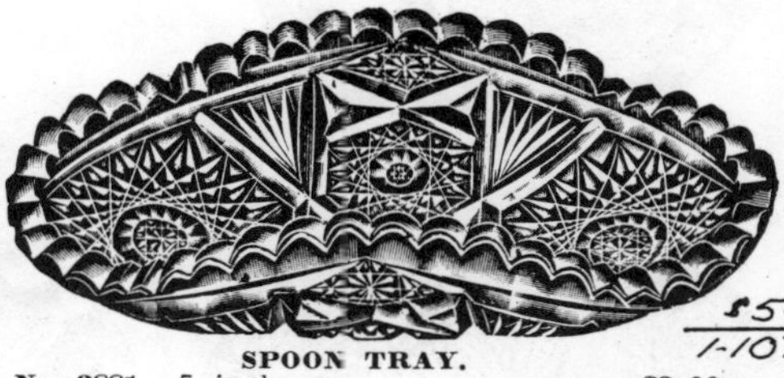

$50
1-107-7

SPOON TRAY.
No. 2881. 7 inch $3.00

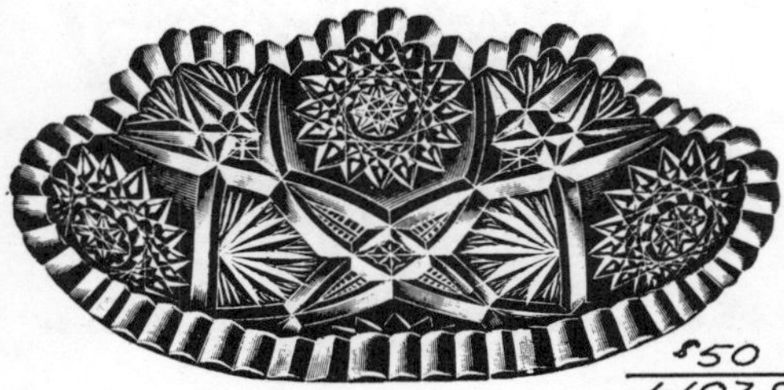

$50
1-107-9

SPOON TRAY.
No. 2883. 6¾ inch $3.35

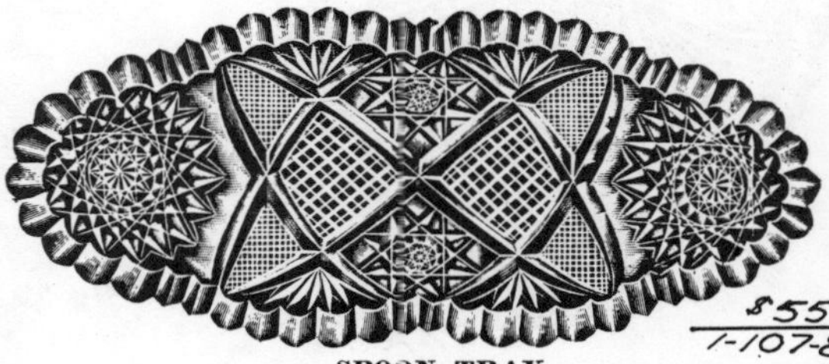

$55
1-107-8

SPOON TRAY.
No. 2884. 7½x3¼ inches $3.10

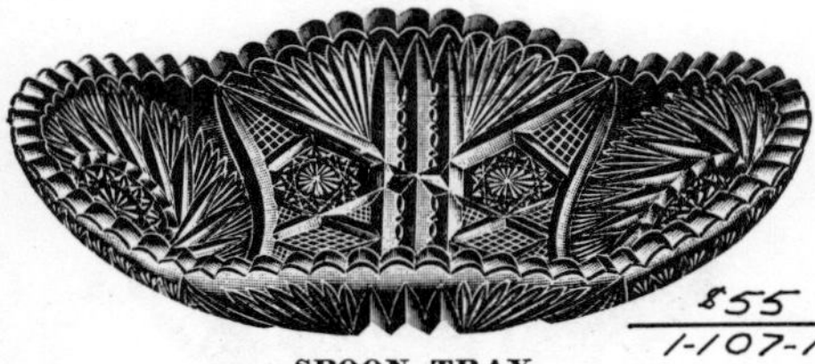

$55
1-107-10

SPOON TRAY.
No. 2885. 8 inch $3.13

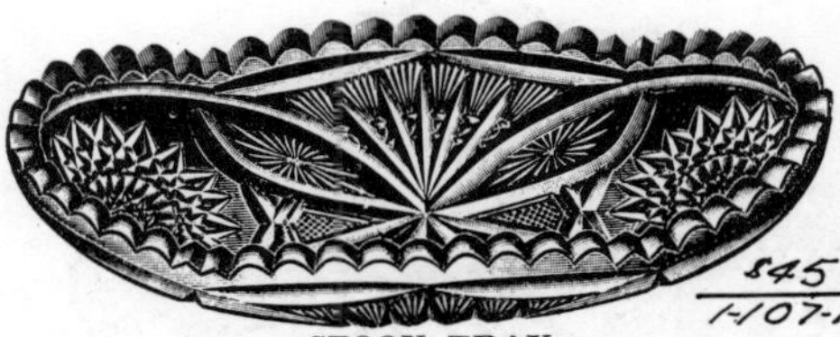

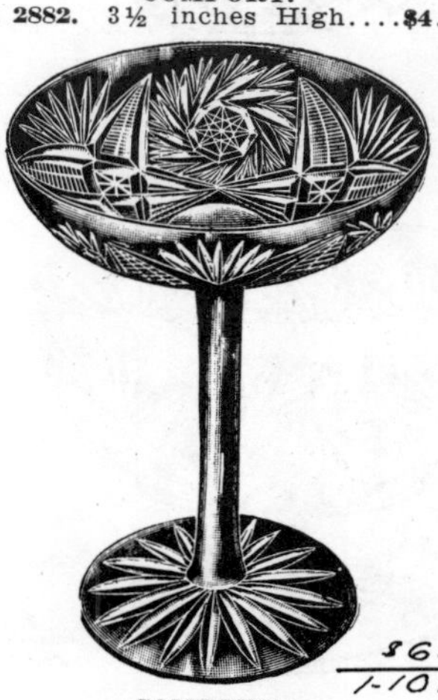

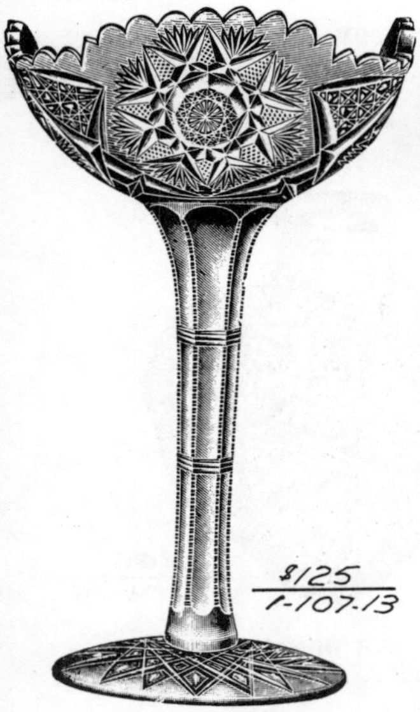

$45
1-107-12

SPOON TRAY.
No. 2887. 7½ inches $2.82

$65
1-107-11

COMPORT.
No. 2886. 6½ inches High....$4.00

$125
1-107-13

COMPORT.
No. 2888. 7½ inches High.$11.25

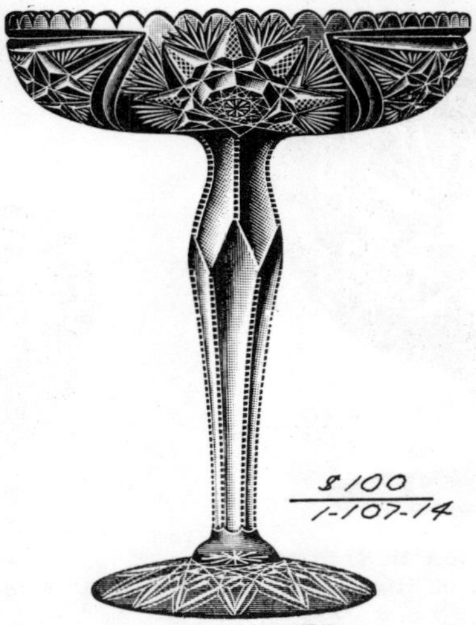

$100
1-107-14

COMPORT.
No. 2889. 6 inches High...$8.13

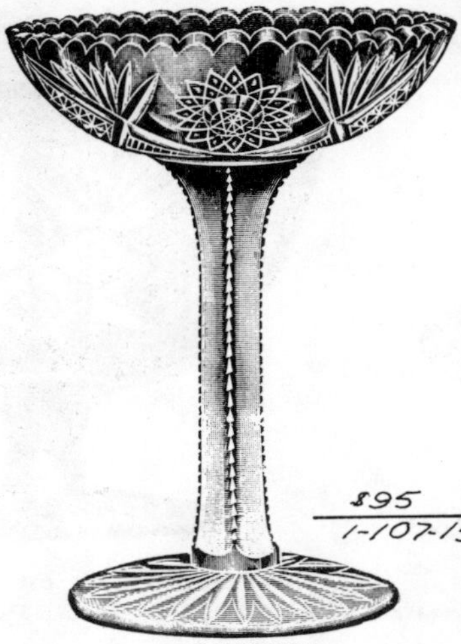

$95
1-107-15

COMPORT.
No. 2890. 6 inches High...$7.49

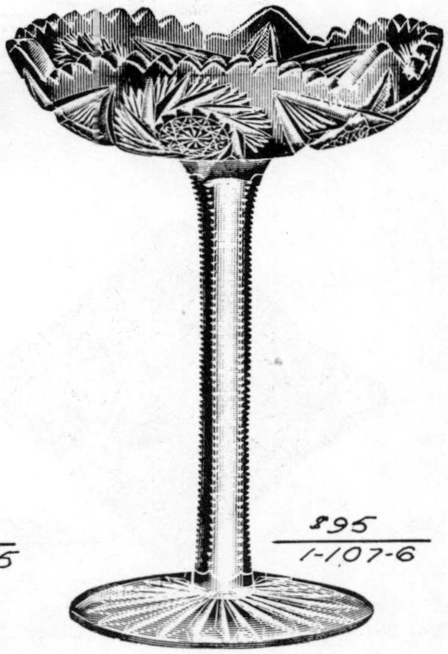

$95
1-107-6

COMPORT.
No. 2891. 9 inches High...$5.50

FINE, RICH DEEP-CUT BON BON AND OLIVE DISHES.

ILLUSTRATIONS ARE REDUCED SIZE.   PRICES EACH.

N.A. & Co.   1909

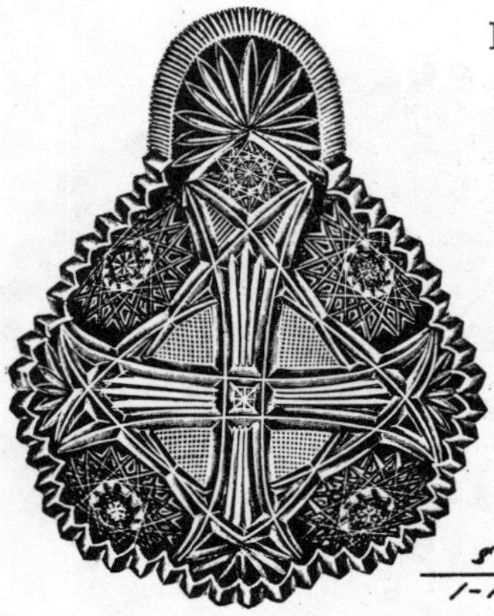

$65
1-108-2

BON BON.
No. 2862.   7½ x 5¼ inches $5.40

$45
1-108-3

BON BON.
No. 2863.   6¾ x 4½ inches $3.34

$70
1-108-1

No. 2861.   HANDLED BON BON. $5.40

$45
1-108-4

BON BON DISH.

No. 2865.   7 inch $3.50

$40
1-108-5

OLIVE DISH.
No. 2864.   6 inch $3.50

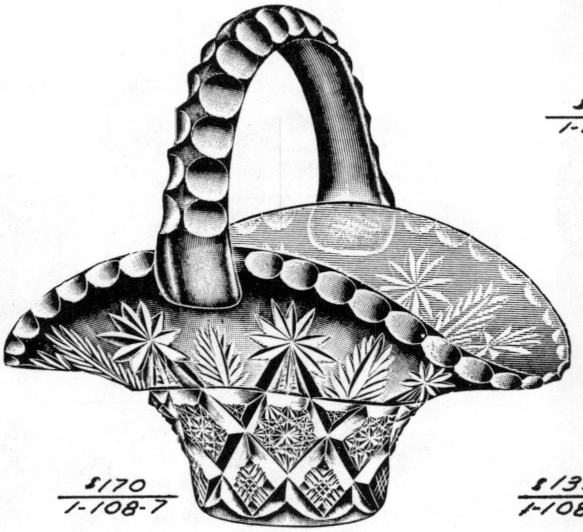

$170
1-108-7

BASKET.
No. 2867.   6¾ in. Long, 4½ in. Wide, 6 in. High......$12.00

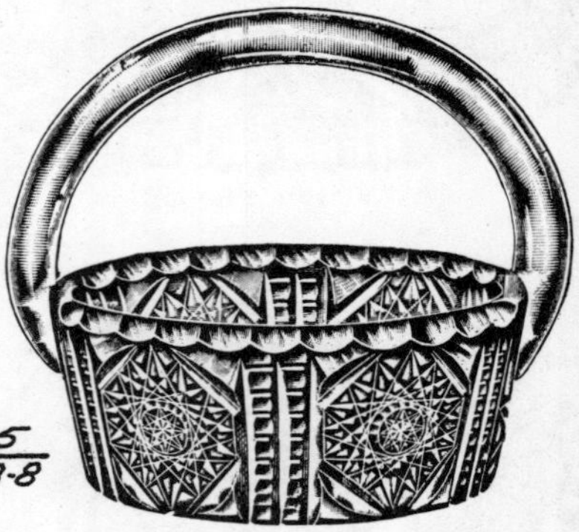

$135
1-108-8

BON BON.
No. 2868.   3½ x 3½ inches $3.34

$70
1-108-6

HEART BON BON.
No. 2866.   6 inch $5.40

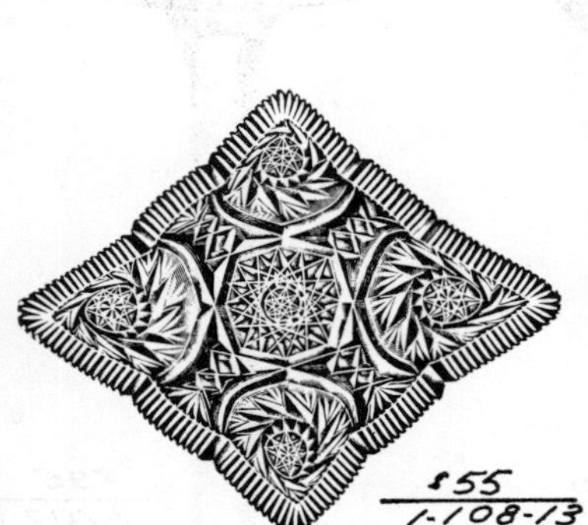

$40
1-108-9

BON BON.
No. 2869.   5½ inches Long...........$3.34

$70
1-108-10

FOOTED JELLY OR BON BON DISH.
No. 2870.   5 in. Diam., 3¼ in. High.....$4.00

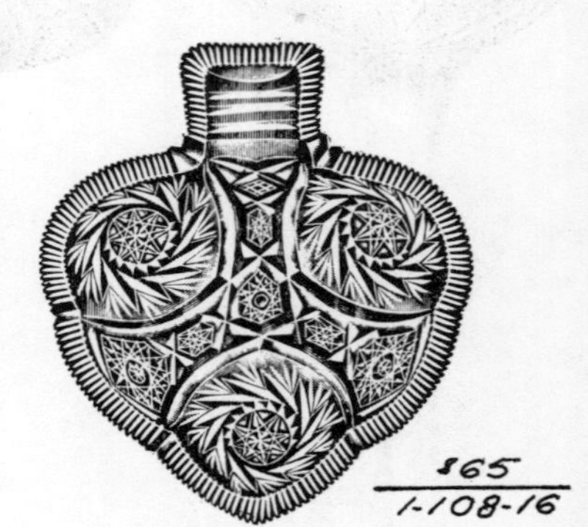

6" $35
1-108-11

7" $40
1-108-12

BON BON OR OLIVE DISH.
No. 2871.   6 inch $2.70
No. 2872.   7 inch 3.34

$55
1-108-13

DIAMOND BON BON.
No. 2873.   6 inch $1.86

$70
1-108-14

FOOTED JELLY OR BON BON DISH.
No. 2874.   5 in. Diam., 3¼ in. High.....$3.06

$65
1-108-16

SPADE BON BON.
No. 2875.   6 inch $1.86

FINE, RICH, DEEP-CUT GLASS WATER SETS AND COMPORTS.

N. A. & Co.
1909

ILLUSTRATIONS ARE REDUCED SIZE.   PRICES EACH.

COMPORT.

No. 3017.   8 inches Wide, 7½ inches High...........$17.40
No. 3018.   9 inches Wide, 8   inches High........... 21.40
No. 3019.   10 inches Wide, 8½ inches High........... 24.00

No. 3020.   WATER SET.   8 Pieces. $14.75

No. 3021.   Carafe $4.50
No. 3022.   Tumblers, ½ Dozen................................ 6.50
No. 3023.   Plateau 3.75

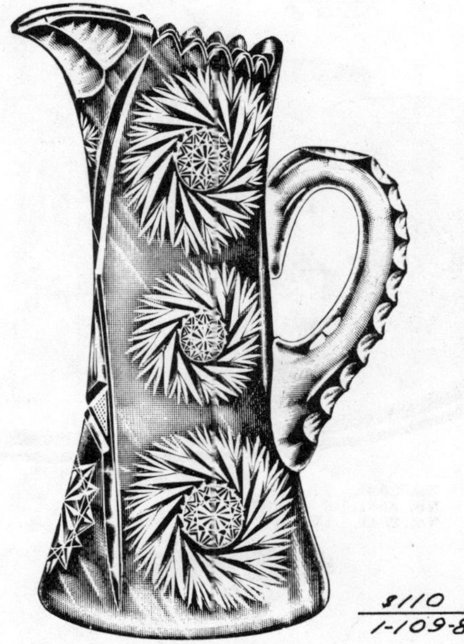

No. 3028.   PITCHER. $9.40
2 Quarts.   Height 10¾ inches.

No. 3024.   WATER SET.   8 Pieces. $19.40

No. 3025.   Carafe, 1 Quart.................................$6.00
No. 3026.   6 Tumblers...................................... 8.70
No. 3027.   Plateau, 14 inch............................... 4.70

No. 3029.   WATER SET.   8 Pieces. $16.88

No. 3030.   Carafe, 1 Quart.................................$6.88
No. 3031.   6 Tumblers...................................... 6.25
No. 3032.   Plateau, 14 inch............................... 3.75

No. 3033.   WATER SET.   8 Pieces. $42.40

No. 3034.   Carafe, 1 Quart................................$12.00
No. 3035.   6 Tumblers..................................... 20.70
No. 3036.   Plateau, 14 inch.............................. 10.70

FINE, RICH, DEEP-CUT GLASS WATER SETS AND PITCHERS.

ILLUSTRATIONS ARE REDUCED SIZE. PRICES EACH.

No. 3037. PITCHER. 2½ Pints. $8.13

No. 3038. PITCHER. 2½ Pints. $8.13

No. 3043. PITCHER. 3 Pints. $11.25

No. 3039. WATER SET. 8 Pieces. $21.25

No. 3040. Pitcher, 3 Pints...$11.25
No. 3041. 6 Tumblers 6.25
No. 3042. 14 inch Plateau.. 3.75

No. 3044. WATER SET. 8 Pieces. $28.13

No. 3045. Pitcher, 3 Pints...$13.75
No. 3046. 6 Tumblers 10.63
No. 3047. 14 inch Plateau.. 3.75

No. 3648. PITCHER. 3 Pints. $17.59

American Cut Glass

Abraham & Straus, Inc.
Brooklyn, N.Y.

George L. Borden & Company
(Krystal Krafters)
Trenton, N.J.
Groveville, N.J.

Cut Glass Corporation of America
(Quaker City Cut Glass Co.)
Philadelphia, Pa.

C. G. Alford & Company
New York, N.Y.

Crystal Cut Glass Co.
141 S. Clinton St.
Chicago, Ill.

American Wholesale Corp.
(Baltimore Bargain House)
Baltimore, Md.

Buffalo Cut Glass Co.
Buffalo, N.Y.

Corona Cut Glass Company
Toledo, Ohio

Clark

T. B. Clark & Co.
860 Broadway
New York, N.Y.

J. D. Bergen Company
Meriden, Conn.

Crystolyne Cut Glass Company
Brooklyn, N.Y.

C. Dorflinger & Sons, Inc.
White Mills, Pa.

George Borgfeldt & Co.
New York, N.Y

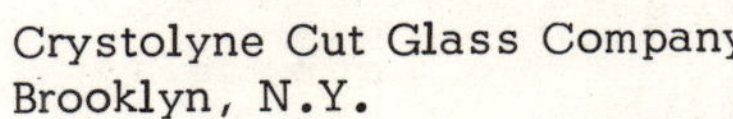

SILVART

Deidrick Glass Co.
Monaca, Pa.

AMERICAN CUT GLASS.

TRADEMARKS

O. F. Egginton Company
Corning, N.Y.

A. H. Helsey & Co., Inc.
Neward, Ohio

Hope Glass Works
Providence, R.I.

Empire Cut Glass Company
New York, N.Y.
Flemington, N.J.

Imperial Glass Co.
Bellaire, Ohio

H. C. Fry Glass Company

Rochester, Pennsylvania

L. Hinsberger Cut Glass Company
New York, N.Y.

Irving Cut Glass Co., Inc.
Honesdale, Pa.

J. Hoare & Company
Corning, N.Y.

T. G. Hawkes & Company
Corning, N.Y.

Lansburgh & Bro.

Lansburgh & Brother, Inc.
Washington, D. C.

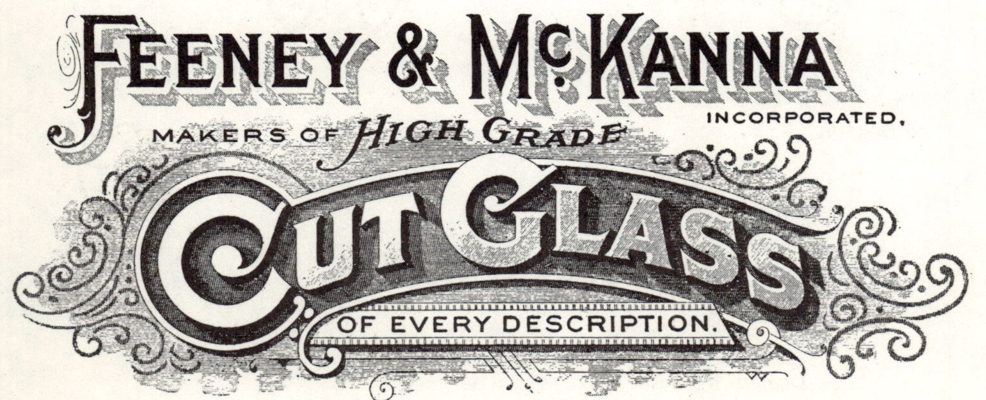

McKanna Cut Glass Co.
Honesdale, Pa.

1892-1896:

TRADE MARK

Meriden Cut Glass Company
Meriden, Conn.

Lotus

Lotus Cut Glass Company
Barnesville, Ohio

1896-1906:

1901:

Mt. Washington Glass Company
(Pairpoint Corporation)
New Bedford, Mass.

Lyons Cut Glass Company
Lyons, N.Y.

1906-ca. 1913:

PRESCUT

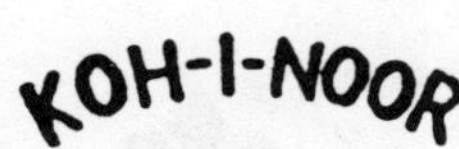

Richard Murr
Chicago, Ill.
San Francisco, Cal.

McKee-Jeannette Glass Works
Jeannette, Pa.

1919-1930:

J. S. O'Connor
Hawley, Pa.

Maple City Glass Co.
Honesdale, Pa.

1933-1935:

J. S. O'CONNOR, HAWLEY, PA.,
Sole Agents, Geo. Borgfeldt & Co.,
18 Washington Place,
NEW YORK.

PITKIN & BROOKS CHICAGO.

W. L. Libbey & Son
(Libbey Glass Co.)
Toledo, Ohio

DiamonKut

Pope Cut Glass Co., Inc.
New York, N.Y.

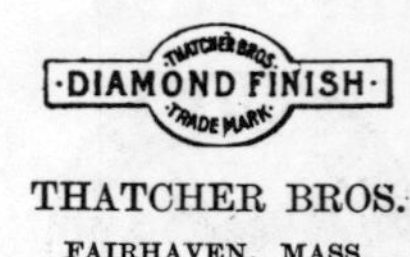

THATCHER BROS.
FAIRHAVEN, MASS.

OHIO CUT GLASS COMPANY

NEW YORK SALESROOM, 66 West Broadway.

CHICAGO SALESROOM, Silversmiths' Building.

ST. LOUIS SALESROOM, Holland Building.

Standard Cut Glass Company
New York, N.Y.

Tuthill Cut Glass Co.
Middletown, N. Y.

Steuben Glass Works
(Corning Glass Works)
Corning, N.Y.

Van Heusen, Charles Co.
Albany, N.Y.

Unger Brothers
Newark, N.J.

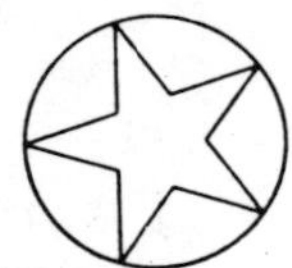

L. Straus & Sons
New York, N.Y.

E. J. S. VAN HOUTEN,
74 Park Place,
NEW YORK.

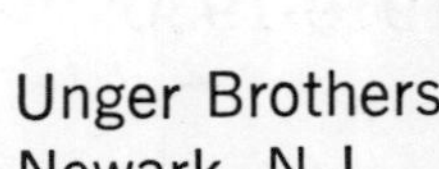

SINCLAIRE

H. P. Sinclaire & Co.
Corning, N. Y.

Taylor Brothers Co., Inc.
Philadelphia, Pa.

Hunt Glass Company

Corning, New York

C. E. Wheelock & Co.
Peoria, Ill.

COMMENTS ON CUT GLASS

The prices shown in script are the prices I feel the piece is worth today.

Many things go into making a piece of cut glass bring a good price. I will

try to list some of them.

QUALITY: Clear and sparkling, and the heavier the better in most cases.

PATTERN: This is very important. It determines beauty and identifies
the maker. For instance, Russian or Royal (Royal is shown on page 42),
which are among the more famous and desirable. This enables a collector
to collect a set of dishes of one pattern.

SIGNED AND UNSIGNED CUT GLASS: To a beginning collector I would
say to be more concerned as to whether the piece is old or new than if it
is signed or unsigned. I have seen in shops and shows new pieces
which have been fake signed with old makers trademarks. I have even
purchased old pieces which were fake signed, but they were excellent
pieces and I did not pay the high price an original signed piece would
cost. True, the old original signed pieces are more desirable and bring
a much higher price to an advanced collector than an unsigned piece.
However, I feel quality and pattern and workmanship are more important
to consider first before purchasing a piece of cut glass than if it is
signed or unsigned.

TRADEMARK: Many makers identified by cutting their mark with acid
somewhere on the article itself. Some used paper labels and, of course,
they came off. A piece will sell for 25% to 50% more with an original
sign. See pages 111 and 112 for cut glass trademarks.

POLISH: Hand or wheel polishing is the best. Acid polishing is not
as desirable.

The retail prices shown in my book are for unsigned pieces. A price guide of

any kind is limited to what it can do, but it will tell you which pieces are the

best and the price range. How much can an individual with cut glass to sell

expect to get from a dealer? If the value of the bowl for example is $50 to $100,

he can probably get 50% of the retail value. If the punch bowl on the other hand

is worth $750 retail, he might get as much as $500 to $600 from a dealer if the

115

dealer has a ready sale for it. A dealer must have a considerable markup in

order to operate. You can get more by selling to a collector, but this is very

time consuming.

REPRODUCTIONS. A few words about this. Most of the cut glass shown

in my book was made during the so-called "Brilliant Period". A special effort

has been made to show the covers from the books in which they were offered

for sale, in order for you to know the date. Cut glass has always been made

from very old to the present. Glass that is being made now is not a reproduction

as such, although many of the patterns are copied from old glass.

New cut glass is expensive. It is mostly found in gift shops and large

department stores in every city in the U.S. A trip to one of these will help you

tell the old from the very new. Reputable dealers in good antique shows will

seldom show new cut glass. Old cut glass is a very good buy at today's prices

when compared with what it cost when new, if you consider that wages were

$2.00 per day or less and a bowl cost $10.00. That same bowl is a terrific

buy at $100.00 now.

Old cut glass prices are going up and probably will continue to do so for

some time yet, as more and more people are finding out it's value and beauty.

No attempt has been made to identify the makers of the cut glass shown in

my book. It would, of course, be interesting to know who all the makers are.

Many of you who read this will know. If you would drop me a line and identify

the piece thus: $\frac{\$2,000}{1-7-8}$ (this will tell me it is from Book 1, page #7, item #8,

value $2,000), I will include the information in Book 2.

I have about enough pictures for another one-half book now. If you

have any old original pictures like the ones shown in this book that you would

like to see published, send them to me. I will not damage them, only

photograph them and return the original to you, or I will buy them from you.

Cut glass prices vary somewhat in different parts of the country and more

so by dealers. Some dealers price high if they don't know the value so as to

be sure they don't make a mistake. Some dealers price their cut glass

according to what they have to pay for it. Some follow price guides as best

they can. There are a number of dealers and shops in the U.S. who specialize

in cut glass. Prices will generally be higher here in these shops and higher

still in the shows. These shops and show dealers provide the cream of the cut

glass pieces to the discriminating and affluent collectors.

The prices in this book are retail and are based on the piece being free of

chips and of good color and quality. These prices are the prices a collector

with the money will pay a knowledgeable dealer. All other transactions will be

somewhere below the price shown in the book.

* * * * * * *   ALL PRICES IN THIS BOOK ARE RETAIL * * * * * * *

ALPHA LEE EHRHARDT

We wish all who see this a very Happy New Year and a good business during the next twelve months.

The pieces illustrated show two new patterns now ready; also a New Star (patents pending) which is the most brilliant and attractive in design we have ever brought out.

Yours truly,

PITKIN & BROOKS.

RICH CUT GLASS

We issue
no
CATALOGUE

Write us
for
our proposition

Made in
MERIDEN

The Cut Glass City
by
practical men
with a life-long
experience
in
cutting glass

THE J. J. NILAND CO.
MERIDEN, CONN.

No. 4134.   Ice Cream Tray "Elsie."   Price, $6.50

Quality First
H. C. Fry Glass Co.
Rochester, Pa.

A Rare Exhibit of Cut Glass
at New York Sample Room, 66 Murray Street
Don't overlook it when you visit New York City

GLASS THAT SELLS

Fry Glass is pure and brilliant.   The cutting is deep and artistic.

ACKNOWLEDGED TO BE THE BEST CUT GLASS

No. 4406.   Plate and Saucer "Keystone."   Price, $2.25

H. C. Fry Glass Co.
Rochester, Pennsylvania